FIFTY SHADES OF BLACK AND WHITE

Anatomy of the Lawsuit behind a Publishing Phenomenon

Mike Farris & Jennifer Pedroza

Fifty Shades of Black and White: Anatomy of the Lawsuit behind a Publishing Phenomenon

Other books by Mike Farris

The Bequest
Isle of Broken Dreams
Manifest Intent
Rules of Privilege
Kanaka Blues
Wrongful Termination
Every Pig got a Saturday
A Death in the Islands: The Unwritten Law and the Last Trial of Clarence Darrow
Call Me Lucky: A Texan in Hollywood (with Robert Hinkle)
Poor Innocent Lad: The Tragic Death of Gill Jamieson and the Execution of Myles Fukunaga.

© 2018 Mike Farris and Jennifer Pedroza
All Rights Reserved
Print ISBN 978-1-941071-89-2
ebook ISBN 978-1-941071-90-8

STAIRWAY PRESS—APACHE JUNCTION

Cover Design by Guy D. Corp, www.GrafixCorp.com
Cover Copy created by BlurbWriter.com

STAIRWAY≡PRESS

www.StairwayPress.com
1000 West Apache Trail #126
Apache Junction, AZ 88120 USA

Mike's Dedication

To Susan, with fifty shades of love.

Jenny's Dedication

To my mom and dad—with your love, even when I'm making you guys crazy, I feel like I can do anything.

And to Mickey—your support and wisdom have meant more to me than I can ever express. You hold me up so I can fly. I love you.

To my favorite son—thank you for always loving your mom, even when I'm embarrassing.

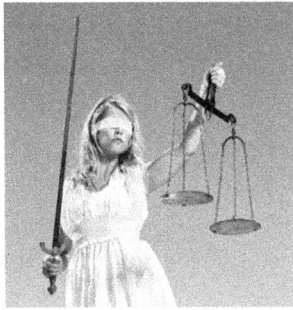

Acknowledgments—Mike

THIS BOOK CAME out of what started as an attorney-client relationship and ended up being a friendship. Without Jenny Pedroza and Christa Beebe, none of this would have come to pass, so I thank both of them for being great clients and even better friends.

Brent Turman was my co-counsel on this case from start to finish, and I knew that I could always count on him. But, more than that, he, too, became a friend, and that's even more valuable.

To my agent, Donna Eastman, who works tirelessly on my behalf, I am eternally in your debt. I also want to thank the great people at Stairway Press—Ken Coffman, Stacey Benson, and Chris Benson—for their hard work in helping to bring this book to fruition.

And of course, I thank my wife Susan for putting up with me while the litigation consumed me, and for her encouragement and support throughout not only the lawsuit, but also the writing process. I couldn't have done any of this without her.

Acknowledgments—Jenny

THIS BOOK WOULD not have been possible without the encouragement and support of all my family and friends. Christa, Kera, Missi, Jody and Lauren—you women are the best friends I could have ever asked for. You each bring something different into our friendship, and I can't imagine my world without you. Thank you for always listening, having my back, and knowing just when to send the mojo. I love you all.

To my sister, and second mom. Becky, I'll always be your little sister getting into trouble, and I'm so thankful I have a sister that always has my back. You have been the best defense against bullies, and I'm so grateful God gave me you.

Thank you to Julia for giving me a tutoring job in the middle of the school year, and then, knowing what was coming, keeping me on as a teacher. I hope I can live up to the faith you have in me.

Thank you to all my Nash, Rosen, and Facebook friends that keep me laughing and are always sending good vibes and prayers when times got tough.

Also a huge thank you to Milli Brown, Jeff Prince, Alexandra Allred, and all the author friends I have made along the way. You each had a part in this story, and I thank God everyday for putting you in my life.

None of this would have happened without Erika. I doubt this will ever make its ways into your hands, but I sincerely want you to know how happy I am for you and all that you have accomplished. You took a fun and sexy story and turned it into a global phenomenon. I'm thrilled to have been there at the beginning, and wish you nothing but continued success in everything you do.

Mike Walker—I wish you were still with us to see this book published. You would have loved this, and I miss talking with you so much.

And to Brent Truman—we were truly blessed to have you on the case with us. You are an amazing lawyer, but even more, you are a wonderful person. Thank you for being my life coach during the trial. Your smiles, hugs, and words of wisdom made each day of the case bearable. Thank you for going through my thousands of emails and not thinking I'm a crazy person. You and your family mean so much to me, and I believe in my heart the world has not seen the last of you. I see great things in your future.

And finally: Mike Farris. How can I acknowledge everything you mean to me? I have told you before how I believe God put you in my path, and there isn't a day that goes by that I don't give thanks that I know you. Your faith and friendship, during what has been to date the hardest part of my life, means more than I can ever express. Your unwavering belief that my story deserved to have a different ending, makes you more than "my lawyer",you are my friend, my author, and my greatest champion. You and Susan have now become honored members of my family, and I look forward to many years of happiness shared between us all.

PART I: PRELUDE TO THE STORM

CHAPTER ONE: The Storyteller

If you wish to influence an individual or a group to embrace a particular value in their daily lives, tell them a compelling story.
—Annette Simmons

February 10, 2015, 9:15 AM

Mike's Story

EVER SINCE CAVEMEN gathered around campfires and regaled others by recounting their hunting exploits, humans have told stories. Plato said, "Those who tell stories, rule society." Filmmaker George Lucas added, "Storytelling is about two things; it's about character and plot."

Sitting at a table, waiting to speak, my heartbeat pounded in my ears. Perspiration coated my forehead, and a drop of sweat trickled down my side. I knew it would soon soak through the fabric of my suitcoat and betray my anxiety. My hands tingled down to the tips of my fingers. Part of me wanted to flee, but the better part kept me in place. I had to stay because I had a duty to speak. I had a story to tell. It had characters, and it had a plot.

It was, at its heart, a simple story: Four women partnered together to publish one of the most successful book series of all time, but one of the partners absconded with the profits.

The story begged for a different ending. It cried out for a

different ending. It *demanded* a different ending. In the plot, one of the partners had betrayed another, who was now demanding her fair share of the profits. The success or failure of my storytelling would be revealed in the ending 12 hearers would write. If the story I told was compelling, they would write my preferred ending and the betrayed character would be vindicated. If not, I would be left to wonder where I had failed her.

Judge Susan McCoy addressed me from her bench. "Mr. Farris, do you wish to give an opening?"

My heartbeat quickened. I felt a flush rising in my face. I took a deep breath, slid my chair back, and stood. "Yes, I do, Your Honor."

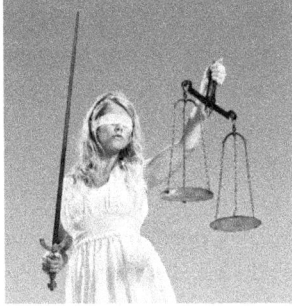

CHAPTER TWO: Lost

Not until we are lost do we begin to understand ourselves.

—Henry David Thoreau

Mike's Story

IN JANUARY OF 2014, by the time I entered my thirty-first year as a lawyer, I had fallen back into a routine that was disrupted less than a year earlier, leaving me with doubts about my future. I had been "Of Counsel" with the law firm of Vincent Lopez Serafino Jenevein[1] since August of 2010, with offices on the 41st floor of Thanksgiving Tower in downtown Dallas. My practice primarily involved representing banks, which were the firm's largest clients, and the occasional "one-off" commercial litigation case, with a little bit of entertainment law thrown in, but nothing had really captivated my imagination for a long time.

Vincent Lopez had spun off from the Dallas firm of Vial Hamilton Koch & Knox a few years earlier, which sent that firm into its death throes. I got my start at Vial Hamilton, then one of the largest firms in Dallas, in 1983 after graduating from Texas

---

[1] Now known as Vincent Serafino Geary Waddell Jenevein.

3

Tech University School of Law.[2] I worked with a group of lawyers, under the leadership of Jim Knox, representing fidelity insurers and surety companies in litigation involving the worlds of financial institutions and construction.

I found fidelity work to be the most interesting, sometimes tiptoeing up to the line of criminal law. The firm represented insurance companies that provided financial institution bonds, commonly called fidelity bonds, which insured financial institutions against various types of losses, including losses caused by employee dishonesty, counterfeiting, and other nefarious activities. As a third-year associate, I got involved in a federal court case in which a savings-and-loan in the Dallas suburb of Irving filed a bond claim for in excess of twenty million dollars in loan losses they claimed were caused by employee dishonesty. Nearly 75 depositions, tens of thousands of pages of documents, three different federal judges, four different plaintiffs (the first plaintiff was Irving Savings Association, followed, after Irving Savings failed, by the Federal Savings and Loan Insurance Corporation, then the Federal Home Loan Bank Board, and finally the Federal Deposit Insurance Corporation), three trips to the United States Court of Appeals for the Fifth Circuit in New Orleans, and, finally, ten years later, when I was a sixth-year partner in my thirteenth year of practice, the case finally came to a close with a victory upheld by

---

[2] I obtained a B.A. from the University of Texas at Arlington in 1977 in political science, then worked on a Master's degree in American history, stopping short of writing my thesis when I was accepted into law school. I would be remiss if I didn't also mention that I am a proud Wildcat from Dallas's "Heisman High" —Woodrow Wilson High School, which has the distinction of being the first high school, and still the only public high school, to produce two Heisman Trophy winners in football, neither of whom was me: Davey O'Brien (winner in 1938 at TCU) and Tim Brown (winner in 1987 at Notre Dame).

the Fifth Circuit.

The most meaningful case I had handled, though, was a *pro bono* matter I took on in the early 1990s for a friend who attended the same Baptist church as I, and who was in the Sunday School class that I taught. She had a young son who had been born with significant physical disabilities and, during a transition period when her employer moved from one group insurer to another, her son had inadvertently been left uncovered because of those pre-existing conditions. Working closely with my friend, and an attorney who represented the insurance company, we ultimately tailored an insurance contract specifically for her son that covered all of his medical conditions, including a number of surgeries he would be required to have. Although the boy died not long after that, and the insurance question became moot, the fact that I could put my experience and education to use to help him and his mother was enormously rewarding for me.

I left law practice at the end of 1997 and, over the next decade, spent most of my time writing and traveling with my wife, Susan, before easing back into law practice with a small Dallas firm in 2007. In 2010, I moved to Vincent Lopez, where I rejoined a number of lawyers with whom I had formerly worked at Vial Hamilton. But after my return to practice, I didn't find anything that grabbed my imagination nearly as much as those fidelity cases back in the 1980s and 1990s. In fact, the world of fidelity law inspired one of my first published novels, called *Manifest Intent*.

Then, in February of 2013, dissatisfied with law practice and creeping up on my 60th birthday, which was a little over a year away, something happened that caused me to rethink my career and my future. Like seemingly the rest of Dallas that winter, I caught a cold, accompanied by a sore throat. I thought I was finally over it after about a week, but on Tuesday, February 19, as I walked around the house and at the office, I noticed a strange tightness in my legs, particularly my thighs. I brushed it off, thinking it was due to having worked out the preceding two days after laying off a week because of the cold. But by Wednesday, the feeling intensified. I felt wobbly when I walked, with weakness in my knees. I thought maybe I was relapsing, or maybe even that I was getting a touch of the flu. Having been sick in the first place was rare for me, so a relapse was just about unheard of.

I left the office early on Wednesday and went home to the house Susan and I shared in the town of Sunnyvale, just east of Dallas. We had met in law school and got married one week after graduation. In 2013, she was working in the Dallas office of the State Bar's Disciplinary Counsel, prosecuting attorney misconduct. As I always liked to joke, that was what you called job security.

I didn't express any undue concern to her because I didn't think it was anything to worry about. She knew I'd been sick the week before, so she agreed it was probably just a relapse. That evening, as I entered our home office, my knees buckled. I dropped to the floor but kept from falling face down by catching myself on extended arms. Weird, I thought. What was weirder was that I felt a strange sensation on certain areas of my skin, legs, and arms that were sensitive to touch. I simply chalked it up to weakness from being ill. Maybe I really was coming down with the flu.

While Susan went to work, I stayed home the next day and spent most of Thursday in bed. I still felt wobbly and weak-kneed but seemed to be able to maneuver around the house just fine when I needed. By Friday morning, the sensitivity to touch had intensified, and I now felt a tingling sensation in my hands and feet. After Susan left for work, I staggered to the kitchen to get coffee, then returned to sit in bed and watch the morning news shows. As I lifted the cup for my first sip, I lost control of my right hand and poured hot coffee on my chest.

At that point I panicked. I tried to set the cup on a nightstand but could barely accomplish that. Both hands had begun to quiver, and I had no ability to still them. I called Susan home, and she drove me to the emergency room at Baylor Hospital on the eastern fringe of downtown Dallas. We arrived around 9:45 and, all through the morning and into the afternoon, I remained in a private room while doctors and nurses consulted, ran tests, and tried to figure out what was wrong. By 4:00, I was unable to walk and could barely stand due to weakness in my legs. The quivering in my hands had given way to a very noticeable, and frightening, shaking.

Still, because none of the tests produced any diagnosis, and a CT scan ruled out stroke, lesions, and tumors, the ER was ready to discharge me, with instructions to call a neurologist Monday morning.

That was when a "sea change" occurred: I attempted to stand, both knees buckled, and I fell, dislocating the pinkie finger on my right hand. Ideas of discharge went out the window. The ER called a hospitalist who specialized in neurology, who ordered a lumbar puncture—a particularly insidious form of torture—to drain spinal fluid to rule out infection, but also to look for elevated protein levels.

Meanwhile, Susan and I were entertaining nightmare scenarios: ALS (Lou Gehrig's Disease), multiple sclerosis, even Parkinson's, although the sudden onset of symptoms, instead of gradual, seemed to rule those out. Around 7:00 PM, we met with an internal medicine doctor, as well as the neurologist, who told us they were operating on a working diagnosis of Guillain-Barre Syndrome, a rare auto-immune disorder that affects only about 1 in 100,000 people annually. Although the actual causes of GBS were unknown, the doctors informed us that it can be triggered by a cold or upper respiratory infection, or even by a flu shot. I had not had a flu shot, so my recent cold appeared to be the likely culprit.

Before midnight, they admitted me to the stroke ward at Baylor Hospital. The doctors ran more tests on Saturday and Sunday, which included confining this claustrophobe in a full-body MRI machine for about three hours, and the neurologist commenced treatment for GBS on Sunday. Even though he had not yet confirmed the diagnosis 100%, he was sure enough that he wanted to get a jump on arresting the progression of the disorder.

My fall in the ER and the quick diagnosis were two strokes of good fortune that befell me in the process. GBS is a rapid onset auto-immune disorder in which the immune system attacks the patient's own tissue.

In a typical case, it attacks the sheath that encapsulates the nerves (much like the outer coating on a wire), and in even rarer cases, it attacks not only the sheath, but also the nerves, themselves. I should have bought lottery tickets because it turned out that I had the rare form of this rare disorder.

GBS is an ascending disorder, which means it starts at the extremities and ascends upward through legs and arms, ultimately reaching the diaphragm and face, unless it can be arrested in time. Damage caused from the disorder disrupts the nerves' ability to transmit impulses from the brain to the muscles, causing loss of motor control and, if allowed to progress unchecked, paralysis.

Forty percent of GBS patients require mechanical ventilation in order to breathe—not all that long ago, that meant an iron lung—and forty percent require speech therapy due to impaired speech. Some patients end up fully paralyzed and, even after recovery, may have lingering symptoms and even partial paralysis. It can also cause high, or fluctuating, blood pressure and abnormal heart beat. In extreme cases, particularly those involving breathing difficulties, it can be fatal.

There is a school of thought that President Franklin Roosevelt, wheelchair bound, actually suffered from GBS and not polio.[3]

Due to a quick diagnosis in my case, and prompt start of treatment, ascension of the disorder was arrested before it reached either my diaphragm or my face. Treatment consisted of a high-dose immunoglobulin infusion administered over the course of four days, about six hours per day. By the end of the second day, it appeared that progression of the disorder had been arrested. After that, it was just a matter of waiting for the effects to reverse themselves.

After three weeks and one day of hospitalization and in-patient occupational and physical therapy, where I re-learned to walk and use my hands, I finally returned home, eleven days earlier than predicted by the doctors and therapists. Their goal was to have me walking on a walker when I left Baylor Institute for Rehabilitation, but when I left, I was able to walk unassisted—although I bore more than a passing resemblance to Peter Boyle in *Young Frankenstein*, performing "Putting on the Ritz" with Gene Wilder. I used a cane on occasion for balance, before weaning myself off of it completely. Five more weeks of out-patient physical and occupational therapy later, the ataxia, or trembling, in my hands had subsided, and I finally went back to work, full-time, on May 1, after having been out of commission for more than two months.

So, as I sat in my office in January of 2014, pondering my future and questioning whether I truly wanted to continue practicing law, I came to a realization that I needed another case

---

[3] "The diagnosis at the onset of [FDR's] illness and thereafter was paralytic poliomyelitis. Yet his age and many features of the illness are more consistent with a diagnosis of Guillain-Barre syndrome, an autoimmune polyneuritis." Armond S. Goldman, Elisabeth J. Schmalsteig, and Daniel H. Freeman, Jr., "What was the Cause of Franklin Delano Roosevelt's Paralytic Illness?" *Journal of Medical Biography* (Nov. 1, 2003).

that I could believe in, as I had believed in the *pro bono* insurance case I handled, and I needed a client I could believe in.

Both walked through my door before the month was over.

Jenny's Story

Driving away from the Omni Hotel in downtown Dallas in the summer of 2012, I was lost. There are many ways a person could be lost, and at that moment I was all of them. First, I had absolutely no idea where I was going; I just recognized a sign that said Loop 12 and went that direction. Nothing looked familiar as I drove, but that didn't mean much. Directions and landmarks have never been my friends. Secondly, I was crying so hard that my vision was lost in a sea of tears. I knew I should pull over but, again, I didn't know where I was. If my dad taught me anything, it was not to pull over in an unfamiliar area unless I saw a sign with a double set of golden arches or an orange W. Seeing neither a McDonald's nor a Whataburger in the passing landscape, I continued to drive as I wiped my eyes.

After weeks of uncertainty, the final pieces of a puzzle that floated loosely in my mind were finally fitting together to bring the full picture into focus. I had lost my friend. I knew down to my bones that our relationship would never be the same. Only one of us would walk away with our dream, and it wasn't going to be me.

Like I said...I was lost.

The dream began three years before this fated trip to Dallas. Amanda Hayward, Jenn McGuire, and I started a company called The Writer's Coffee Shop ("Coffee Shop"), and we went on to publish one of the biggest book series of all time—the erotic *Fifty Shades* trilogy, sometimes referred to as "mommy porn," which consisted of three books: *Fifty Shades of Grey*, *Fifty Shades Darker*, and *Fifty Shades Freed*. We were all excited and scared, but we were in it together. We were going to make this work, and for a little over two years we did an amazing job. Within a year, we were on a fast track to success, and I soon quit the teaching job I had held for over 12 years to devote full time to Coffee Shop. This was not an easy decision, but it was one that I made because I believed in our company, and I believed in *us*.

Amanda lived in Australia, while Jenn and I both lived in Texas, so we talked on Skype often to discuss our hopes and aspirations. We envisioned new houses, sending our kids to private schools, and setting up our families with enough savings to last a lifetime. The impossible dream was becoming possible. But somewhere along the way, the dream became less and less "ours" and more and more "Amanda's."

Beginning in December 2011, and carrying over to January of the next year, movie companies began courting Erika Leonard Mitchell, who, writing under the pen name E. L. James, was the author of the *Fifty Shades* trilogy, for film rights to the books and, in March, Coffee Shop sold publishing rights to the trilogy to Random House. It was shortly after that, in the early summer of 2012, that Amanda and Cindy Bidwell, also of Australia, flew to Dallas and asked Jenn and me to join them at the Omni Hotel to discuss plans for the company's future. Cindy was a friend of Amanda and had recently started working for the company as her assistant. Her role was not clearly defined, but it appeared that she took on the jobs that Amanda didn't want to tackle.

From the moment they walked through the hotel doors that weekend, I knew something was wrong. As hours turned to days, the weekend seemed to last forever. Amanda told us that we needed to "restructure" the company to save on taxes. We had been talking about different business structures for some time so this, alone, didn't alarm me. We had already set ourselves up as a partnership in the United States, obtained an employer identification number (EIN) from the Internal Revenue Service, and even filed a partnership tax return for the company. However, with the number of books we were selling, we needed a more formal structure. I had looked into how to accomplish this and even got the paperwork started. Then, when Random House bought the rights to the trilogy, our little dreams became big dreams.

What I didn't know then was that, while I was still researching potential business structures, Amanda was already hard at work setting up something far more complicated and, I later learned, far different from what we had discussed. She didn't tell us exactly what that something was, but she assured us that she was following her lawyers' and accountants' advice in order to minimize taxes. With the sale of the *Fifty Shades* trilogy, we were all going to make a lot of money, she said, so tax planning was critical. We just needed to trust her.

While the concept of reducing taxes made sense, it also set off muted alarm bells in my mind. Amanda's behavior over the past couple of months had been odd. Right after Random House acquired the publishing rights, she dropped off the radar, unreachable and unresponsive to my communications, before resurfacing to request this meeting. All this talk of taxes, something none of us knew much about, combined with that period of silence concerned me. But I couldn't fit the puzzle pieces together in my mind.

Amanda made her unknown plan sound innocent. We simply needed to do what was "best for the company" so that everyone could still have a job—and she was apparently to be the sole arbiter of what was best. Those muted alarms now rang with gusto in my mind. Still have a job? Hadn't we closed a deal with Random House that should be sufficient to ensure the success of the company for years to come? We didn't yet know how profitable that deal would be, but we all believed it would earn our little company millions of dollars. I had no idea then that it would ultimately be tens of millions of dollars.

The weekend was a mixture of Amanda telling Jenn and me

that we needed to be on board with what her lawyers required her to do, with Cindy nodding knowingly in agreement, and the continued drumbeat of how we needed to trust her. If we didn't all agree on the new structure, she said, then the company would be in trouble. When I voiced concerns about people losing their jobs, Amanda told me not to worry, that she would take care of everything. All Jenn and I needed to do was sign some simple paperwork that her lawyers were preparing and all would be well. We just had to trust her. That seemed to be her mantra.

I couldn't see how financial jeopardy was possible, but I didn't have anything to base that on other than speculation as to how much we would make from the Random House deal. I had never seen the contract with Random House. Amanda told Jenn and me that the publisher required her to sign a non-disclosure agreement, so she couldn't show it to us. But again, I simply needed to trust her.

In hindsight, I remember feeling trapped in that small hotel room, unable to call anyone for advice. If I got on the phone, others would hear my conversation. If I went into the hall, I felt sure that at least one of them would follow to get ice or see what I was doing or what was taking so long. Amanda told us that the lawyers would handle everything and repeated her mantra—"just trust me"—because she had our best interests at heart.

I didn't know if Amanda did it deliberately, but she managed to isolate me even with three others in the room. I was a trusting person, but I knew something was wrong. I knew things were taking a bad turn, but I didn't know what was wrong or what to do about it, or even *if* I could do anything about it. So, instead of balking or protesting, at the end of the weekend I simply left the hotel—in tears.

In an attempt to control my emotions, I called my mom almost as soon as I left the hotel parking lot. That's what we good Southern girls do when we have problems. Moms always have sage words that can solve just about any problem. If they can't fix it, then they at least cry with you until you feel better. Moms are like that, and my mom was no different.

But it was my dad who answered the phone.

"Hey, Jenny! How was the weekend with the girls? Did y'all have a good time?"

He was completely unaware of what was coming his way. At the sound of his overly chipper voice, I said, through sobs and hiccups, "I'm lost and I can't see and Amanda just kicked me out of the company."

Dad didn't miss a beat. "Here, you better talk to your mother."

Dad has never been fond of any of his girls crying. Living with three females for most of his adult life, plus growing up with three sisters, you would think he'd be able to handle a few tears, but that just wasn't his way. I heard a shuffle and a quiet murmur of "Jenny needs to talk to you."

Mom's soft voice calmed me a bit. "Jenny, what's going on? Where are you? Do we need to come get you?"

"I don't know where I am, but I just left the hotel and I think Amanda is trying to force me out of the company. I don't know what to do."

"First things first, let's get you someplace where you can talk. You're going to have to stop crying so we can figure out where you are. Can you do that?"

I shook my head, but no one could see me.

"Honey, did you hear me? You need to stop crying."

"Okay." I sniffed. "I think I just passed a sign that said 183 North. Should I take that?"

It took several attempts to get me going in the right direction, but soon enough I finally headed West on I-30, in the direction of Fort Worth. Just fifteen more minutes and I would be safely at their home, and then we could talk about everything that had happened over the past three days. Ray Milland's *The Lost Weekend* had nothing on me.

Looking back, the pieces to the puzzle were all there. They were just scattered about so that a cohesive picture wouldn't appear. As I mentioned, after the sale of the *Fifty Shades* trilogy, Amanda disappeared for weeks at a time, cut off from Jenn and me in Texas. When she popped up to talk briefly or email, all I got were cryptic messages about lawyers and accountants and how she hated all the stuff they were telling her to do. I should have been able to put the pieces together. Unfortunately, I couldn't. I wanted too much to believe in my friend. I wanted her to know that I still believed in the dream. *Our* dream. And that I trusted her. I'll admit that I had a few doubts, but I wanted to believe her, so I ignored the signs and turned a blind eye to the puzzle pieces.

On that June day as I left the Omni Hotel, there was no more hiding from the truth. Things were changing rapidly, and if I didn't do something, I might lose everything. On top of a weakened grip on the company I had quit my job to help build, there were other reasons I needed Coffee Shop to continue with me as part of it. My parents both worked for the company. Mom and Dad had recently sold their business, and Amanda and I offered them jobs distributing books. It didn't pay much, but it supplemented their retirement. They enjoyed doing it, and I enjoyed giving them that.

Then there was Christa Beebe. Christa had been my best friend for over a decade. We started teaching with each other in 2002 and, although we got off to a rocky start, we soon learned that we shared a love of laughter and teaching. She was truly one of the smartest people I knew. When Amanda and I needed help with marketing, we brought Christa into the fold.

Now, here's the thing with Christa: she can see through people better than most. She was leery of Amanda almost from day one, but because I was a co-owner of the company, Christa shared my belief in our dream. She knew I would never betray her trust and, to this day, I feel guilty for involving her. Don't get me wrong, working with my friend was a great experience. We created a strong book marketing team from scratch. She researched how to market books, and together we made it happen. A lot of what we did was uncharted territory, and we seemed to break new ground every day. The indie author was just starting to make its mark on the publishing industry with the explosion of e-books and print-on-demand books. I like to think that, with our work on the *Fifty Shades* trilogy, we had something to do with the growth of independent publishing. Only time will tell.

Now I was on the precipice of what was supposed to be the beginning of my brilliant future, the culmination of many months of hard work. Instead of basking in it, I had to worry whether my parents and my best friend would still have jobs, or whether even I would have a job. Amanda's words echoed in my mind: "Just sign the paperwork and everything will keep working like it always worked. No one will lose his or her job, and everything will be fine. Just trust me." I didn't see that I had a choice. What could I do? My parents were counting on that extra money, and Christa had a family to support. If I fought it, my family and my friend would suffer. I felt trapped.

Mom and Dad, and later my husband, repeatedly told me not to sign anything Amanda put in front of me until I had a lawyer review the paperwork. But I didn't have a lawyer, nor did I know how to find the right lawyer. One shoe had already dropped, and I was afraid that, if I questioned Amanda, the other shoe would fly right by. I wish I had known Mike Farris then. I wish I could have called and asked for his advice. He would have given me the strength to stand up for myself but, sadly, I wouldn't meet Mike for more than a year. I had to make this decision alone. I wanted to believe that our dream was still alive.

I wanted to believe in Amanda.

So, against my better instincts, I did what Amanda said. I signed a contract that I never should have signed, determined to make the company a continued success. I never dreamed the end was so near. I never thought for one moment that I would have to fire my parents and see my best friend lose her job in the middle of the school year, far too late to get a new one.

In June of 2012, at the Omni Hotel in Dallas, I became lost. But as I began my free fall to reality, I learned that sometimes you have to get lost in order to find your way again.

CHAPTER THREE: Going Downtown

When you're alone and life is making you lonely, you can always go downtown.
——Tony Hatch

Jenny's Story

WHEN I THOUGHT of lawyers, lawsuits, and litigation, my understanding was limited to television and movie lawyers giving dramatic but poignant speeches that brought justice to the world. My father's version of the perfect lawyer was Perry Mason. To this day, he quotes old cases from the show. To me, lawyers were either the good guys defending justice, like Tom Cruise in *A Few Good Men*, or on the flip side, lawyers out to hide the truth and help the wealthy keep their money, like Jon Voigt in *The Rainmaker*. Of course, courtrooms and lawsuits were not in my realm, so my views were limited and a bit biased. When I found that I actually needed a lawyer, I was intimidated, feeling lost and alone.

Standing on the ground level of Thanksgiving Tower in downtown Dallas, waiting for an elevator to the 41st floor offices of Vincent Lopez Serafino Jenevein, Christa Beebe and I anticipated the worst. I had spoken with Mike Farris on the phone, and I admit to Internet stalking him before the meeting, but I couldn't come to grips with the idea of actually meeting a lawyer so he could, possibly, represent me. It sounded ridiculous. How had my life come to this? Two months prior, I was just an out-of-work teacher trying to manufacture enough handmade soap to keep my family fed. In fact, I don't recall ever being in a high-rise building before, at least not for business reasons. I suppose you had to count once in Sears Tower in Chicago for a sightseeing experience, but that was an entirely different story. I was most assuredly out of my element.

Still lost.

Christa and I had been colleagues for more than ten years, since I returned to work after the birth of my son in my second year as a third-grade teacher. We didn't get along when we first met. We team-taught that year, with her as the math and science teacher, while I was the reading and social studies teacher. The students spent half the day with Ms. Beebe and the rest of the day with me. Christa was someone who knew what she wanted and how she wanted it, and she didn't want help nor did she appreciate someone else suggesting how she should teach. So, there were many opportunities for us to clash.

And clash we did.

She and I were both very passionate about our students and, when we look back now, we know our hearts were in a good place. We both believed in what we were doing, which is what unified us in the end. In order for Christa to truly trust someone, she needed to know that the person was smart enough to stand up to her and worthy enough to earn her trust. Over the course of that first year, we proved both these things to each other and, from that point on, became best friends.

Christa, and now Kera, her wife, have been with me through some of my darkest times. Not only with the trial in this case, but also those normal family and life dramas that play out on a daily basis. Besides my husband, they are the first people I call with good news, and they are the first people I trust when I need an ear or a shoulder to lean on. This closeness is one of the main reasons why losing our jobs in the middle of the school year crushed me. I felt like they trusted that I would always have their backs, and now they were struggling because of my inability to recognize the betrayal that had swirled around us.

When Christa and I worked on projects together, there was little we couldn't accomplish. She was the research-and-know-how woman, and I was the put-it-into-action-and-move-forward woman. We had been a great marketing team with Coffee Shop, so it seemed logical to take what we learned from that experience and try our hand at a new publishing company. We believed it would help us get out of the hole in which we found ourselves. The drawback was that darn service contract that Amanda had made us both sign. The one she told us was simply something to get the accountants and lawyers off her back. The one with a convenient non-compete clause. The one that got us both terminated. Neither Christa nor I understood the nuances of the verbiage, but we didn't want Amanda Hayward suing us for breaching those nuances. That was primarily why we stood in the lobby of Mike Farris's office building.

Another reason came from our "jump the shark" effort to move on with our lives. After we were terminated, neither of us could find teaching jobs, since it was the middle of the school year. Looking for a creative way to earn some income, we decided to try our hand at making soap. Yes, it was a bit of a leap from teaching to soap-making, but we were desperate. So, in the middle of all this craziness, we started The Soap Barista. We felt sure that we had a great product, we had the social media marketing experience, and we had the drive. Surely, we could succeed.

At this point, I would have done anything to help my friend. Christa and Kera were struggling to raise two kids on one salary, with a mortgage and bills to pay. Every day, a knife of guilt twisted in my gut because I had helped put them in that spot. Luckily, my family had a cushion for a short while as my husband, Mickey, cashed in some of his 401k shares, but for how long? The worry was real.

In early January, our friend Alexandra Allred introduced us to a mogul in the Dallas publishing world, Milli Brown, owner of Brown Books Publishing. She had heard about our marketing on *Fifty Shades of Grey* and was interested in our experience. We spent a few hours telling her about ourselves, and she was utterly enthralled with our story. She said that we should be telling it to the world, and she gave me the name of a friend who just happened to be a lawyer. She said that, if we needed any advice on publication law, Mike Farris was a great person to ask. I took the card she offered but didn't think I would need it. Our focus was on making The Soap Barista profitable, not legal stuff, and we didn't believe for one second that Amanda Hayward would interfere with that. Boy, were we wrong.

The first interference came when several authors from Coffee Shop contacted us about ordering soap as a way to market their books. The idea was that they would pick a fragrance that complemented their novel, put a picture of the book cover on the soap, and give it away as a prize for blog giveaways or at book signing events. We were excited to help some of the friends we had made in the publishing venture as well as to have a new avenue through which to sell our soap. And so, the idea of custom soap orders was born, and we began marketing to authors on the Internet.

Unfortunately, Amanda and Cindy Bidwell got word of this venture and told their authors that they could not use The Soap Barista as a marketing tool. Coffee Shop owned the copyrights to the covers, they said, and they wouldn't let the authors use Coffee Shop material on our soap. This didn't stop authors from buying the soap for marketing ideas; we just had to get creative on how we packaged the product.

Additionally, this forced Christa and me to understand that we had eyes on us. We were trying to move on, but it appeared spies watched our every move. The authors were afraid to publicly cross Amanda, fearing that she would retaliate. Having been on the receiving end of Amanda's wrath, I understood that, and I was thankful for their support, even if it had to be behind the scenes.

We still needed exposure for our fledgling company, so when *Fort Worth Weekly*'s Jeff Prince asked to interview us for a story about how we went from teachers to soap-makers, Christa and I thought it would be great free advertising. *Fort Worth Weekly* was not a large publication, boasting a circulation of only about 75,000 people in the Dallas-Fort Worth area, but we thought the article would target our geographic market. We didn't have ulterior motives or grand schemes of vengeance against Amanda, but we wanted to get our company into the public eye.

So, we sat down with Jeff Prince for the interview, but the more we talked, and the more Jeff revealed what he already knew from his own research, the more worried we became. It was as if he were shining a light on all the dark details of what had transpired over the last couple of years, and it illuminated some difficult memories. Christa, Kera, my husband, and I also worried about what Amanda, who could be vindictive, might do when the article was released. Then I remembered the card that Milli Brown had given me, and I left a message with Mike Farris to schedule a meeting.

Mike returned the call promptly and, sitting in a car in the parking lot of Target, Christa and I spoke to him for about thirty minutes. He was straightforward and gave us some good advice, so we scheduled to meet with him the following week. We needed to talk about the non-compete clause and, more importantly, we needed to know what could happen when the article hit the virtual stands.

As Christa and I stood on the ground floor of the enormous skyscraper, I thought how appropriate the setting was. We were starting a journey against what looked to be insurmountable odds. We wanted to move forward with our lives, but neither of us wanted to keep looking over our shoulders, wondering when Amanda would strike. But what could we do if she did?

Maybe Mike would have some ideas.

Mike's Story

I didn't know what to expect when Jenny Pedroza and Christa Beebe arrived at my office. I knew only that they were interested in setting up a book publishing venture and were concerned about the implications of a non-compete agreement they had signed while with a previous publisher. I had no idea our discussion would involve the publishing blockbuster *Fifty Shades of Grey*, which, I feel compelled to add, I hadn't read and didn't intend to.

I greeted them in the firm's reception area when they arrived. Jenny, who I would later learn possessed a naturally buoyant and bubbly personality, seemed subdued, as did Christa, when I led them to my office. We sat at a table by the window that looked north, through which I could literally look down into the office on the 15th floor of Republic Bank Tower, now part of what is called Republic Center, that I occupied when I first started practicing law at Vial Hamilton Koch & Knox more than 30 years before. After some opening pleasantries, they got to the heart of what brought them to see me.

"Christa and I used to work for a publishing company that published e-books and print-on-demand books," Jenny said, "and we want to open a company of our own, but we signed contracts that have clauses that say we can't compete. Milli thought you could tell us if there's any way to get around that."

"That depends on what the clause says. For it to be enforceable, it has to be reasonable both in geographic area and duration. Do you have the contract with you?"

She handed me a copy of what was titled a "Service Agreement" that she had signed with a company called TWCS Operations Pty Limited ACN. On the front page, it also contained a logo for something called The Writer's Coffee Shop Publishing House.

"What's TWCS Operations?" I asked.

"It's a new company that was set up to take over the publishing business from The Writer's Coffee Shop. That was the first publishing company."

I had never heard of a "Pty Limited" company, so I asked, "What kind of company is TWCS Operations? What country is it in?"

"It's in Australia."

Surely, I thought, the non-compete clause was at least limited to Australia, and it shouldn't cause Jenny and Christa any problems if they formed a company in Texas. Or so I thought.

I flipped through the agreement until I came to page four and a section entitled "Post Termination Restraint." I read through it, amazed at how broad it was, on its face. The time restraints were likely reasonable—24 months or less—but the area restraint was not.[4]

The contract provided:

Restraint Area means the area bounded by:

(a)   Global; or if that is found to be unreasonable by a

---

[4] I later dealt with an Australian lawyer who represented Amanda Hayward, and who may have been responsible for drafting this contract. If so, his correspondence with me was consistent with the quality of this contract.

court of competent jurisdiction the period[5] in clause (b) below.

(b)   Australia; or if that is found to be unreasonable by a court of competent jurisdiction, the period in clause (c) below

(c)   New South Wales; or if that is found to be unreasonable by a court of competent jurisdiction the period in clause (d) below

(d)   100 kilometres from Cherrybrook, NSW; or if that is found to be unreasonable by a court of competent jurisdiction, the period in clause (e) below

(e)   15 kilometres from the Service Provider's place of work with the Customer

Think about the implications of that language. It showed that the draftsman already knew that the geographic area was unreasonably broad, since it continually referred to a lesser area if the prior one was "found to be unreasonable by a court of competent jurisdiction." That told me that Australian law imposed the same "reasonable" geographic area restrictions as did Texas law, so the fact that the agreement mandated that Australian law applied raised no concerns.

Who can doubt that "global" was unreasonably broad? The successive lesser areas—Australia, New South Wales, and Cherrybrook—freed Jenny and Christa, who wanted to set up their business in Texas. If you got to it, though, the last area might be problematic: 15 kilometers from the "service provider's" place of work. By definition in the respective

---

[5] This was probably supposed to be "area" instead of period, but let's not quibble over small mistakes. Let's save the quibbling for bigger things.

agreements, Jenny or Christa was the "service provider," while TWCS Operations was the "customer." In other words, this clause prohibited Jenny and Christa from competing with Amanda within 15 kilometers of their (Jenny's and Christa's) homes. This was either a simple error in draftsmanship or incompetence. Either way, I doubted if a court would enforce it.

The bottom line was that I didn't believe my office visitors had anything to fear from the non-compete clause.

The next question that Jenny and Christa asked was a little more unclear. "We started a soap-making business out of Christa's house," Jenny said, and "we're talking to a reporter for *Fort Worth Weekly* who is interested in writing a story about our soap business. But he's also interested in the work we did for The Writer's Coffee Shop when it published *Fifty Shades of Grey* and how we got fired. What can we say that won't get us sued?"

That was a helluva question. "If someone wants to sue you, it doesn't matter what you do or don't say. All you can do is try to minimize the chances, but there are no guarantees."

"How do we minimize it?"

"Well, tell me what happened."

For the next half hour or so, Jenny and Christa outlined a tale that had my mind reeling. I would find out more details in the coming months, but the story, in a nutshell, was this:

Coffee Shop was formed a few years earlier by Jenny and Amanda Hayward—who lived in Sydney, New South Wales, Australia. At some point, two other women became involved: Jennifer McGuire, of Waxahachie, Texas, and Lea Dimovski, also of Australia. Jenny and Amanda originally formed Coffee Shop as a fan-based website to discuss books, to blog, and to help writers get published, and it soon started publishing e-books and print-on-demand books (POD).

Christa later went to work for Coffee Shop as an employee, and at some point, both Jenny and Christa quit their teaching jobs to work at Coffee Shop full-time.

Between mid-2011 and early 2012, Coffee Shop published *Fifty Shades of Grey*, *Fifty Shades Darker*, and *Fifty Shades Freed*, all by E.L. James, as e-books and POD paperbacks. In March of 2012, Coffee Shop sold the publishing rights to all three of the *Fifty Shades* books to Random House in a seven-figure deal, plus a share of the sales proceeds for a certain period of time. Jenny wasn't sure of the exact terms because Amanda never showed her the contract.

Although the women (Amanda, Jenny, McGuire, and Dimovski) operated Coffee Shop as a partnership, they didn't have a written partnership agreement. Jenny had prepared one and circulated it to her partners in November of 2011, but it was never fully executed. Still, the IRS had issued an employer identification number to Coffee Shop as a partnership in February of 2011, and Coffee Shop filed a partnership tax return for 2011.

In the summer of 2012, Amanda Hayward started telling her partners that the partnership needed to be restructured into some other type of business entity for "tax reasons." She said that her lawyers and accountants told her this was the only way to minimize taxes on the company, particularly now that the *Fifty Shades* publishing rights had been sold. In late 2012, Amanda set up a company called TWCS Operations Proprietary Ltd. and, in November, Hayward sent "service agreements" to both Jenny and Christa, which essentially made them independent contractors of TWCS Operations.

Amanda told Jenny that she would funnel her share of profits from the Random House deal to her as salary, along with a signing bonus of fifty thousand dollars, which would help her tax-wise.

The service agreements, identical except for the job titles and compensation terms, both contained a clause that permitted Amanda to terminate either, or both, of them without cause on seven days' notice. The termination clause bothered both Jenny and Christa, and Jenny asked about it in an email. Amanda responded that she "would NEVER do that to you even if we fall out and have a huge fight. Out of respect to you and our friendship. I swear on my daughters [SIC] lives...."

Putting their trust in Amanda, Jenny and Christa both signed agreements in November of 2012, and Jenny received the fifty thousand dollar signing bonus. Less than a year later, in the fall of 2013, Amanda terminated both of them after the school year had already started so that it was too late for them to find teaching jobs for that year.

By the time they finished their story, I couldn't believe what I had heard. "Was the partnership ever dissolved?" I asked.

"No," Jenny said.

"Were you ever formally expelled from the partnership?"

"Well, she terminated me."

"Yeah, from TWCS Operations, but that's not The Writer's Coffee Shop."

"No, nothing from The Writer's Coffee Shop."

"Did you ever sign any documents to convert the partnership to this other company?"

"No. I think she just set that up as a new company on her own."

I sat quietly for a second, collecting my thoughts. Finally, I said, "It sounds to me like The Writer's Coffee Shop not only was a partnership, it's still a partnership. That means you're still a partner. Do you know how much money the partnership has been paid by Random House?"

"No. Amanda wouldn't tell me."

"Let me look into this a little more, okay? For now, I think I can safely say that the non-compete in the service agreements shouldn't be a problem. And as far as the interview, like I said, there are no guarantees. But as long as you don't say anything defamatory, like accusing Amanda of dishonesty or committing a crime, and just stick to what happened, without characterizing her in any way, I think you're on safe ground."

I paused, and then added, "And let me give the whole partnership thing some thought. It doesn't sit right with me."

Jenny's Story

As we sat with Mike in his office and told him the whole, unvarnished story, it was hard for me to recount everything that had happened. Not because I didn't remember, but because it meant admitting to him and to Christa, and ultimately to myself, how blinded I had been.

I had acted like a fool.

Even when I knew better and should have sought help, I continued to trust Amanda.

That was not an easy pill to swallow, but to lift myself up, I had to start at the bottom.

Amanda had been responsible for putting us here, and she was still making our lives difficult. We were trying to make the best of a bad situation, but it seemed as if she was always there to keep us from moving forward.

I didn't think I could have gotten any further to the bottom than I was that day.

CHAPTER FOUR: Lawyer and Letters and Threats, Oh My!

Lions and tigers, and bears, oh my!
  —Dorothy in *Wizard of Oz*

Jenny's Story

A FEW DAYS after meeting with Mike, Christa and I spoke again to Jeff Prince of *Fort Worth Weekly*. Almost as soon as I finished the interview, and feeling pretty proud of myself, my husband looked at me and said, "Really? Jenny, what are you doing? You know she's going to find out about this, and you're going to hear from her. I give it twenty-four hours after publication."

I honestly didn't see that Christa and I had done anything wrong. We had simply told the story of how two veteran teachers quit their jobs to help market the biggest-selling romance book in the world, and how I had helped to build a company that took on the author and worked to get her on the top of *The New York Times* best sellers list. That had to be newsworthy. But after listening to my husband, I started worrying. Mike had told me anyone can sue for anything if they felt slighted, even if there was no legal basis for it. You might be able to win the lawsuit, he said, but you couldn't keep them from filing it.

Mickey suggested I call Jeff and see how he was going to spin the article, which I did. He was a very nice man, listening patiently as I had a mini-breakdown on the phone. When I finished telling him my concerns about retaliation, he said, "Man, this almost sounds like an abusive relationship."

That statement brought me to my knees. Here was a man who knew only what he had found on the Internet about the publication of *Fifty Shades of Grey*, plus what I had told him about my time with the publishing house, and even he saw right through the dysfunctional relationship I had been blind to. I didn't know if our conversation caused him to change anything in his article, but he assured me he would post only facts he had found on his own, plus my feelings on my tenure and release from the company. He, of course, didn't have a crystal ball, but he would do his best to write the story as innocuously as he could.

Well, darned if Mickey wasn't right. Not 24 hours after the article, called "Soap Opera," hit the Internet, I received a threatening cease-and-desist letter, attached to an email, from Cindy Bidwell. A few days later, I received a second cease-and-desist, this time from an Australian attorney writing on Amanda's behalf.

Christa and I knew we needed legal help. So, with a small retainer fee, Mike Farris became our attorney, and our version of Tom Cruise was on the case.

Mike's Story

A few weeks after I first met with Jenny and Christa, I heard from them again. Unfortunately, it was not to tell me they had successfully set up a publishing business of their own or that their soap-making venture was going great guns. It was not even to tell me how well their interview had gone with *Fort Worth Weekly*. Instead, they had heard from "down under"—threats of a lawsuit.

On February 10, Jenny emailed me:

Good Morning Mike,

Christa Beebe and I came to your office in January with our story about The Writer's Coffee Shop Publishing House. We were being interviewed by Fort Worth Weekly and wanted to know our legal rights under the contract we signed. The article did run, and as you can probably suspect, we have been given a Cease and Desist Notice from TWCS.

We would like to retain you as our lawyer in helping us not only decipher these documents, but also counsel us as to how to move forward.

I am attaching the two Cease and Desist Notices to this email as well as giving you the link to the article from Fort Worth Weekly.

Link to article —
http://www.fwweekly.com/2014/01/29/soap-opera/

We will call you later this morning, but I wanted to get these to you first so that you would have them as we talked.

The Breach Letter was sent first by Cindy Bidwell.
The TWCS Operations Pty. Limited was sent yesterday.

Jenny Pedroza

My first emotion was curiosity: What had they said to the reporter to generate a cease-and-desist letter? Not just one cease-and-desist letter, but *two* cease-and-desist letters. I knew they were uneasy about Amanda Hayward and how she might respond to the interview but come on! Amanda was literally on the other side of the world; Jenny and Christa had been booted from the business; Jenny had been (in my opinion) screwed out of her interest in a very profitable partnership; they were both out of work and scrambling to generate income for their families; and both appeared understandably despondent and subdued when I talked to them in my office. What could they possibly have said in a limited circulation local paper to spark any kind of response from Australia?

I clicked on the link to the *Fort Worth Weekly* article, titled "Soap Opera," and began reading what was a pretty straightforward account of Jenny's and Christa's time with Coffee Shop. Far less detail than they had given me. By the time I finished, I was shaking my head. There was nothing defamatory in the article as far as I could see. I read it a second time, focusing now simply on negative comments, even if true. There were occasional statements that might reflect poorly on Amanda, but even those were inferential, at worst, and appeared to be entirely factual. And even most of those were the writer's words, not Jenny's or Christa's.

For example, writer Jeff Prince started this way:

Fifty Shades of Grey became 50 shades of blush for an Arlington woman who made a bad business deal. Jenny Pedroza helped introduce the masses to one of the hottest sellers in the history of books. Now she's embarrassed that she wound up with almost none of the money after being "outmaneuvered" by a former business partner.

"You live and you learn," Pedroza said. "Don't just take a handshake."

If anything, that was a back-handed compliment to Amanda for being a savvy businesswoman.

33

The article described a restructuring of the business to show that Amanda was a sole proprietor, something she said was "for tax purposes." When Amanda approached Jenny and Christa with documents to sign, Jenny said, "I never got a lawyer. I just trusted." And, when the publishing rights to *Fifty Shades* were sold, the amount of money Jenny received was "unfairly small." Prince went on to write Jenny felt "silly that she didn't hire a lawyer to protect her interests...." Again, nothing defamatory there, just a retrospective acknowledgement that Amanda had, again, "outmaneuvered" her. Maybe you could read something into "I just trusted," but it was a stretch to interpret that as defamatory.

In the latter half of the article, Jenny and Christa acknowledged the business restructuring "created red flags," but "they considered Hayward a friend who was looking out for all of their best interests." The article quoted Jenny as saying, "I trusted blindly." Again, perhaps an inference Amanda hadn't acted in a trustworthy fashion but, still, simply more of a reflection on being outmaneuvered.

I thought I must have missed something somewhere in the article. Time to read the cease-and-desist letters, to see if they might direct my attention to something specific in the article I had overlooked.

The first letter, dated February 1 and addressed to both Jenny and Christa, was written on TWCS Publishing House letterhead and bore Amanda Hayward's name at the bottom of the second page. It quoted the confidentiality clause of the respective service agreements they had signed with TWCS Operations, including language that stated that "you are bound by this even after the cessation of your's [SIC] and TWCS's relationship." The letter concluded:

In view of this, I must ask you both to cease and desist using TWCS and it's [SIC] association with Random House, E.L. James and The Fifty

Shades of Grey Conglomerate or any other information protected by the above clauses as fodder for your own self gain or for any other purpose. Failure to comply with this request will result in TWCS taking appropriate legal action.

The service agreements defined "confidential information" as "any information relating to the business or operations of a Party which is of a confidential or commercially sensitive nature." Not only was no "confidential or commercially sensitive" information contained in the *Fort Worth Weekly* article, nor did the letter point out what was alleged to be confidential or sensitive, but the bulk of the article discussed the history of events with Coffee Shop, not TWCS Operations. It was TWCS Operations that was the other party to the service agreements, though, not Coffee Shop.

Maybe, I thought, the lawyer's letter will be more helpful, or at least more specific, so I could figure out what the complaint was. It came from "Fontgalland Lawyers" in Sydney, Australia, and was signed by someone with the overly-complicated name of Gaurav de Fontgalland as "Managing Director/Solicitor." The word solicitor told me that he was what I would call an office lawyer—dealing with non-litigation matters—and not a trial lawyer, which would have been a barrister.

de Fontgalland quoted extensively from the service agreements, and then listed specific information that he contended was confidential. He said that Jenny and Christa "have revealed the Confidential Information to third parties, namely Jeff Prince, who has published the Confidential Information in a recent article in Fort Worth Weekly titled 'Soap Opera' (the **Article**)."

He claimed that, because of the article, his client lost six book titles that were scheduled to be published, as well as future authors, and its reputation had been damaged. He then made this demand:

We are instructed to hereby demand that you undertake the following by no later than 5 pm on Monday, 17 February 2014 (the Due Date):

(i)   cease and desist all communication regarding the Confidential Information:

(ii)   cease and desist any claims in the ownership rights in the Intellectual Property;

(iii)   cease and desist all communication with any customer of the Company;

(iv)   cease and desist all reference to the Article on media forms, including, but not limited to, your website; and

(v)   provide us with a written undertaken (the Undertaking) confirming that you have complied, and will continue to comply, with the actions set out in [(i)-(v)].

If Jenny and Christa failed to comply, the letter concluded, he would file suit against them on behalf of his client and would seek "injunctive relief and/or damages."

When Jenny and Christa first called me to talk about the letters, I pressed them for more information about the interview process. I learned that the bulk of what de Fontgalland claimed was confidential information was actually information that the reporter, Jeff Prince, had learned for himself through Internet research, and that he came armed with questions based upon that. Neither Jenny nor Christa had "revealed" it to him. Instead, it was already publicly available information.

I could tell, though, that the letter had scared Jenny and Christa, and why wouldn't it? A threatening letter from a lawyer with a fancy name was intended to do just that: scare someone into submission. And if the person who received such a letter had done something wrong, maybe she needed to be scared. But not these two women. They had done absolutely nothing wrong or improper. The mere fact that Amanda had been behind sending two cease-and-desist letters showed me that she was a bully. Jenny and Christa had been terminated and left jobless, and now Amanda was kicking them when they were down.

I asked them to send me additional documentation, including copies of the service agreements, so that I would be better informed when I responded to de Fontgalland's cease-and-desist. Jenny emailed those to me and raised an additional question about the proposed publishing venture she and Christa planned to launch. Even though I had already told her I believed the non-compete provisions in their service agreements were not enforceable, these letters upped their concerns. As Jenny put it, "We would just like to revisit that in light of all of this."

So not only was Amanda kicking them when they were down, she had her foot on their throats and was refusing to let them get on with their futures.

It pissed me off royally!

I prepared a response letter, ran it by Jenny and Christa to approve, then sent it via email to de Fontgalland on February 14. I started by taking a jab at the language of the service agreement, and I pointed out that it was poorly worded, defining "confidential information" as information that is of a "confidential or commercially sensitive nature." In other words, it defined "confidential information" as information that is confidential. Brilliant!

I then rebutted, point by point, his claims that Jenny and Christa had disclosed confidential information.

For starters, much of the information contained in the article by Jeff Prince that you referenced was information Mr. Prince uncovered on his own and then simply followed up with questions, as opposed to information that was "revealed" by Ms. Pedroza or Ms. Beebe. Assuming for the sake of argument, though, that it was information they provided, your use of the term "revealed" is a misnomer as the information was already public knowledge before the interview was given.

Let's take them one at a time:

"5(i) information regarding the establishment of the Company, including but not limited to, funding, demonstrated in the Article by the discussion of an investor in the Company." The "discussion" you refer to is one simple line: "The Aussie investor Dimov began handling more managerial duties." No attribution is given to Ms. Pedroza or Ms. Beebe as being the source of that information, but the fact of Ms. Dimov's role and involvement in The Writer's Coffee Shop ("TWCS") was easily found on the Internet long before the article was published.

"5(ii) information regarding the Company's confidential agreement with Random House Incorporated demonstrated by the statement in the Article that 'the (Company) sold the rights to Random House for seven figures and a percentage on future e-book sales." Again, there is no attribution made to Ms. Pedroza or Ms. Beebe as the source of this information, but it was widely available on the Internet and print media long before the article. In fact, Amanda Hayward even gave an interview in which she corrected the interviewer who referred to the sale as having been for one million dollars by saying, "It wasn't one million dollars; it was a seven million dollar figure. . . a seven number figure." A slip of the tongue, perhaps, in stating that the price was seven million dollars, but it's clear that Ms. Hayward, herself, has been comfortable discussing the terms of the deal publicly. That hardly makes the information confidential.

"5(iii) information regarding the Company's confidential agreement with the [sic] Erika Leonard (the Author), demonstrated by the revelation of the Author's confidential name in the Article." Once again, there is no attribution made to Ms. Pedroza or Ms. Beebe as being the source of this information, but it was widely available on the Internet and print media long before the article. Biography.com, for

example, begins its synopsis of the author with the words: "E.L. James was born Erika Leonard in London, England, in 1963."

"5(iv) information regarding the financial earnings of the Company, demonstrated by the statement that 'Hayward collected a million bucks from selling the book rights.'" See the above discussion regarding the public nature of the purchase price and Ms. Hayward's admission that it was actually more than a "million bucks." Once the cat is out of the bag, the information is no longer confidential — particularly when your own client opened the bag.

"5(v) information regarding the policies of the Company, demonstrated by the statement that '(you) were shoved out, along with many of the company's two dozen employees.'" For starters, the Company's "policies" are not defined as "confidential information." Secondly, the Agreements specify that the company's "policies and procedures do not form part of this agreement." And thirdly, nothing in the Agreements suggests that termination of an employee is confidential in nature. The mere fact that, one day an employee works for the company and the next day she does not, pretty much puts a public face on the no-longer-employed status of the now-former employee. In fact, Ms. Hayward disseminated an e-mail on November 1, 2013, to a wide distribution list, including authors who published with TWCS but who were not employees, stating that Ms. Pedroza and Ms. Beebe were leaving TWCS — and that Ms. Hayward was the one who made the decision. Perhaps your client is simply unhappy with the phrase "shoved out," but are you really suggesting that it was Company policy to "shove out" employees?

I addressed a few other points from de Fontgalland's letter, including his claim that, by saying she was "a founder" of the company and the amount of money she received was "unfairly small," Jenny was somehow laying claim to "intellectual property" belonging to TWCS. I pointed out that TWCS, itself, issued a press release that called Jenny one of four women who "created" the company. I also noted there's a big difference between a claim of inadequate compensation and a claim of ownership to the publishing rights to *Fifty Shades*.

I concluded with this paragraph, rattling a saber or two in the process:

The bottom line is that there is nothing from which Ms. Pedroza or Ms. Beebe should cease and desist as they have not violated any terms of their Agreements. Nevertheless, and without any admission, they have removed the link to the Fort Worth Weekly article from their website. What should be of more concern to your client is the conduct of Amanda Hayward in restructuring TWCS from a partnership into a different type of entity under Ms. Hayward's control that disenfranchised Ms. Pedroza as an equal partner and permitted Ms. Hayward to avoid properly accounting for proceeds from the sale of Fifty Shades to Random House. That conduct casts doubt on the validity of the Agreement, in any event.

I didn't want to goad Amanda into filing a lawsuit, but I did want her, and her lawyer, to know that, if she did, Jenny had legal claims of her own.

It didn't take de Fontgalland long to respond, sending me a letter the next day. He started by accusing my letter of containing a "number of inaccuracies, including but not limited to": stating that Jenny and Christa had not disclosed confidential information to Jeff Prince; stating that the confidential information was already publicly known; stating that Amanda Hayward had already disclosed the same information to third parties; and stating that Jenny and Christa had never asserted any ownership rights to TWCS company. Of course, he didn't point to any facts to show that my statements were inaccurate. It was the legal equivalent of a childhood response to a taunt by saying, "Oh, yeah?"

He then repeated his threats of litigation unless Jenny and

Christa complied with his demands.

I had hoped the bullying from down under would cease after my initial response, but the latest letter repeated the prior threats. I knew that, no matter what Jenny and Christa did or didn't do, there was always a chance that Amanda would sue them for some perceived slight or breach. The question was how to head that off. The answer might be a pre-emptive lawsuit.

Jenny's Story

What do you think a girl from Arlington, Texas, does when she gets not one, but two, mean cease-and-desist letters from a country on the other side of the world? It wasn't pretty. Mickey and I had been married for 18 years by this time, and he had witnessed my grumblings about state tests, uncontrollable students, unfeeling administrators, and uncaring parents. It amazed me that he could listen to my stories for so long and often give me good advice about how to proceed. Don't get me wrong, there were nights when he would tell me, "Let's not talk about school tonight."

However, on the whole, he was a very good listener. So, when I got those letters and lost my mind, my husband was right there. I knew he wanted to give me the dreaded, "I told you so," but he waited until years later, when I was writing this book, to remind me to put that in. I thought my life, as I knew it, was over. I had never been threatened with a lawsuit before, and my first thought was, "What could she sue me for? I don't have anything." Then I thought, "Could they just throw me in jail because I don't have anything for her to take?" Maybe that was irrational, but I was a layperson and I didn't know anything about lawsuits. Drastic times called for drama of the highest order.

When I saw the first cease-and-desist letter, I called Christa to see if she had read it. The conversation went something like this:

> Me: *"Have you seen it yet?"*
> Christa: *"Yes."*
> Me: *"What are we going to do?"*
> Christa: *"She's never going to go away. Why won't she just go away?"*
> Me: *"How did she even find out about the article?"*
> Christa: *"What did Mick say? Should we reply?"*
> Me: *"Hell, no! What would we even say? Mickey is freaking out but says not to reply."*
> Christa: *"Should we call the lawyer guy?"*

We didn't respond to Cindy's letter, but we maintained a sliver of hope that, if we took down the article from our soap website, they would leave us alone. On February 10, 2014, we realized they were never going to leave us alone. The second letter was even more terrifying because it came from a lawyer, but this time we sent for reinforcements. Mike's response letter represented the first real moment when I felt someone was on our side. Christa and I both thought it was the best letter we had ever read. It blew each of the Australian lawyer's points out of the water with simple rebuttals. He didn't need thesaurus words to sound smart. His response was brilliant in a "real world" way that made those fancy words sound haughty.

We were both shocked when the second letter from the Australian lawyer came but, once again, it was full of vagueness and ambiguity. And once again, we leaned on Mike. Without him, we would have crumbled. We would have taken one look at those wordy legal drafts and thought we were done. Maybe that was the response they were hoping for but, fortunately for Christa and me, we had a dynamo on our side. He not only understood what they were trying to say, but he could spin it back to them in words we understood. Those cease-and-desist letters changed everything. Without those, we would never have talked again with Mike, and we would never have planted the seed for the groundbreaking lawsuit that followed.

I want to believe that Amanda now looks back on those letters and wishes she had left well enough alone. The public would have forgotten the article in a few weeks' time. Had Amanda not sent those letters, Mike and I wouldn't have met at a coffee house a few weeks later to talk about a lawsuit and, most importantly, she wouldn't have found her name splashed across every newspaper from New York to Saigon, with all the details from the trial.

I am forever thankful for Milli Brown and the card she handed me that day. I am thankful for Mike Farris for agreeing to see us and help us deal with Amanda, and I am utterly thankful that I first took that long elevator ride up to the 41st floor to meet with the man who soon became my friend.

CHAPTER FIVE: Contingency

Hope may inspire and inveigle us, but we cannot just live on hope. Certainly, love can be hope, but it is merely a contingency, since it might either mend our life or break our heart.

——Erik Pevernagie

Mike's Story

NO MATTER HOW hard I tried, I couldn't get Jenny's plight out of my mind. I didn't know how much money Coffee Shop had made from the sale of the *Fifty Shades* publishing rights, but it had to be in the millions. After all, nearly one hundred million copies of the book had been sold by then. I believed, based upon what Jenny told me and the limited documents I had seen, that Coffee Shop was a partnership and Jenny was a partner, which meant she was entitled to her proportionate share of the company's profits, whatever they might be. It was clear Jenny didn't fully understand that but, as I once heard someone say, "Even if you don't know what you have, it doesn't mean you don't have it."

I knew that, if Jenny filed suit to assert her rights as a partner, it would almost guarantee a counterclaim from Amanda. But I also knew it was quite likely Amanda might sue her anyway, probably in Australia. It seemed to me the safest route was to sue first, in Texas. Better to be counterclaimed against in Texas than sued in Australia.

At a weekend construction law seminar in San Antonio in late February of 2014, I discussed Jenny's situation over dinner with my wife, and one of the law firm's partners and his wife. I was mostly looking to bounce ideas off them but also to confirm my thinking about the law of partnerships was correct. All at the table concurred with my opinion.

I then had to consider how Jenny could finance what would be an expensive litigation. One of two things might happen if she filed a lawsuit against Amanda and TWCS Operations in Texas. One was Amanda would ignore it and Jenny would obtain a default judgment. I researched the procedure for enforcing a United States judgment in Australia and was surprised to learn there was no treaty between the two countries that permitted recognition of one country's judgments in the other. Instead, we would have to follow a more complicated procedure, although simpler than relitigating the entire case in Australia.

We would have to file a common law action in Australia to enforce the judgment and would have to show five things:

(1) the existence of a final judgment;

(2) the judgment was for a sum certain, or an amount that could easily be calculated;

(3) the judgment was less than twelve years old;

(4) the action in Australia involved the same parties as the lawsuit in the United States where the judgment was obtained; and

(5) the Australian citizen had submitted to the jurisdiction of the American court.

The problem if we got a default judgment was that it would be because Amanda had not submitted to the American court's jurisdiction—number (5)—so we couldn't enforce it in Australia. Although it would be relatively inexpensive to file suit and obtain a default judgment, it would still cost thousands of dollars, and it didn't make sense for Jenny to incur that expense for an unenforceable judgment.

The other thing that might happen if we filed suit in Texas was Amanda would hire a Texas lawyer and contest the lawsuit. If that happened, it would be expensive to litigate the full case, likely hundreds of thousands of dollars in attorneys' fees and expenses. Maybe even a million dollars. But at the end of it, we'd at least have a judgment we could enforce in Australia, because Amanda would have submitted to the American court's jurisdiction. There was no way Jenny could afford the fees, though.

Unless my law firm took the case on a contingency.

I was reluctant to raise the issue with Jenny unless I first had a commitment the firm would agree to a contingency *and* would front the expenses, which themselves could be high. In addition to filing fees, there would be depositions, including possible travel to Australia to conduct discovery, as well as experts' fees. The costs, alone, might easily be six figures, so it would be a major commitment from a 25-lawyer firm like ours, not to mention the risk of pouring thousands of non-billable hours into a case with no guarantee of success. Even if we ended up with a judgment enforceable in Australia, the likelihood existed Amanda might have hidden her assets so we'd still come up empty.

Before I presented it to firm management, though, I needed to determine how strong the case was. That meant hours of research (for which I would not be able to bill) to ensure I had covered every possible legal issue that might arise. When I was satisfied, I drafted a memo to the firm's managing partner, and outlined a "possible contingency case." I attached a number of documents to the memo as exhibits.

Fifty Shades of Black and White

I started this way:

We represent two clients, Jenny Pedroza and Christa Beebe, who were involved with an entity called The Writers Coffee Shop (TWCS), which was the company that discovered and first published the novel Fifty Shades of Grey. The company was originally set up as a partnership of four women, including Ms. Pedroza, but when money appeared on the horizon, one of the partners, Amanda Hayward, duped Ms. Pedroza into going along with a change from partnership to an Australian business entity. For her role in discovering, editing, and marketing Fifty Shades of Grey, Ms. Pedroza was given $50,000 and shown the door. Ms. Beebe, who quit her teaching job to work for TWCS, was also terminated.

I noted that I had not yet discussed a lawsuit with Jenny and Christa, and "at this point, they're a little worried about whether TWCS and Hayward might sue them for allegedly breaching their contracts with TWCS. They also don't have the wherewithal to fund a lawsuit, but if handled on a contingency basis, they may well be willing to go forward."

I included a fairly detailed statement of the facts and a description of how the clients came to my attention.

I first got involved earlier this year when Ms. Pedroza and Ms. Beebe were referred to me by another client, Milli Brown of Brown Books. They were considering whether to open a new publishing company and were concerned that they would be violating the non-compete agreements in their contracts. There was nothing to be done at that point – it was just an initial consultation – then they gave an interview in the Fort Worth Weekly (Exhibit 7) that resulted in their being sent cease and desist letters by an attorney in Australia on behalf of Amanda Hayward. I responded to the letter, and that's when I first began looking a little deeper into this and realized how badly they had been mistreated and that they, or at least Ms. Pedroza, had legitimate claims that could be

47

asserted against Hayward and TWCS.

I concluded with a discussion of these potential causes of action that we could assert if we filed suit:

I think a decent argument can be made that the service agreements were induced by fraud and are void ab initio. If we filed a lawsuit, I would want to assert that and to seek a declaratory judgment invalidating the contracts. That would also entitle us to recover our attorney's fees.

I also believe that Amanda Hayward has breached her fiduciary duty, as a partner, to Jenny Pedroza and that Ms. Pedroza is entitled to her partner's share of any income streams arising out of Fifty Shades and any other book published by TWCS when she was a partner. She has told me she believes that TWCS has gotten at least $20,000,000 from Fifty Shades, but she doesn't know what happened to it — Hayward has not made an accounting, but she has apparently been living high on the hog since the money started flowing. I would want to include a claim for an accounting.

It looks like there is ample ground to assert jurisdiction in Texas: the 2011 Partnership Tax Return for TWCS shows the partnership's address as being in Arlington; Ms. Pedroza and Ms. Beebe both carried out their duties on behalf of TWCS from their homes in Tarrant County; Hayward has made trips to Texas as part of TWCS business, and personally fired Ms. Beebe at her home in Arlington.

I delivered a copy of the memo to the firm's management. After several follow-up conversations, they gave me the go-head to discuss with Jenny and Christa their options and the firm's openness to undertake the case on a contingency basis. I emailed Jenny on April 9 and said, "Just wanted to touch base and see if you've heard anything else from TWCS or Amanda. I'm leaving town tomorrow on vacation but would like to talk to you about a couple of things when I get back."

After Susan and I returned from a week-and-a-half in west

Texas, including five days of strenuous hiking through beautiful Big Bend National Park, I made arrangements to meet with Jenny on Tuesday afternoon, May 6, at a Starbucks in Mansfield, Texas, near her home. Over coffee, we talked more about her time at Coffee Shop, Amanda's actions and threats, and what I believed was a strong claim by Jenny that she was entitled to share in the profits from Coffee Shop's sale of the *Fifty Shades* publishing rights to Random House.

"If that's something you're interested in," I said, "I think the firm will agree to take the case on a contingency, including fronting all expenses. I'm not authorized to promise that right now, but I need to know if you're interested in proceeding."

Jenny paused before answering. "What worries me is that Amanda may try to retaliate."

"That's always a possibility. She could file a counterclaim, but it might prevent her from filing a pre-emptive lawsuit in Australia. I've done some research on whether we could get an injunction to prohibit her from filing a suit against you down there, and I think the law is on our side."

"What if she files a lawsuit in Australia, anyway?"

"She could do that even if you don't sue her here."

"I'm going to have to think about this. The other thing that worries me is, what if Amanda retaliates by doing something to Christa or my parents? They've already lost their jobs. I don't want to get them sued just because Amanda does something in retaliation."

I knew from my prior conversations with Jenny and Christa that, not only had Christa quit her teaching job to work for Coffee Shop, but she had also passed up an opportunity to go back to work as a teacher based upon a guarantee from Amanda, made in writing in an email in the spring of 2013, that she would have her job for at least the 2013-2014 school year. Amanda then terminated her in mid-fall of 2013, leaving Christa unemployed for the rest of the school year.

"I can't guarantee she won't," I said, "but it might make sense for Christa to be part of a lawsuit here. She wasn't a partner, but I think she has a claim for breach of contract. She would be a plaintiff, too."

"Can I think about it and talk it over with Christa and my mom and dad?"

I knew I had left Jenny with some serious thinking to do. It can be just as scary to be a plaintiff in a lawsuit as it is to be a defendant, especially if the lawsuit invited a counterclaim. I believed that this one would. After all, Jenny had already been threatened with a lawsuit simply for giving an interview to *Fort Worth Weekly*. If she and Christa proceeded with setting up a publishing company, I had no doubt that Amanda, once she got wind of it, would do her best to shut them down, one way or the other. If we could bring together all of the potential issues involving the partnership question and the enforceability of the service agreement into one lawsuit in one place at one time, we might be able to resolve, finally, the rights and relationship between Jenny and Amanda and remove that uncertainty from Jenny's future.

Jenny's Story

Reading Mike's story above was the first time I knew how hard he went to bat for us. He and the firm were putting everything on the line for a potential nightmare. I was humbled by their faith in my story and their willingness to help. Cynics have said it's always about the bottom line for lawyers but, when the big picture was in front of them, the bottom line was far away. How do you ever repay someone for taking a chance on you like that?

Right after meeting with Mike at the coffee house, I called my new principal, Julia, who had just given me a job as a fourth-grade reading teacher. I was poised to start teaching again in

August, and I wanted her to know what was coming and the media attention it might garner. I had worked with her at my previous school, and she and I had been through some rough times together. I respected her opinion, and I was grateful for the job, so I didn't want her to regret hiring me after the story broke.

Immediately, she was on board, but she said that she would have to talk to her superiors to make sure there was not a contractual problem. As it turned out, everything was fine. I have now been teaching under her for several years, and I appreciated her support from the beginning.

The idea of a lawsuit not only terrified me, but it also worried me about the future of my family and friends. Amanda knew how much Christa and my family meant to me. It didn't take a genius to figure out that hurting one of them would, in turn, hurt me. Christa, Kera, Mickey, and I talked for hours about what to do. We discussed what might happen if we moved forward but, more importantly we talked about what might happen if we didn't. Amanda's threats to sue over something as inconsequential as an article about soap was a wake-up call. We felt Amanda would hover over us for the rest of our lives, ready to pounce at the next perceived slight. We realized that, if we didn't take a stand, we would never be clear of that.

I wish I could say we made our decision and never looked back, but there were many times, after we decided to move forward, that we all stopped and thought, "What are we doing?" I needed to be sure that, during this process, the rest of my world didn't come crumbling down.

Mike's Story

At 7:50 that evening, Jenny emailed me:

My mind is running as you can imagine. I am so very thankful that we walked into your office that day, and I really appreciate you coming to meet with me...I don't want to put my family or friends in a worse situation than we have been in since November of last year. I have complete faith that you know what you are doing and can see this through.

However, I am most worried about the "ripple effects" of what this will cause. I know you said that she could sue me in Australia, but does that mean your office will help me with that too? I also mentioned Amanda coming after Christa. Is there a way we could make sure her legal fees as a result of any type of counter maneuver on Amanda's part come out of the lawyer fees from this case? The point being that Amanda would not have ever sued her in the first place if she hadn't felt the need for retaliation.

I guess what it boils down to is...if we open this can of worms, will your firm cover those "ripple effect" cases as well?

The next morning, Wednesday, I talked with the firm's managing partner, who agreed that the firm would handle any retaliatory action that Amanda might take. I emailed Jenny back:

I confirmed with our managing partner that, if Amanda were to sue you in Australia, or even counterclaim against you here, we would treat that as part of representing you. As for Christa, it might make sense for me to have a conversation with her about having her join in the lawsuit. She does have a claim for breach of contract, or fraud, based upon Amanda's guarantee of a job until the following school year. If she were part of the lawsuit here, we could include her in our efforts to obtain an injunction to enjoin, or prevent, Amanda from enforcing the service agreements — we would want to specifically include hers.

I spoke to Christa later that day to discuss her options. She had a lot of questions, obviously concerned that, if she joined in the lawsuit, she might stir up vindictive passions in Amanda, but she also realized that could happen anyway, even if she and Jenny did nothing more than simply try to move forward with a publishing business.

Saturday evening, I got their decision. "Christa and I have spent countless hours weighing the pros and cons," Jenny said, "and have agreed that we are both ready to move forward. We appreciate your patience in this. So, I guess, what is the next step? We are ready."

That next step was for me to prepare identical contingency fee contracts for both Jenny and Christa that would commit the firm to taking on Amanda Hayward and TWCS Operations for them.

The "purpose of representation" in the contracts provided:

Client hereby retains and employs Attorneys to sue for and recover all damages and compensation, including attorney's fees, (the "Action") to which Client may be entitled arising out of her involvement with, and/or employment by, The Writers Coffee Shop and/or TWCS Operations Pty Limited and/or Amanda Hayward. This includes defending counter-claims that may be asserted in the Action or asserted separately in another action.

The contracts also committed the firm to "advance all Expenses in connection with Attorneys' representation of Client under this Agreement," and promised that the attorneys—specifically me:

...will represent Client effectively and professionally in the Action. Although Attorneys may offer an opinion about possible results regarding the Action and the subject matter of this Agreement, Attorneys cannot guarantee success or any given result but will strive to represent Client's interests vigorously and efficiently in accordance with the Texas Rules of Professional Responsibility. Client acknowledges that Attorneys have made no promises about the outcome of the Action and that any opinion offered by Attorneys in the future will not constitute a guarantee.

Although the contracts were between Jenny and Christa, respectively, and the firm and me, individually, I felt as if the responsibility rested solely on my shoulders and not the firm's. Once they were signed, I was committed.

Now it was time to get to work.

PART II: JENNIFER LYNN PEDROZA, ET AL V. AMANDA HAYWARD, ET AL

CHAPTER SIX: Fifty Shades of Greed

There is no fire like passion,
there is no shark like hatred,
there is no snare like folly,
there is no torrent like greed.
— Gautama Buddha

Mike's Story

I NEEDED TO gather all the information Jenny and Christa could provide me about their history with Coffee Shop, from the time Jenny and Amanda first "joined forces," as Amanda said in an Internet post in October of 2009, until Amanda terminated the two of them on October 29, 2013. I drafted the Plaintiff's Original Petition with two goals in mind: first, to be as accurate as possible; and second, to be as detailed as possible. Although Texas law requires a petition to include a sufficient statement of facts to put the defendant on fair notice of the basis for the lawsuit, I had seen plenty of lawsuits with sparse factual statements, sometimes nothing more than bare bones, intended simply to get the case into court.

But I wanted Amanda and her lawyers—assuming she contested the lawsuit—to realize we had a solid basis for everything we claimed. Not that it would scare them into submission, but it would evidence how serious we were.

I also had to research the law. Not just Texas law, to see what causes of action I could support with the facts, but also Australian law, in case the defendants argued that the partnership question was controlled by the law where Amanda lived. For starters, I needed to determine whether a Texas court had jurisdiction over an Australian resident.

Texas law provides its courts with "long-arm" jurisdiction—the ability to reach a "long arm" beyond Texas borders—over foreign citizen in two instances. One is "general jurisdiction," which means the foreigner has continuous or systematic contacts with Texas, such as operating a business in Texas. The second is "specific jurisdiction," which means the foreigner has taken actions in, or which involve, Texas that are specifically tied to the subject matter of the lawsuit.

I believed Texas clearly had specific jurisdiction over Amanda. She was a partner (at least under our view of the case) with two Texas partners; their partnership filed a U.S. Return of Partnership Income in the name of Coffee Shop with a given address in Arlington, Texas; the partnership obtained a partnership EIN from the IRS with an address in Arlington; Amanda contracted with Texas residents, Jenny and Christa; Coffee Shop maintained a post office box in Waxahachie, Texas; and Amanda made several trips to Texas promoting Coffee Shop books and authors, including attending the Texas Book Festival in Austin and appearing on the television morning show *Good Morning Texas* in Dallas. If that weren't enough, she physically sat in Christa's house in Arlington, Texas, when she fired both Jenny and Christa.

I wanted to enjoin Amanda from collecting additional

royalty payments from Random House for any of the *Fifty Shades* books. I feared that, if the money got to Australia, a Texas court might not be able to reach it even if we got a judgment. I also wanted to prevent her from spending or hiding whatever money she had already received. I didn't want to win the lawsuit only to find she had successfully secreted everything away.

Additionally, I wanted to prevent Amanda from suing Jenny and Christa in Australia. So, in addition to freezing any assets under Amanda's control that she had gotten from Random House, I wanted an "anti-suit injunction." Texas courts, as a general rule, don't like to interfere with courts in other jurisdictions, and they certainly don't like to tell other courts they can't handle lawsuits that might be properly filed there. The Texas Supreme Court has, however, recognized it is appropriate to enjoin lawsuits in other jurisdictions in certain limited circumstances, including when there might be a threat to a Texas court's jurisdiction. The concern was, if separate lawsuits on the same subject matter proceeded in separate jurisdictions, you might end up with inconsistent rulings, and one of the parties might then "cherry pick" favorable rulings from each court.[6]

Most importantly, I wanted a declaration that Coffee Shop was a partnership and Jenny was a partner. If I could get that, then it followed that Jenny was entitled to her share of Coffee Shop's profits, including whatever money Coffee Shop received from Random House. That figured to be millions.

Texas law defines partnership as "an association of two or more persons to carry on a business for profit as owners...regardless of whether:

(1) the persons intend to create a partnership; or
(2) the association is called a 'partnership,' 'joint venture,'

---

[6] *Golden Rule Ins. Co. v. Harper*, 925 S.W.2d 649 (Tex. 1996).

or other name." [7]

In the absence of a formal written agreement, the courts considered five separate factors in determining whether a partnership existed between "two or more persons":

(1) the persons' receipt or right to receive a share of the profits;

(2) the persons' expression of an intent to be partners in the business;

(3) the persons' participation or right to participate in control of the business;

(4) the persons' agreement to share, or sharing, losses of the business or liability for claims against the business; and

(5) the persons' agreement to contribute, or contributing, property or money to the business. [8]

I committed these five factors to memory because everything I did going forward would revolve around them. I had to view everything—documents, emails, testimony—through that prism. I didn't have to prove all five to establish a partnership, but the more I could prove, the stronger our case. I already strongly believed Coffee Shop was a partnership. The question would be whether I could prove it through anything other than testimony, which Amanda would surely contradict, leaving us a "she said, she said" swearing match. That was another reason why I wanted to create a detailed, accurate statement of facts for the petition to initiate the lawsuit. The more I could document the claims up front, the better equipped I would be later on.

To help me, I enlisted the assistance of an associate in the firm, Brent Turman. Brent was a new, somewhat inexperienced

---

[7] *Texas Business Organizations Code* §152.051(a).

[8] *Texas Business Organizations Code* §152.052.

lawyer, having graduated from SMU Law School just two years prior. He had several things going for him, though, including a burning interest in all phases of entertainment law. The big one, though, was that he was extremely bright and motivated. I would lean very heavily on him throughout the litigation, and I came to know, quickly, that I could count on him for whatever the case needed. He would prove to be invaluable, not only to me, but also to Jenny and Christa, in the days ahead.

When Jenny gave me the go-ahead for the lawsuit, I started working on the petition. I went through various drafts, always running it by Jenny and Christa for their approval. I knew that, once the lawsuit was filed, one of three things would happen. As I discussed before, the first was Amanda would ignore it. The second was Amanda would defend the lawsuit and hire a Texas lawyer to represent her—good for me because that would mean she had submitted to the Texas court's jurisdiction—but then remove the case to federal court. I didn't have any problem with that although it might complicate the procedure a little bit. The third thing was she would simply defend the lawsuit in Texas state court, which was my hope.

I also knew the case was likely to attract media attention merely because of the controversial erotic subject matter. *Fifty Shades of Grey* and its progeny, *Fifty Shades Darker* and *Fifty Shades Freed,* had already sold in figures approaching, if not surpassing, one hundred million copies. E.L. James, the books' author, topped the *Forbes* list of highest-earning authors for the period from June 2012 to June 2013, coming in at $95,000,000, besting such notables as John Grisham, Dan Brown, and Stephen King.

That was another reason why I wanted to be as accurate and detailed as possible in the statement of facts, and why I attached, as exhibits, many of the documents that supported my statements. Not that I wanted to try the case in the press, but my words would be under scrutiny by a lot of microscopes, and my credibility, as well as the credibility of my clients, was at stake.

The petition, itself, ended up being 50 pages and, with exhibits attached, it was 147 pages. I hoped that, if reporters or others bothered to check the filing, they would at least read the start of the petition and then the headings and subheadings I used throughout, to gain a general knowledge of what the lawsuit was about. For that reason, I started with a brief overview, designed to grab attention, that said this:

I. OVERVIEW: FIFTY SHADES OF GREED

This is a case about greed and self-dealing by Amanda Hayward in conning her business partner Jenny Pedroza out of her rightful partnership interest in advances and royalties flowing from the *New York Times* best-selling *Fifty Shades of Grey* trilogy and in fraudulently inducing both plaintiffs into entering into contracts with a sham entity. It appears that Hayward also defrauded, among others, Random House and E.L. James, author of the *Fifty Shades* trilogy.

Pedroza and Hayward, along with two others, were partners in The Writers Coffee Shop ("Coffee Shop"), which was the original publisher of, and owner of the publishing rights to, the *Fifty Shades* trilogy. Without consulting her partner Pedroza, and without complying with Texas law, Hayward tried to convert Coffee Shop into TWCS, an Australian sole proprietorship that she, alone, owned. She signed a contract with Random House (the "Random House Deal") for the rights to the *Fifty Shades* trilogy, in exchange for millions in advances and future royalties but, because of her chicanery, all payments flowed to her and not to the partnership.

The petition contained these causes of action:

(1) It asked the court to declare that Coffee Shop was a Texas partnership, subject to Texas law, and Jenny was a partner entitled to her share of Coffee Shop's profits;

(2) It asserted Amanda had breached her legal duties as a partner and asked for an accounting of the partnership's profits;

(3) It asserted Amanda and TWCS had fraudulently induced Jenny and Christa into signing their respective service agreements, and they had also committed common law and statutory fraud against Jenny and Christa;

(4) It asked the court to rescind, or void, the service agreements;

(5) It asserted Christa was entitled to compensation, under various contract and quasi-contract theories, for Amanda's termination of her after guaranteeing her employment;

(6) It asserted Amanda had converted, or stolen, Jenny's share of partnership profits;

(7) It asked the court to impose a constructive trust on any money Amanda had taken that belonged to the partnership, including any property she had purchased, or investments she had made, with that money;

(8) It asked for punitive damages; and

(9) It asked for a temporary restraining order to be followed by a temporary injunction that would freeze all assets in Amanda's hands, or under her control, that could be traced to profits belonging to the partnership, and also to enjoin, or prevent, Amanda from filing a lawsuit against Jenny or Christa in Australia or anywhere else.

Jenny's Story

As Mike moved into the investigation phase of the case, Christa and I first met Brent. My first impression was that he was young and pretty darn handsome, and almost immediately he jumped into the case. As the days went by, he became a sounding board to not only Christa and me, but also to Mike. Now, Mike was always a cool customer. He never let on that he was worried about any aspect of the case. He did let us in on his concerns about Amanda, but he wasn't worried about them, just aware of them.

He seemed to have a bigger picture in mind. To me, he thought of the case like a giant chessboard. If Amanda made this move, he would counter with that move. He was always looking at the end game and making sure our pieces on the board never got trapped in a checked play. When he talked to us about upcoming pitfalls, he always had an alternate strategy to counteract her next move. If I had not been in the middle of the fight of my life, I would have stepped back just to admire both Mike's and Brent's work. They really seemed prepared for everything.

After Brent joined the team, next came the arduous task of sifting through my thousands of emails to find old conversations that might help prove our case. This was difficult and time-consuming, but more than that, it was hard to look at the evidence of a friendship that incinerated over time. My first emails and Skype conversations with Amanda, and then later with Jenn, were happy and full of promise. Amanda and I had been co-writing a fan fiction story on another site. She had actually started the story some time earlier and asked if I would help her finish writing it. We had a fan base that grew each day. Ours was one of the first stories we published on the Coffee Shop site, and it brought with it a huge following.

Jenn worked hard to set up the website and build the library. She really did a great job learning the coding and making banners for stories. This helped bring new people to our page, and those new views increased advertisement revenue. As Jenn and I worked to bring in more readers, Amanda worked behind the scenes to attract authors that we wanted to publish. Some demurred, but others were interested and we wanted to be able to accommodate them.

Jenn, Amanda, and I worked well together, and we viewed ourselves as equals. I believed in what we were creating, and the three of us shared a joint vision of a bright future full of good books, great stories, and fun times. We each participated in all major decisions about the future of the company, and we leaned heavily on each other. Soon, we started making plans to visit in each other's homes, me traveling to Australia and Amanda to Texas. She and I became very good friends. I enjoyed getting to know her family, and I really enjoyed getting to know her.

There was no way three women from across the globe would ever have been able to start a company like that twenty years ago, but the Internet shrank the world. Since we lived in different hemispheres, our interaction was well documented in hundreds of emails, Skype messages, and I-messages, which detailed the trust we had in each other from the beginning. Unfortunately, the task of sifting through all this meant going back to the beginning of each chain, finding all the conversations, creating folders to document each encounter, and then sending them to Brent to evaluate as potential evidence. It was a tremendous undertaking.

I had most of the beginning conversations, although not necessarily full chains. But Christa...well, Christa doesn't *ever* delete emails. She had over one hundred thousand saved emails the last time I checked. She claimed she kept them just in case she ever needed to find something, and this was one of those times I was glad she did. She was able to find some great references to the partnership, and to Amanda and Jenn talking about the partnership, in those early messages.

So, you can imagine that poor Brent was inundated with countless hours of reading our correspondence. We didn't know much about starting a business or running a publishing company, and that meant many of the emails were about crazy ideas and random life bits that we sometimes talked about for hours. I imagine that, by the end of the first day, he was ready to throw his computer out the window, but he never let on how inane our conversations may have seemed to him. Christa and I noticed a few times, though, that he smirked when we talked about a particular email chain or a chat. I knew he thought I was crazy, but he was always nice about it. I'd like to believe he found our ideas endearing rather than idiotic, but that may just be wishful thinking.

The bottom line was that the emails and other conversations evidenced that we started this operation on a leap of faith in each other as partners. We dreamed of making a living from our hard work, and we relied heavily on each other for support and guidance. We were all in and ready to take on the world.

It took about two months to review all of the messages, and still there were times I double-checked to ensure I hadn't missed anything. We ended up with a mountain of evidence that clearly proved, at least to Mike, Brent, Christa, and me, that both Amanda and I believed that Coffee Shop was a partnership, that we acted like a partnership, and that we portrayed our company to the world as a partnership, from the very start.

Armed with this information, Mike opened his Queen's Pawn Game on the chessboard: He filed the lawsuit.

Mike's Story

On Thursday morning, May 29, my secretary electronically filed our Plaintiff's Original Petition in Tarrant County, and the case was assigned to the 153rd Judicial District Court in Fort Worth, which was presided over by Judge Susan Heygood McCoy. Judge McCoy had been elected to the court in 2012 as a Republican after a 20-year career as a litigator, initially practicing in Dallas after her graduation from the University of Houston Law School and then opening her own firm with a partner in Fort Worth. I had never been in her court but, before this case was over, would spend countless hours there and would develop great respect for her as a judge.

Once the lawsuit was filed, and a court assigned, I emailed a copy to Amanda's Australian attorney, de Fontgalland, at about 12:30 PM. our time, which was 5:30 AM the following morning his time, and told him:

You and I have previously corresponded in matters regarding your representation of Amanda Hayward and TWCS Pty Ltd., and my representation of Jennifer Lynn Pedroza and Christa Beebe. This is to advise you that Ms. Pedroza and Ms. Beebe have today filed the attached lawsuit in the 153rd District Court of Tarrant County, Texas, and will be seeking, this afternoon, (Texas time) to obtain entry of a temporary restraining order against your clients as set forth in the attached pleading.

I figured this would be a mighty fine wake-up present for him that morning, not to mention for Amanda, to whom, I presumed, he would forward the lawsuit.

After lunch, Brent and I drove to Fort Worth to present the application for a temporary restraining order to Judge McCoy. When we arrived, the court clerk told us to wait in the courtroom while she went back to speak to the judge. After about an hour or so, she came back with the TRO signed, not by Judge McCoy, but by Judge Ken Curry, who had been McCoy's predecessor in the 153rd. It was not uncommon for courts to assign visiting judges, who were often retired, to handle matters in the absence of the presiding judge. What was unusual, though, was that Judge Curry had not permitted us to speak to him.

Ordinarily when presenting an application for a TRO, if the defendant is not represented by counsel, the plaintiff's lawyer is permitted to orally present the application.

It is a rare exception to the general rule against *ex parte* communications with a judge, which, translated from Latin, means "of or from one side or party." [9] In other words, only one side is present when the communication is made. Interestingly, though, Judge Curry apparently wanted to make it clear he had not talked with us without the other side present. He handwrote on the order, "Matter considered outside of the presence of all counsel."

That was the only change he made to the order, which I had drafted. It recited the necessary elements for obtaining a TRO, including findings that, unless the TRO was granted, "there is no adequate remedy at law to address the threat to this Court's jurisdiction, [10] or the irreparable injury, loss, or damage as set forth above."

The TRO concluded:

IT IS THEREFORE ORDERED, ADJUDGED AND DECREED that Defendants Hayward and TWCS, and their officers, directors, agents, employees, successors, assigns, representatives, affiliated entities, and any other person or entity acting in concert or participation with them who receives notice of such orders and injunctive relief by personal service or otherwise, be temporarily restrained from:

(a) Enforcing, or attempting to enforce, the Pedroza and Beebe Agreements[11] in any other jurisdiction or court.

---

[9] *Ballantine's Law Dictionary*.

[10] This was what we needed for the anti-suit injunction.

[11] This was a reference to the service agreements that Jenny and Christa had signed with TWCS Operations.

(b) Collecting money from any source, including Random House, Amazon, and Barnes & Noble, that is owed, or will become owed, to Coffee Shop, Hayward, and/or TWCS arising out of the Random House Deal or any publishing contract to which Coffee Shop is or was a party.

(c) Dissipating funds they have already received from any source, including Random House, Amazon, and Barnes & Noble, owed, or to be owed, to Coffee Shop, Hayward, and/or TWCS arising out of the Random House Deal or any publishing contract to which Coffee Shop is or was a party.

(d) Transferring, moving, disposing of, alienating, destroying, or concealing any cash, certificates of deposit, and bank accounts, including all savings and checking accounts, stocks and bonds, mutual funds, and any other intangible assets traceable to the Random House Deal.

(e) Transferring, moving, disposing of, alienating, depleting, destroying, or concealing any tangible assets traceable to the Random House Deal, including real and personal property.

(f) Destroying, altering, concealing, or moving any books, records, accounting records, tax returns, invoices, contracts, and ledgers of Coffee Shop and/or TWCS.

The TRO required us to post a $1,000 bond, and it scheduled a hearing on our application for temporary injunction for June 12, 2014. A TRO was good for only 14 days, which was why we needed the temporary injunction hearing set so quickly. It could be extended once, for an additional 14 days, but otherwise, if you hadn't moved forward with obtaining an injunction, which would last until the end of the lawsuit, then the TRO would lapse. You could still get a hearing set on a temporary injunction later than 14 or 28 days after the start of the TRO, but the risk was that, if the TRO lapsed prior to the hearing, the defendants could then do any or all of the things they had been prohibited from doing until and unless you got a temporary injunction.

To extend a TRO beyond the 14- or 28-day period, you needed an agreement from the other side. As of the date of the TRO, I didn't know if Amanda would hire a lawyer and contest the case or not, so I prepared to go forward with the injunction hearing on June 12.

As part of getting the TRO, I had also asked the judge to order Amanda to produce certain documents, including financial records, that we needed to prepare for the hearing, and he also signed an order granting that request. After Brent and I returned to the office, I emailed de Fontgalland with copies of both orders, and asked if he would accept service of formal process on his clients. He tersely responded, "We are not able to accept service. You will need to organize [SIC] for service to be effected directly on the relevant parties."

He signed his email, "Kind Regards." I suspected his sign-off was insincere, something he proved a few days later when he sent another threatening letter.

Jenny's Story

As soon as Mike told us the lawsuit had been filed, Christa and I were on pins and needles waiting for the other shoe to drop. We knew Amanda would retaliate, causing both of us sleepless nights. We both had witnessed her reactions to others she thought had wronged her, and none of those people had threatened her with an actual lawsuit. That had been the source of our reluctance in deciding whether to sue in the first place: What would Amanda do? We knew her reaction would be angry and it would be fierce. It's why I hadn't stood up to her when she coerced me into signing the service agreement nor later when she terminated Christa and me from TWCS Operations.

But now, Christa and I had lost our jobs and neither of us could get new teaching jobs in the middle of the school year. Our families were suffering, and I felt as if I had nothing else to lose. The difference, this time, was that I had people at my back and truth on my side. Still, we knew a tidal wave of retribution was coming. We just hoped we could hang on.

CHAPTER SEVEN: The Battle is Joined

It is a pleasant world you live in, sir, a very pleasant world. There are bad people in it, Mr. Richard, but if there were no bad people, there would be no good lawyers.

—Charles Dickens, The Old Curiosity Shop

Mike's Story

THE DAY AFTER we filed the lawsuit, the first report hit the press. Reuters filed a story under the headline "Texas women sue 'Fifty Shades' publisher for royalties, advances." The article relied on language in the petition, stating that Jenny and Christa had filed a lawsuit "seeking money from the global best-seller that they allegedly were tricked into surrendering by their Australian partner." That wasn't entirely accurate, since neither Jenny nor Christa had surrendered any money, but close enough, I suppose. The article went on to say, "The suit alleges that Hayward cut the two Texas women out of money generated by the novels through an agreement with Random House, which saw payments flow to Hayward and not her partners."

By the end of the day, I had fielded calls and emails from a number of media outlets, as the Reuters article made the rounds. If Amanda was concerned over negative press in the small, local *Fort Worth Weekly*, she was in for a huge disappointment over what would soon become international coverage. Over the next few days, I was twice interviewed on local television stations in Dallas and by print reporters both locally and abroad. Barry Shlacter's article in the Fort Worth *Star-Telegram* led with "Arlington woman seeks millions in royalties from 'Fifty Shades of Grey.'" Shlacter was the first, but not the last, to pick up on the correlation between the cease-and-desist letters and the lawsuit. I'll admit I helped him along with that a little.

He wrote:

Farris said he is arranging to have Hayward served with a copy of the suit in Australia. He said he had informed her Sydney lawyer, Gaurev de Fontgalland, of the litigation by email. It was de Fontgalland who threatened Pedroza and Beebe with legal action in February, after the Fort Worth Weekly published a lengthy article about the Fifty Shades dispute.

Had Amanda not chosen to bully Jenny and Christa after that article about their soap-making business, everything would likely have blown over and she could have gone on her merry way. Now she was facing a publicity hurricane of her own making. In her backyard, the *Sydney Morning Herald* ran an article by reporter Linda Morris under the headline "Fifty Shades of Grey's Aussie publisher Amanda Hayward 'tricked us out of cash,'" complete with a picture of Amanda, captioned "Sitting pretty...*Fifty Shades of Grey* has made Amanda Hayward a wealthy woman," and a picture of her new multi-million dollar home with the caption "The Dural house in NSW [New South Wales, Australia] that bondage bought."

Morris asked me what I thought our chances were at trial and quoted my answer: "I believe that the law, the facts, and the equities are in our favour [SIC—she spelled it the

British/Australian way, but I spoke it in Texan], although I never like to speculate on the outcome of a case. However, I like our chances in front of a jury."

Other media outlets that picked up the story included *USA Today*, *Chicago Tribune*, *Los Angeles Times*, *PublishersLunch*, *Latin Post*, and even *Fort Worth Weekly*, which had gotten the ball rolling in the first place.

Jenny's Story

When we first filed the lawsuit, I knew that our story would garner attention, but I never thought it would reach as far as it did as fast as it did. Early on, I told Mike that neither Christa nor I wanted to talk to the media. Although Amanda's lawyer claimed otherwise, this was never about media attention. I never sought to direct a spotlight on Amanda. When I told Jeff Prince the story for *Fort Worth Weekly*, I thought it would be heard by only a few thousand locals who might want to buy soap. But, while that was my intent, things don't always work out as intended.

Mike did a great job with the first interviews, and I figured that, within a week, they would all be talking about something new. At least I hoped so. It wasn't lost on Christa or me that media attention might embolden Amanda to fight back, so we closed ranks and didn't talk much about the lawsuit to anyone. We received emails and messages from friends and acquaintances, saying they were proud of us and wishing us well. We also got a few that told us to watch our backs. But we never went public with our story from this point forward. Or so we thought.

What I didn't know then was that the media watches court proceedings. Once filed, those legal papers became public record. So, each time Mike or Brent filed a motion or attended a hearing, the possibility existed that the media would be right there to pick up the story. That was particularly true later on during the case, when the story kept coming back into the spotlight, but it was never our side sending the word out. There were a few times when someone strange called me, but if I didn't know the number, I refused to pick up. My husband even got a call from a reporter on his cell phone one night. Mickey told him in no uncertain terms that we were not interested in talking; the reporter got the message and never called back. That didn't stop me from worrying, though, about waking up to find the media on my front lawn or surrounding my school.

Thankfully that never happened.

Mike's Story

With the assistance of a law firm in Sydney, Australia, we were able to get both Amanda Hayward and TWCS Operations Proprietary Ltd. personally served with the Plaintiff's Original Petition, as well as with the two orders signed by Judge Curry. Then came the waiting. Would Amanda respond and, if so, how? I had confidence in what Jenny had told me, particularly because I had seen dozens of documents and emails that supported it, and I knew her story by heart. But I also knew that, in every lawsuit, there would be a different story from the other side. As I once heard it said, "No matter how thin you slice the baloney, there are still two sides to it."

On Wednesday, June 4, I received a letter from de Fontgalland, responding to the allegations in the petition. Not only did he send it to me, via email, but he also sent it directly to Jenny—a violation of the ethical rules for lawyers in Texas and, it turns out, in Australia as well.

He started his letter this way:

The Application [his shorthand for the Original Petition and Verified Application for Temporary Restraining Order and Temporary

Injunction] appears to be nothing more than a frivolous and opportunistic attempt by both you and your clients to seek a share of funds to which you have no entitlement whatsoever. We have no doubt that this intention will surface in the very early stages of any proceedings which your clients prosecute, if they are even able to do so.

Ms. Beebe's claims rely heavily on false and nonsensical allegations by Ms. Pedroza. We are firmly of the view that both claims are bound to fail.

He went on to say that he had been instructed to "reject the basis for the Application in its entirety"; to "strenuously reject the claim…that there was, at any time, a partnership in existence"; to note that the lawsuit is "wholly baseless, without merit, and an abuse of process"; that his clients "vigorously oppose the Application"; and that his clients "have provided us with a substantial body of evidence which appears to refute every cause of action set out in the Application."

In other words, "Oh, yeah?" Or, "You're wrong; no, I mean really wrong; no, really, really wrong." The "strenuously" rejecting was particularly effective. Or, maybe not.

He demanded that Jenny and Christa pay for his clients' legal costs and, anticipating they wouldn't be able to, demanded they place $500,000 in security into his firm's trust account. He said if Jenny and Christa didn't, he would seek an "order that the Application be dismissed with prejudice." That might have been scary if the lawsuit had been filed in Australia, and Australian rules applied, but Texas didn't recognize a "loser pays the other side's fees" rule.

But here was where de Fontgalland went off the rails. He knew, obviously from Amanda, that Jenny and her husband had filed bankruptcy in 2007 and were discharged in 2012. He accused Jenny of bankruptcy fraud for supposedly not disclosing to the trustee her interest in a partnership that he and his client denied existed. In a particularly condescending manner, he told me, "It appears that you may require some assistance in understanding the implications of the Non-Disclosure for Ms. Pedroza." If I needed some assistance, and I didn't, I would have gotten it from my law firm's bankruptcy expert, or from my own research, but not from this know-it-all.

The line I considered most damnable was this: "18 U.S. Code §152(1) sets out the penalties for knowingly and fraudulently concealing any property belonging to a bankrupt estate, which, we note, are criminal penalties which provide for up to five (5) years in prison, together with substantial fines." He went on to say that, unless we immediately dismissed the lawsuit, he would "notify the [Bankruptcy] Trustee of Ms. Pedroza's Non-Disclosure." In other words, dismiss the lawsuit or he would see to it criminal charges were brought against Jenny. I thought what made it particularly insidious was that he sent the letter directly to her. His obvious intent was to scare her. Had he sent it to me, alone, I would have shared it with Jenny but only after first talking her through it and allaying her fears. de Fontgalland's goal appeared to be to deprive me of that opportunity, so as to inflict the maximum psychological damage.

Jenny's Story

I don't look good in orange, nor do I want to ever don a jumpsuit of any kind.

This letter was absolutely terrifying. I expected retaliation but to threaten me with prison was absolutely mind-blowing. My bankruptcy was over. I had paid my dues and presented my tax returns to the bankruptcy trustee for five years, including the 2011 return that reflected my partnership interest, with attached K-1 from Coffee Shop. I hid nothing, nor did I do anything wrong. Once Mike had the information, he looked into the situation and saw that I did everything the way I should have. Even though I already knew this, because I had talked with my own bankruptcy attorney prior to my discharge, I almost had a nervous breakdown, and I cried on my husband's shoulder. "I don't want to go to prison!"

He tried to talk me down, but there was an irrational fear in the back of my mind that said, "What if you missed something? You're doomed. Say goodbye to your family. Your son is going to grow up without a mother." I was convinced that I had brought this on myself and that I was going to be wearing an orange jumpsuit for the next five years.

Okay, so I was being dramatic, but it was really scary. Finally, Mickey told me to call Mike. He knew that Mike could calm me down. I was worried because it was almost 9 o'clock and that was late to call anyone, but Mickey said, and he was right, that Mike would want me to call. I needed to relax so I could sleep.

When I heard Mike's voice over the phone, I almost couldn't talk. I was inconsolable. I think I babbled something about jail and maybe this was a bad idea. Once he started talking, I heard the anger in his voice. He was mad, not at me, but *for* me. That lifted my spirits quite a bit. I honestly had not thought about the bankruptcy when we discussed filing the lawsuit. What really disappointed me was that Amanda knew how intimidated I had been about the bankruptcy. I had spoken to her several times about wanting to be sure I did everything right. She knew I was trying hard to dot my i's and cross my t's, and now she used that fear against me.

It was a low blow, one that almost knocked me to my knees.

Mike's Story

Because of the time difference between Texas and Australia, de Fontgalland's letter arrived after business hours. I don't remember exactly when I received it but, before I could call

Jenny, she called me on my cell at shortly past 9:00 PM. When I answered, I could tell right away she was in tears. Breathless and sobbing, she was upset because she had not told me about the bankruptcy, and she was afraid she had done something wrong and might go to prison for it. As best I could, I explained to her how wrong the letter was, how she had done nothing wrong, and that it was, in fact, de Fontgalland who had done something wrong.

"I'm sorry," she said. "I just didn't think the bankruptcy was relevant, and I forgot all about it."

She was right; it wasn't relevant.

"Don't worry about it," I said. "I'll deal with him." I might have used a stronger word to describe de Fontgalland, but I don't recall. But if I had, it would have been justified.

A short while later, after I had a chance do a little research to confirm my thoughts, I emailed Jenny at 10:35: "I think you can put your mind at ease."

Shortly before 11:00 p.m., Jenny responded.

Seriously, I cannot tell you how much your answering your phone meant to me tonight, and then this too. I feel like we are battling the school yard bully, and man it's tough. I think what got me was the five years in prison. You were so right when you said she is trying to scare me. She has done it before, and I'm sure will do it again. I will work on getting a bit tougher. (No promises) but I will try to keep the crying phone calls to a minimum. Lol

I really appreciate you, and all you are doing for us. I am so sorry I forgot about the bankruptcy. I just didn't think it was relevant. Thanks again and have a good night.

I was so pissed off when I went to bed that I couldn't sleep. I would deal with de Fontgalland in the morning.

Jenny's Story

Anyone who has spent time with me knows that I am a rule follower. I didn't buck the system, nor did I try to pull the wool over anyone's eyes. I read the rules, I followed the rules, and if I made a mistake, I worked hard to fix it. Filing for bankruptcy had not been an easy decision for either my husband or me. Throughout college, and into young adulthood, we had lived beyond our means. We blamed ourselves, but something also has to be said about the ease with which we could get credit cards when we had no business getting credit. The real problem was that, once you've started down the debtor's path, it is almost impossible to come back. We both had good jobs, but the interest alone ate through our monthly paychecks.

My dad had often told me that only losers, who were trying to find an easy fix, filed bankruptcy. He owned his own business for 35 years, so he had seen his fair share of people screw him over by filing Chapter 7 and leaving their debts unpaid. I didn't want to let go of my responsibility, so Mickey and I agreed to a payment plan. We worked hard for five years to fulfill our promise to the plan, and we were discharged early.

Amanda and her lawyer capitalized on my fear that maybe I had forgotten something or made a mistake. She made me doubt myself, even for a short time, and, for a person who once called herself a friend, I thought that was a pretty low thing to do. I felt horrible that I had not given Mike, ahead of time, the necessary information regarding my bankruptcy. I honestly didn't consider it an issue, because it was a part of my past and I didn't think it would be used against me now. But I should have remembered who I was dealing with. This proved to me that she would seek out, and use, any weakness she perceived in me. Mike assured me he would look into it, figure out a plan, and send a reply letter.

When we got off the phone, I was much calmer. I knew Mike was angry that I had been sent the letter in the first place. He said that once a person has hired an attorney, all further communications should go through the attorney, and that letter never should have been sent directly to me. Once again, their scare tactics were evident. How did you deal with someone who was willing to do anything to scare you? This was an unsettling thought, but with Mike on my side, I felt like it would all come out all right. That night, as I tried to sleep, my mind wouldn't turn off. I kept rehashing the threat in the letter. I wanted to let go and simply believe that Mike would fix it, but that was a hard thing to do when you think you might go to prison.

About 10:30, I heard my phone chime, indicating that I had a new email message. My stomach dropped. What if it was something new from the Australian lawyer? What if someone had talked with my second-grade teacher and found out that I had copied Shirley's spelling test that one time? Or something else equally as ludicrous?

As I grabbed for my phone, I saw it was a message from Mike, with some of his research about the claims Amanda's attorney had made. After reading that reply, I kid you not, I read it to my husband, sent Mike a quick reply email, rolled over, and slept the rest of the night like a baby.

In the days that followed, I thought about anything else Amanda might use against me. I talked with Christa to be sure I had covered everything, and I told Mike all that I could come up with. I didn't want to leave any stone unturned, and I vowed that there wouldn't be any more surprises. It wasn't as if I had any dark secrets, but with Mike shuffling his chess pieces around the board, he had to know every detail. The bankruptcy was the largest blip on my past, but I still told him each bit of trivia I felt he needed to know in case Amanda decided to use something else as a way to scare me. By the time we were finished, I think Mike knew me better than I knew myself.

Mike's Story

By the time I got to the office Thursday morning after a sleepless night, I had calmed down a little—but not much. I had three basic problems with what de Fontgalland had done. First, he communicated directly with Jenny, which, at least under the applicable ethical rules for Texas lawyers, was prohibited since she was represented by counsel, a fact de Fontgalland knew. I didn't know at the time if that was a no-no in Australia, but I suspected it was. I made it a point of my research before responding.

Secondly, he used the threat of criminal charges, wrongheaded though it was, to try to gain an advantage in a civil lawsuit. Even though he obviously didn't know that Jenny had, in fact, disclosed her interest in Coffee Shop, he flat-out said he would tell the trustee that she hadn't, which he believed might put Jenny in prison, unless she dismissed her lawsuit. That meant he was trying to use the threat of prison in order to end the lawsuit. That violated the Texas ethics rules; I would find out how it played under Australia's rules.

And thirdly, Jenny's bankruptcy, which ended two years earlier, was totally irrelevant to any of the issues in the lawsuit.

In my opinion, he was simply trying to embarrass her by threatening to bring it up in the context of the lawsuit. There was no shame in filing bankruptcy during a time when tens of thousands were forced to do that very thing during a rough patch in the U.S. economy.

Still, it could be embarrassing, and de Fontgalland must have known that. I suspected he had been put up to this by Amanda, who knew of the bankruptcy through her friendship—now irrevocably broken—with Jenny. In fact, de Fontgalland proved that when he said, in his letter, "Our clients have also discovered that during the Bankruptcy Period, Ms. Pedroza has not disclosed to the Trustee…"

de Fontgalland tipped his hand that Amanda was, indeed, bothered by the publicity the lawsuit had garnered, particularly, I suspect, by articles in her local newspaper.

He wrote, "It appears, given the substantial media attention both you and your clients sought to garner, since filing the Application, that Ms. Pedroza will have to prepare herself for a criminal investigation into the Non-Disclosure."

Neither Jenny nor I had "sought to garner" media attention; the media had contacted me, not vice versa. Still, it was interesting to see what a sore spot it was for Amanda.

Once I had done my research, I started a response letter.

I was shocked to see that…you communicated directly with my client, Jennifer Lynn Pedroza, and threatened to institute criminal action against her if she does not comply with your demands in this civil matter. Obviously the intent of your sending the letter to her was to bully and intimidate her. Both actions by you—communicating directly with my client and threatening to present criminal charges to gain an advantage in a civil matter—are unethical and are barred under the Texas Disciplinary Rules of Professional Conduct. Rule 4.02(a) prohibits communication with a party represented by counsel without that counsel's consent, and Rule 4.04(b)(1) prohibits threatening to present criminal charges in order to gain an advantage in a civil matter. Because this conduct is prohibited in Texas, I delved into the New South Wales Professional Conduct and Practice Rules 2013 (Solicitor's Rules) to see if it is likewise prohibited in Australia, and I discovered that it is.

I quoted the Australian rules that applied to all three of my complaints. New South Wales Solicitor's Rule 33.1 prohibited an attorney from dealing directly with the client of another attorney without the other attorney's consent.

Rule 34.1.2 forbade an attorney to "threaten the institution of criminal or disciplinary proceedings against the other person if a civil liability to the solicitor's client is not satisfied."

And Rule 34.1.3 forbade the use of "tactics that go beyond legitimate advocacy and which are primarily designed to embarrass or frustrate another person."

One of the things I didn't address was de Fontgalland's threats to my law firm. In his letter, he wrote:

Finally, we suggest, as a professional courtesy, that you consider your own position carefully, bearing in mind the implications for you and your firm should Ms. Pedroza be charged as a result of the Application.

Professional courtesy, my ass!

That was a threat.

But I didn't want to distract from my anger at his treatment of Jenny, so I let it pass. I concluded my response by demanding that he direct all future communications directly to me, and not to communicate directly with either Jenny or Christa in the future.

Those would be my last dealings with de Fontgalland. A new attorney was about to enter the picture.

Jenny's Story

I knew Mike was mad, but now I knew he was pissed. I envisioned that the Australian lawyer thought he was dealing with a backwoods Texan, wearing a cowboy hat and driving a truck, or perhaps getting to work each day on the back of a horse.

I could assure anyone that Mike was not one of those people. He is from Texas, though, and I was damn glad he was. There was a grit and determination in his reply that de Fontgalland would still be feeling weeks later. Whereas de Fontgalland had chosen to intimidate, Mike simply threw the law at him.

We had now drawn a line in the sand, and it should have been clear to Amanda that we were not going away. It was her turn to understand, maybe for the first time, that what she did was wrong and that at least a handful of people in Texas knew it.

Before it was over, the whole world would know.

CHAPTER EIGHT: Crossfire

The minute you read something that you don't understand, you can almost be sure that it was drawn up by a lawyer.

—Will Rogers

Mike's Story

WHEN MY OFFICE phone rang on Wednesday, June 11, and I saw the name of the law firm "Jones Day" on the readout screen, I knew what was coming. Jones Day was one the world's largest law firms, boasting more than 2,500 lawyers on five continents, including Dallas. They also had an office in Sydney, Australia. I answered and the caller said:

This is Bob Kantner at Jones Day in Dallas. I've been hired by Amanda Hayward to represent her and TWCS Operations Proprietary in the lawsuit you filed in Fort Worth on behalf of Jennifer Pedroza and Christa Beebe.

I didn't know whether de Fontgalland had somehow pinpointed him in Dallas and referred the case to him, or if perhaps someone in Sydney's Jones Day office had made the referral. Regardless of how it happened, I now knew that Amanda planned to defend the lawsuit, which meant that she would "submit to the jurisdiction" of the American court. That is, unless her lawyers figured out it was in her best interest to ignore the lawsuit, leaving me to pursue a default judgment I would be unable to enforce in Australia.

While we talked, I looked up Kantner on his law firm's website, to get an idea of who I was dealing with. That was a standard practice I followed in all new cases. I learned over the years that knowing opposing counsel could be just as critical as knowing the opposing party and knowing the judge. I found that Kantner obtained his B.A. from the University of Virginia in 1977, followed by a J.D. from Harvard University in 1980. He touted himself on the Jones Day website as "an experienced trial lawyer who handles intellectual property and business cases."

Kantner wanted to push back the hearing date for the temporary injunction, which was set for the next morning. That made sense, since both sides wanted to take depositions before the hearing, so I agreed and prepared a proposed order to send to the court, which the judge signed and reset the hearing until August 11. The order also extended the TRO "until the hearing on Plaintiffs' Application for Temporary Injunction has been completed and *a ruling thereon issued* by the court." That language was important because, if the judge held the hearing but didn't immediately rule, but instead took the matter under advisement, I didn't want the TRO to lapse in the interim.

Kantner also wanted an extension of the deadline to produce documents that Judge Curry, acting on behalf of Judge McCoy, had ordered his client to produce, and he wanted me to produce documents from Jenny. Both requests seemed reasonable at the time, so I agreed to them. Later, I came to view these two requests as the first steps in a pattern of delay that persisted to the very end of the case.

In a subsequent phone call a few days later, Kantner suggested we jointly ask the court to enter a protective order that would allow either side to designate documents they produced as "confidential" or "highly confidential." In my 30+ years as a litigator, I could count on one hand the number of cases in which that had been done, and I would still have fingers left over. After all, this wasn't a corporate espionage or trade secrets case with a heightened need to protect documents from both outside scrutiny and the opposing party. But as long as it didn't handicap Jenny's case or our ability to introduce evidence to the court, it wasn't worth a fight. I have found that, in litigation, it's better to choose your battles than to engage in scorched earth tactics on every issue.

The protective order Kantner drafted, which the court ultimately entered on July 18, forbade the lawyers from disclosing "confidential" documents outside of the lawsuit. It also forbade disclosing "highly confidential" documents not only to outsiders to the case, but also to the clients, at least until the documents were used in court. Kantner ultimately designated nearly every document he produced throughout the lawsuit as either confidential or highly confidential, including email correspondence that Jenny was a party to and Australian public records, such as real estate documents and trademark registrations.

The delays continued in the way Kantner chose to handle his initial production of documents that had been ordered by Judge Curry. He asked for two extensions of time to produce those documents, the first extending the deadline until June 20. On June 18, he asked for an additional two-week extension because of a medical issue involving his mother. I agreed to both requests. Then, the day production was due under the second extension, he called to ask for yet another extension, albeit a shorter one. He spoke to Brent on the phone, who, acting on my instruction, denied the third request. Kantner had already gotten more than an additional four weeks to produce the documents, and I thought I had been lenient enough already.

In response to the denial, Kantner abruptly hung up on Brent. Then, instead of producing all the documents, on the last day, he filed a motion attacking the order, something he could have done at the start, without the need for two extensions of time. I believed he had an obligation to file that motion, and obtain a ruling, before the deadline, rather than simply withhold documents he had been ordered to produce. Instead, he delayed for more than four weeks before filing the motion.

In the meantime, I had agreed to voluntarily produce documents to Kantner, even though no order required it, if he would send me a list of categories he wanted. Because we were doing this by agreement, with shortened time frames to accommodate the temporary injunction hearing set for August 11, I didn't require that he send a formal request for production of documents under *Texas Rule of Civil Procedure* 196. I didn't make a *carte blanche* agreement to produce everything he asked for, though, because I needed to review the requests, first.

In the same email of June 18 in which he asked for the second extension of time, he sent me his list of document categories. After I reviewed his list, I told him I would produce all of the documents he asked for with the exception of Jenny's income tax returns for the years 2009-2013, as well as some documents relating to Jenny's bankruptcy. I didn't believe they had any relevance to the issues in the lawsuit. Besides, in order to obtain tax returns, Texas law dictated that the requesting party first had to prove the returns were not only relevant, but also "material." And, as one Texas court stated it, tax returns were "not material if the same information can be obtained from another source." [12] The only information on the returns that could possibly be relevant, I thought, was any gain or loss from Coffee Shop that Jenny might have listed on her returns. And

---

[12] *In re Williams*, 328 S.W.3d 103, 116 (Tex. App. – Corpus Christi-Edinburg 2010, orig. proceeding).

Amanda already had that information. After all, she was the record keeper for Coffee Shop.

When I objected to producing Jenny's returns, Kantner filed a motion asking the court to order me to produce them. In that motion, he attached a personal declaration he had signed, which attached copies of the schedules from Jenny's bankruptcy that had been filed in 2007, before Coffee Shop even existed. It seemed to me Kantner was simply reminding Jenny of de Fontgalland's letter that threatened her with prison time. I didn't like it any better when Kantner did it than I had when de Fontgalland was the culprit. As part of my response to Kantner's motion, I filed a motion of my own and asked the court to sanction Kantner for doing this. I put it this way:

*Notwithstanding that bankruptcy filings are matters of public record, Kantner has seen fit to dredge up records from a bankruptcy that was filed **seven years ago**, and in which the debtors were discharged two years ago, and to file them with this Court. One of only two possible purposes for dragging these documents back out into the open **seven years later**, particularly when they aren't even the subject of Defendants' Motion, is to embarrass and harass Pedroza.*

A second possible purpose hearkens back to a letter written by Hayward's Australian counsel, in which he referenced the same bankruptcy records, contended erroneously that they involved bankruptcy fraud, and directly threatened Pedroza with a criminal investigation unless she dismissed this lawsuit. While attaching the records to Kantner's Declaration may be more veiled than Australian counsel's blatant violation of his ethical duties, it is nevertheless intended as a threat by reminding Pedroza of the prior letter, and this time makes the threat in a public forum. Lest there be any doubt as to who is responsible for the current threat, one merely has to note that the records are attached to the Declaration of Kantner, Hayward's Texas counsel.

It is a violation of [Texas Civil Practice & Remedies Code] Chapter 10 to file a pleading for any improper purpose, including to harass. It is a violation of [Texas Rules of Civil Procedure] 13 to file a pleading that is groundless and brought in bad faith or for the purposes of harassment. It is a violation of Disciplinary Rule 4.04(a) for a lawyer to use any means that has "no substantial purpose other than to embarrass" a third person. It is a violation of Disciplinary Rule 4.04(b)(1) to threaten criminal charges to gain an advantage in a civil matter. Kantner has violated all four provisions; violations of the latter two constitute the very kind of improper purpose, bad faith, and harassment contemplated by the first two.

Although Judge McCoy later denied my motion for sanctions,[13] I believe the reason was it was still early in the case and she didn't want to fall into a pattern of sanctioning the lawyers. I still felt it was worthwhile to file the motion to put Kantner on notice I would scrutinize his every move. I once heard an anecdote about baseball great Carlton Fisk, catcher for the Boston Red Sox that, whether true or not, illustrates my point. The anecdote says Fisk once berated a home plate umpire for failing to call a game's first pitch a strike. When the umpire questioned why Fisk became so irate on the first pitch, Fisk answered, "If I let you get away with it on the first pitch, you'll do it all game."

Although Kantner's answer to the lawsuit was due on June 30, I agreed to give him an extension to July 8.[14] When he filed it, he asserted a number of affirmative defenses, although he didn't outline the factual basis for any of them. Interestingly, he

---

[13] Judge McCoy ordered me to produce the tax returns to Kantner, but only after first redacting, or blacking out, all financial information on them other than Jenny's income or loss from Coffee Shop. That was information that Amanda, and thus Kantner, already knew from Coffee Shop's financial records that were in Amanda's possession. I was fine with the compromise Judge McCoy offered on that.

[14] See how the delay thing works?

did not initially include a statute of frauds defense, although he added it when he filed an amended answer on September 11. The statute of frauds, which requires certain contracts to be in writing or else they are not enforceable, became the linchpin of Kantner's defense for the rest of the case, on up to the appeal that was ultimately dismissed when the case was finally settled. I'll talk much more about it later.

On July 28, Kantner filed counterclaims against both Jenny and Christa, asserting that they breached their respective contracts—the service agreements—simply by filing the lawsuit. The identical counterclaims relied upon language in Sections 15(b), 15(c), and 15(e) of those agreements, which said:

(b) The Service Provider [Jenny and Christa] irrevocably releases the Customer [TWCS Operations], its predecessor and its related parties (including without limitation Amanda Hayward) from any other claims, entitlements or interest that it might allege was derived from their previous engagement by [TWCS Operations] prior to this Agreement.

(c) [TWCS Operations] or its related parties may use this Agreement as a bar to any proceedings based on previous employment or engagement or [Jenny's or Christa's] role in respect of the business known as The Writer's Coffee Shop.

...

(e) [Jenny and Christa] indemnifies [TWCS Operations] and its related parties in respect of any claim commenced contrary to the above acknowledgements.

I had studied the service agreements, and these provisions in particular, before filing the lawsuit, and I felt we were in a strong position, both factually and legally. Under this language, Jenny and Christa released only claims based on their "previous engagement by [TWCS Operations] prior to this Agreement." TWCS Operations was part of a complex business structure (see the chart in Chapter 9) Amanda set up in the latter half of 2012. It didn't exist before that, nor had Jenny or Christa been "previously engaged" by TWCS Operations "prior to" signing the agreements. That meant that neither of them had released anything.

The only language that caused me a little concern was the "bar" language in 15(c) that referred to Jenny's and Christa's "role in respect of the business known as The Writers Coffee Shop," but I thought that was incredibly vague and likely would not be enforceable. What I learned as we proceeded in the case was that Amanda contended that Coffee Shop was not, and never had been, a partnership; rather, she was always a "sole trader," the Australian equivalent of a sole proprietorship. How, then, could this language have barred Jenny from making claims as a partner in what was, to Amanda's mind, a non-existent partnership?

What this language really did was suggest to me Amanda's intent, all along, had been to get Jenny, in particular, and Christa to give up any claims they had from working at Coffee Shop, even though, as we'll see, she concealed the value of Jenny's ownership interest in Coffee Shop. That meant, when she coerced them into signing the agreements (something I'll discuss more later), she was consciously trying to deprive Jenny of her rights as a partner.

Jenny's Story

Oh goody, the counterclaim. Mike had warned me to expect it, so it wasn't a surprise. He said that the counterclaim would help us to understand their thinking and to be able to anticipate what to expect in my and Christa's depositions that were coming up soon. In retrospect, it also helped me walk into the next phase of the lawsuit with a game plan.

Mike's first interaction with Bob Kantner was civil, and he even mentioned that, based on the Jones Day website, he appeared to be a good trial lawyer. I hoped he was a fair man who knew the law and would apply it to defend his client rather than simply find loopholes for her to squeeze through. I hoped he was more like Mike and Brent and less like *The Rainmaker*'s Jon Voigt.

But, as the case moved along, hostility grew. Kantner hanging up on Brent when he was denied more time didn't strike me as very lawyerly. I mean, I never saw Perry Mason hang up on another lawyer.

Soon enough, I would have my own experience with Bob Kantner.

CHAPTER NINE: Truth Fears No Questions

Truth is such a rare thing, it is delightful to tell it.
—Emily Dickenson

Mike's Story

THE INJUNCTION HEARING had been reset for the morning of August 11, so obviously we needed to conduct depositions prior to that. Scheduling them should have been easy, but I had a few contentious moments with Kantner doing that. Both sides also wanted documents from the other, to help prepare witnesses, but that didn't prove to be straightforward, either. We responded to Kantner's informal document request by producing 971 pages and didn't designate any of them as confidential or highly confidential. On the other hand, Kantner, whose client should have had more documents than Jenny since Amanda maintained all of Coffee Shop's business records, initially produced only 272 pages, and later supplemented to bring the total to 393 pages prior to the injunction hearing. He designated all but a handful of them as either confidential or highly confidential.

He failed to produce documents in two of the categories listed in Judge Curry's order. Those two categories were:

Financial records, including bank statements, deposit slips, wire transfer transactions, checks, or other documents that reflect payments made by Random House to Coffee Shop and/or Hayward and/or TWCS arising out of the Random House Deal, or payments from any other source, including without limitation Amazon and Barnes & Noble.

Documents reflecting purchases by Hayward and/or TWCS in the amount of $10,000 or more utilizing funds received by Hayward and/or TWCS arising out of the Random House Deal.

According to Amanda's accountant, David Wayling, who signed a declaration to excuse producing them, it would cost "at least $100,000 to identify and produce all such documents." When I later took his deposition in Australia in December, he testified the basis for that figure was simply, "That's what I quoted to do it," and "I don't have to justify how I get to my billing system."

What was more disturbing was Amanda's own written declaration that companies in which she and her husband owned an interest had made more than 200 transfers of $10,000 or more and:

...it may or may not be possible to trace funds that I received from Random House or other funds I received in connection with The Writer's Coffee Shop and invested in these other businesses into and out of these accounts.

In other words, she had concealed and commingled the Random House payments, and she was arguing she shouldn't have to produce the documents that proved her concealment. My argument in response, which I asserted in a motion to compel production, was you can't commit fraud and then hide behind the success of your fraud as an excuse to not produce proof of it.

The line about companies Amanda and her husband owned piqued my interest. Digging into online records of the Australian Securities & Investments Commission, I discovered the existence of a number of companies, including TWCS Operations, that Amanda set up effective as of September 3, 2012, under the umbrella of a holding company called TWCS Investments Proprietary Ltd, which was owned by Amanda's husband, James Hayward. The structure looked like this:

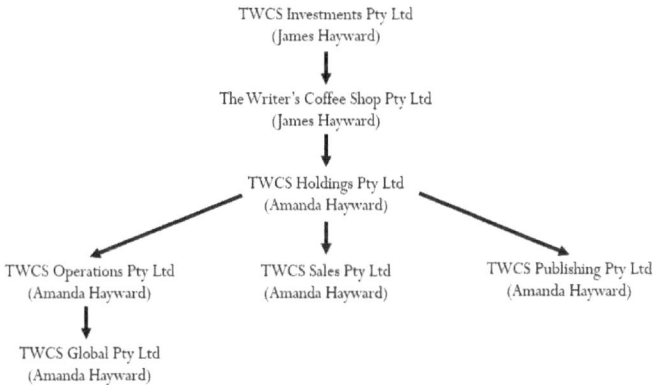

One glance at this structure and I think you see "shell game" written all over it.

Additionally, Amanda had been ordered to produce royalty statements from Random House, but Kantner produced a grand total of only four pages that supposedly comprised those statements. Because I am a writer, and have seen royalty statements before, I knew four pages wasn't a complete production. Rather than fight with Kantner, we subpoenaed the records directly from Random House in New York, which produced the royalty statements in full: 177 pages.

On July 8, I filed a motion to compel production of the financial records Kantner had been ordered, but failed, to produce, but I wasn't able to get a hearing set until after the injunction hearing. That meant I wouldn't be able to use them at Amanda's deposition or at the hearing. Subsequent history revealed that I didn't get most of them until after the trial had ended, which I suspect had been the goal all along—to deprive me of their use.[15]

We scheduled Jenny's deposition for July 28, Christa's for July 29, and Jennifer McGuire's for July 31. Amanda would be coming in from Australia for the temporary injunction hearing, and I wanted to depose her early in the week of August 4, to allow me to get a transcript from the court reporter several days in advance of the hearing. Kantner wouldn't agree, though, but insisted it be the latter part of the week so she didn't have the expense of extra nights in a hotel.

"I think she can afford it," I said, as we talked on the phone.

There was a long pause, after which he said, "Well, that's a rather sarcastic answer that I don't think I appreciate."

I'll admit I was being sarcastic, but that didn't stop it from being true, nor did I care if he appreciated it. I believed Amanda had absconded with millions of dollars that were rightfully Jenny's, so I was plumb out of sympathy for her.

We finally agreed to Thursday, August 7, for Amanda's deposition, which gave me a grand total of three days afterward to prepare for the hearing, while Kantner would have completed Jenny's and Christa's depositions 13 and 14 days, respectively, prior to the hearing.[16]

Jenny's Story

As I stated before, I had already combed through thousands of emails, found hundreds of documents, and created timelines, so all the facts of my story would be clear and concise. I suspected, though, I might have missed some things because it was impossible to find everything. I worried that Amanda's lawyer

---

[15] Once again, see how this delay thing works?

[16] See footnote 15.

might surprise us at the last minute with something I had omitted but, as he and his client dragged their feet and produced only limited documentation to Mike and Brent, it became clear they didn't have anything new to offer. It frustrated me that much of what they deemed confidential were documents I already possessed and had produced, myself. It became glaringly apparent to me that, while I had nothing to hide, they seemed to want to hide everything.

Preparing for the deposition was exhausting. Christa and I researched depositions—what they were and what procedures were followed—because neither of us had done this before, and we didn't know what to expect. We knew generally that Mr. Kantner would ask questions, a court reporter would transcribe the proceedings, and everything would be videotaped. Combining those three things made for high stress. Though I had not met Mr. Kantner, knowing how he resisted turning over documents, and the dismissive manner in which he treated Brent and Mike in phone conversations, I didn't have a good feeling about him.

One shining bit of good news was that, because she was a party to the lawsuit, Christa could stay in the room during my deposition. That gave me a measure of relief. Having Mike, Brent, and Christa, all three, present meant I wouldn't have to face this alone. Although Brent and Christa wouldn't be able to say anything, they could pass notes to Mike.

Mike explained that, under the procedural rules, he was very limited in what he could say during Kantner's questioning. That was tough to hear because it meant Kantner had broad latitude in his questioning. Whether it could be used later was up for debate, but he could still ask. So, Christa and I ran down list after list of what we thought might be on Kantner's agenda. But it was Mike's and Brent's assurances that I simply had to tell the truth that helped the most. By sticking to the facts, I would survive this.

Their confidence reassured me, but I still prepared for the worst.

Mike's Story

On Sunday before the depositions, Brent and I met with Jenny and Christa in the firm's main conference room to prepare, and also to familiarize them with the surroundings where they would be deposed. We met again Tuesday morning, with Jenny's deposition scheduled to begin at 9:00. I knew she was ready, although I could also tell she was nervous. But not worried. Witnesses who have reason to worry are those who can't keep their stories straight, a risk that comes with less than truthful answers.

Kantner would ask the questions, while I would save mine for the courtroom. That meant Jenny would probably not be able to tell her story in a chronological fashion because, when opposing counsel asks questions, it's cross-examination. Kantner wouldn't care about hearing Jenny's straightforward story so much as he wanted to trip her up, so I told Jenny that, if necessary, she could preface answers by setting the context. I also cautioned her to watch out for trick questions, the "have you stopped beating your wife" questions, which are framed so any answer can be twisted against you. My job was to be alert for those and to object to the form of a question if I thought it was improper.

I couldn't coach her on her answers, though. Under the *Texas Rules of Civil Procedure*, lawyers were limited to three very simple objections: (1) "Objection, leading," if you thought the questioner was impermissibly suggesting answers to a friendly witness; (2) "Objection, form," if you thought there was something wrong with how the question was phrased, such as if it was vague or ambiguous, assumed the truth of facts that were not in evidence, was misleading, or argumentative[17]; and (3) "Objection, nonresponsive," if you thought the witness had evaded the question. I would learn a few days later that Kantner apparently didn't think these restrictions applied to him.

I also warned Jenny that some lawyers bully witnesses, while others try to provoke witnesses by making them angry. I once heard a lawyer caution a witness by quoting Prometheus from Longfellow's *The Masque of Pandora*: "Whom the gods would destroy they first make mad."

I had never been involved with Kantner before, so I didn't know what his approach would be.

I had some inklings, though, by such things as his hanging up on Brent, his reaction to my "sarcastic" comment, attaching Jenny's bankruptcy schedules to his declaration, and his recalcitrance in producing documents.

The deposition took place in a windowless conference room at my firm's office, since the main conference room—the one where we prepped Jenny and Christa, with the floor-to-ceiling windows and killer view of downtown Dallas—was in use that day. Jenny sat at the end of the conference table, while I sat to her left and Kantner sat to her right, so he and I faced each other. Christa sat next to me, and Brent next to Christa as we lined one side of the table. The court reporter set up her machine between Jenny and Kantner, and a videographer recorded from the far end of the table, facing Jenny. The deposition kicked off at 9:04 AM.

One of the good things about watching opposing counsel depose your client is you can get a feel, from his questioning, what he thinks is important in the case. Although Kantner had not yet filed his amended answer to assert the statute of frauds as a defense, I knew it would be coming based upon some of his

---

[17] This isn't an exhaustive list of "form" objections, but merely examples.

questions.

The statute of frauds says if a contract is not capable of being performed within one year, then it must be in writing in order to be enforceable. It's irrelevant whether it was actually performed within one year; rather, it is an objective standard as to whether it could have *possibly* been performed within that year. If it was possible, then no writing was necessary unless the agreement fell into some other category, such as contracts regarding real estate, for example.

After Jenny answered initial questions to establish she and Amanda had first started Coffee Shop in late 2009, with Jenn McGuire coming on board later, Kantner asked, "Did you have any time horizon in mind for this partnership? In other words, was this a temporary thing that would last a few months and then end or was it to be extended?"

"No, it was—yeah, it was extended. Yeah, we were supposed to continue on."

"For how long?"

"I don't—"

"Years?"

"Yes, years."

"In other words, when this alleged partnership was formed in 2009, it was not your intention that it could be or would be only a one-year partnership?"

"No."

"It was going to be a multi-year partnership?"

"Yeah."

"And that was part of the plan?"

"Yes."

These were good questions, but they didn't get to the heart of the statute of frauds issue. Even with all the good intentions in the world that a partnership last for years, if it could possibly be performed within a year, then the statute didn't apply. I knew that, sooner or later, I would have to address this issue. We were dealing with a partnership-at-will, which meant that any partner could terminate it at any time. "At any time" included within days or months of its formation, or even up to, but still less than, a year. That meant that it was possible for the partnership to be performed, and ended, within one year. Texas law makes it clear that "at will" relationships, whether partnerships or employment contracts or any other type, aren't governed by the statute of frauds, a truism that Kantner would resist to the bitter end.

Later that morning, Kantner circled back to this issue and, still later, he returned once more. He was focused on it, like a dog with a bone, and I anticipated he would soon file an amended answer to assert it as a defense, which he did.

"The Writer's Coffee Shop had a three-year contract with Erika Mitchell; is that correct?"

"Yes, uh-huh."

"Did The Writer's Coffee Shop commit to promote Fifty Shades of Grey for Erika Mitchell for a full three years when it signed that contract?"

"Yes."

"In other words, you understood you had undertaken a commitment to Erika Mitchell for three years, correct?"

"Yes."

"And so, you couldn't satisfy or complete that contract in less than three years, could you?"

"No. I mean, we were under contract with them, yes."

Here, Kantner demonstrated a basic misunderstanding of the law, at least as I perceived it. Whether Coffee Shop had a three-year commitment to Erika Mitchell was a different question from whether Coffee Shop's partners had three-year commitments to each other. Coffee Shop could have dissolved within a year, and the multi-year contracts with Erika Mitchell and other authors would simply be included among partnership assets to be divided between the partners as part of their settling up before going their separate ways. But unless Jenny and Amanda had agreed to remain partners for the duration of those contracts, they were irrelevant to determining whether the partnership, itself, could be performed in less than a year.

To top it off, the author contracts guaranteed books would be published within six months of the date the contracts were signed. If they weren't, then the contracts were automatically void. That meant that even those author contracts could not only possibly be performed within six months, they *had to be* performed within six months.

Kantner also zeroed in on the release and bar clauses in Section 15 of the service agreement, as well as the termination-without-cause provision. I couldn't tell if he agreed with me that there had been no "previous engagement" of Jenny by TWCS, but he emphasized the vague language in 15(c) that tied the "bar" specifically to "any proceedings based on...[Jenny's or Christa's] role in respect of the business known as The Writer's Coffee Shop."

"I didn't understand what that meant," Jenny said.

So why did you sign it, Kantner wanted to know, if you didn't understand what it meant? Jenny's repetitive answer was Amanda told her to, that this was merely something she had to do for tax reasons, and that Jenny's partnership share of profits would come to her through TWCS Operations.

"Now, is that statement anywhere in this agreement?" Kantner asked.

"No."

"Did you understand the inconsistency at the time you signed this agreement?"

"Yes."

"You were well aware of it?"

"And I asked Amanda about it."

"You were being told something different than what this agreement is, and you signed this agreement anyway, correct?"

"She told me we needed to."

"Okay. And you signed it notwithstanding the fact that you knew there was an inconsistency between what she was saying and what this agreement says, correct?"

"And because I trusted her and she told—she swore on her daughters' lives that she would take care of it."

That wasn't just hyperbole on Jenny's part. When Jenny had questioned Amanda about the termination provision in the service agreement, Amanda emailed:

I would NEVER do that to you even if we fall out and have a huge fight. Out of respect to you and our friendship. I swear on my daughters' lives....

Kantner turned to the termination clause just before ending the deposition.

"You knew it was in there, right, that TWCS Operations Proprietary Limited could terminate you pursuant to the terms of that provision?"

"That company could, yes."

"But your view was in addition to that company, there was still a partnership?"

"Correct."

"But when you were terminated in November of 2013, were you terminated solely with respect to your position as an independent contractor to TWCS Operations Proprietary Limited?"

"So, was I still a partner?" Jenny asked.

"Well, that's another way of asking the same question, but I'll accept that."

"Yes."

"You were still a partner?"

"I was still a partner."

"The termination only related to your contract with TWCS Operations Proprietary Limited?"

"Yes."

Damn straight! Although a partner can be expelled from a partnership, that would take a vote of the partners, and often required that the partnership be dissolved. If Coffee Shop was never dissolved—and it wasn't—then Jenny continued as a partner even after she signed the service agreement with TWCS Operations. When Amanda terminated her in late 2013, it was only from TWCS Operations and not from Coffee Shop. Whatever happened at TWCS Operations was irrelevant to whether Jenny was still a partner in Coffee Shop.

By the time Jenny's deposition ended at 3:15 that afternoon, I felt I had gained more from it than had Kantner. I now understood his thinking on his legal defenses and felt Jenny had done a good job of deflecting them, notwithstanding Kantner's efforts to intimidate her. Sometimes he pointed his finger in her face, and other times he jabbed the table in front of her. He raised his voice, almost to a shout, and if Jenny didn't understand a question, he often just repeated it, almost word for word, but more slowly and more condescendingly. Still, she hung tough.

Tomorrow we would see how he handled Christa.

Jenny's Story

Upon meeting Mr. Kantner, my guard immediately went up. He was nice enough during the introductions, but almost as soon as the deposition started, he went for the kill. Mike had warned me that he might try to trip me up, but I can't fully explain how confusing and overstated his questions were. I wondered whether he even knew the facts of the case, because he appeared confused about the timeline, and he didn't know about some essential emails and contracts. There were even times when I had to correct his misconceptions, which added to my confusion. Why wouldn't he know all the facts? I wasn't sure if this was a deliberate tactic, but I felt as if I gave him more information than his own client had.

Never in my life had I been as mentally drained as I was when the deposition ended. I now know how kidnapping victims feel as they are interrogated. Everything was a test. No matter how many times Mr. Kantner asked certain questions, my answers were always the same: Yes, we were a partnership; yes, the partnership intended to make money; yes, we presented ourselves to the world as a partnership. If he asked a question that took too long for me to answer, he often rephrased the question without giving me time to think. Sometimes he repeated questions in different ways, and he often asked long questions within questions. If I had to look at a document, he implied that I didn't have an answer. He often turned my answers around to another question. And if I didn't understand a question, sometimes he simply repeated it, as if asking a second time clarified it, but at other times, in an attempt to replicate his question, he ended up changing it.

I tried hard to stay calm and, as the hours ticked by, I became almost numb. Through it all, I simply told the truth. And one significant truth that continued to pop up was that I had trusted Amanda to do right by all of us. By the end, I felt like even Mr. Kantner wondered *why* I put so much faith in her. That was the only question he didn't ask, one I wouldn't have had an answer for.

To this day, I don't understand why I chose to believe in

her. Why would I willingly trust that she had all of our best interests at heart when the signs pointed to her self-interest? As I look back, I can only answer that I thought we were friends, and I couldn't believe that a friend would betray me this way. I was disheartened to find out that I had misjudged her.

If Mr. Kantner had asked why I put so much faith in her, my answer would have been, "Because I was a naïve fool."

Mike's Story

The next morning, everyone reconvened at my firm's offices, this time in the main conference room with the outstanding view. As before, the witness—Christa—sat at the end, Kantner across from me, and Jenny and Brent next to me. By the end of the depo, which lasted less than two hours, I was convinced Kantner would, if possible, settle Christa's claims in an effort to keep as much of her testimony from the jury as he could. If Christa was out of the lawsuit, although she could still testify on the partnership issues, damaging facts relating to Amanda's broken promises to her would be considered irrelevant and would likely be excluded from evidence.

Christa testified she first went to work for Coffee Shop, on a part-time basis, in early 2012, to help with marketing once the *Fifty Shades* trilogy took off. She had previously met Amanda, whom Jenny introduced as her "business partner." In May of 2012, at the end of the school year, Christa quit her teaching job with the Mansfield, Texas, Independent School District, as did Jenny, to work full-time for Coffee Shop, starting in June at a salary of $5,000 per month.

"Did you ever learn, in 2012, that there was going to be any change in either The Writer's Coffee Shop or Amanda Hayward's interest in The Writer's Coffee Shop to a sole trader or proprietary company?" Kantner asked.

"I was around when there were those conversations about that, yes," Christa answered.

"And when were those conversations?"

"I believe May or June of 2012."

"I don't know that you can isolate them, but to the extent you can, tell me what you recall about the discussions in May."

"They were discussions about how the company was going to be set up, what our employee status would look like, benefits were talked about, things like my house being paid off were talked about, my interest in the company."

"Your interest in the company?"

"I left my job assuming that I was working for a partnership that Jenny was a part of, and that I was going to be an employee of this company."

"And you based that in part on what Jenny Pedroza told you?"

"That, in part, yes, and then in part—"

"And what Amanda told you?"

"—on what Amanda told me."

"Now with regard to your statement about the discussions about how the company would be set up, were any details offered to you?"

"No, not a lot of details. At some time in there it was talked about becoming independent contractors versus employees, for tax reasons."

Christa confirmed Amanda planned to set up the new structure in Australia but, "My understanding was Jenny was still a partner in this, in the company, but I didn't know what that meant for restructure—or structure of the new company."

She went on to say she was not happy with the change from employee to independent contractor, but Amanda put a hard sell on her to sign the service agreement with TWCS Operations. "I was told, when I started, that this would be a position where I would have a chance to grow with the company that was starting off really strong, and that things would happen, like I could get bonuses and my house would be paid off so my kids could go to any private school I wanted them to, so that was my understanding going into it."

As part of her job with Coffee Shop, she said, she prepared press releases about the company's successes, particularly *Fifty Shades of Grey*. After Coffee Shop sold the *Fifty Shades* trilogy publishing rights to Random House in March 2012, the *Wall Street Journal* asked for information for a story about the sale of those rights. Christa was tasked with responding, and she asked Amanda if there was anything she should *not* say. Amanda responded by email: "The only thing you need not to say is that Jenny and Jenn [McGuire] are partners because we have to say they are business associates for tax reasons."

That was the first time anyone had suggested disclaiming there was a partnership. I thought it was significant that Amanda had not told Christa not to say Jenny and Jenn were partners because they weren't; instead, it was simply for "tax reasons."

The real damning testimony, though, related to Christa's termination from TWCS Operations. In February 2013, Jenny told Christa that, according to Amanda, the company might not be able to keep her on due to financial concerns. As of that date, Amanda had already received a royalty payment from Random House of $16,512,649.73, and she would receive a second payment in April of $15,729,593.23. Jenny didn't know this, of course, because Amanda didn't tell her about the payments.

"Do you recall any more, particularly, what Jenny Pedroza told you?" Kantner asked.

"I just know it had something to do with finances."

"Well, did you ask her, wait a minute, Fifty Shades of Grey is going gangbusters, why is there a problem?"

"Sure, yeah."

"And what did she say?"

"That there was a problem with—she was told there were problems with the Random House money, and that was all she was ever told."

But then Amanda later told Christa that, instead of terminating her, the company would simply reduce her salary. In February and March, Christa exchanged emails with Amanda about the possible termination, then salary decrease, but she "didn't feel it was my place to question their financial situation." It was these emails that I believed Kantner would try to keep from the jury by settling Christa's claim. I have set them out here, typos and all, with some highlighting that I added for emphasis:

Christa Beebe
Thu, Feb 7, 2013 at 2:52 PM
To: Amanda Hayward

*Well, Jenny told me the news. I'm not gonna lie, **I'm pretty much devastated**. I love my job and this company and I feel like we are finally making some good progress with our upcoming titles. As much as I hate this, I understand that you have to do what is right for the company. I appreciate this opportunity and I cannot begin to express how thankful I am that you are keeping me on until August. **My family would be in serious trouble if I lost my job right now.** I will continue to work my hardest to make TWCS successful until it's time for me to go. I wish that it didn't have to be over. I truly love working here. We have all become like family. If there was any way for me to keep my job, ANY way, I would love to talk about it. If not, I understand.*

Christa

Amanda Hayward
Thus, Feb 7, 2013 at 6:21 PM
To: Christa Beebe

I can talk about it with you…honestly my worry is more if I didn't let you know now and I have to let you go and it was too late for you to get a teaching job I would feel even worse..

I needed you to apply for jobs and have another one because if the business keeps going the way it is right now there is not job for you in August..

I can't talk today as I have to go to the bank.. I'm trying to get everything done before I go to Vegas.. I wanted to talk to you about it first but Jenny wanted to be the one to tell you..

If...and I mean if...things pick up way better than we hope then it might (very slight) might change and you can stay for another year (I will only keep you on if I can keep you until the school year goes back I would never do that to you) **I just know that March is a time you need to apply** *I was very careful of that fact and wanted to make sure you and Jenny could go back if ever needed.*

At this stage there is no job in August but it could change.. I hope it does.. but I needed to be fair and let you know.

I love you as a friend this is why it is so hard for me.. I've been pretty upset about a few of the changes but I know it needs to happen.

Christa Beebe
Thu, Feb 7, 2013 at 6:29 PM
To: Amanda Hayward

I appreciate your honesty and your thoughtfulness. Of course I would love nothing more than to stay on, but I also understand that the chances of that happening are small. I have a meeting next week with a coordinator in the district to get things moving.

Please know that I will continue to work my ass off for TWCS.

110

Amanda Hayward
Thu, Feb 7, 2013 at 11:43 PM
To: Christa Beebe

I know honey I am just so sorry I had to do it :(

Christa Beebe
Wed, Feb 27, 2013 at 5:03 PM
To: Amanda Hayward

Jenny just told me about your offer to keep me on at $4000 a month, with the understanding that I would find a part time job as well. I am super excited about this!! **And your sure the company can do this for another school year?** *I don't want to put us in a bad spot...*

I am going to talk to Kera about it and we will try to figure out how to make this work... because I REALLY want it to.

I am sorry that I am such a large expense. If I could take less and still make ends meet, you know I would.

Amanda Hayward
Wed, Feb 27, 2013 at 5:12 PM
To: Christa Beebe

We can definently do it for another year *especially with how I cut the editing money out.. If we are going to do 3-4 books each month I'm also hoping our sales go up.. but even without that we can cover your salary I wouldn't do that unless we could..see what Kera says I'm sorry to muck you around but I am really trying to make this work for the company and you and I didn't know I was going to do what I did with editing.. (my god I have wasted money there I'm glad that is under control now)*

Christa Beebe
Mon, Mar 4, 2013 at 8:26 PM
To: Amanda Hayward

Hey — I hope things are going well over on the other side of the world!

So, Kera and I had some time to talk this weekend and we are both excited about your offer. Again, I am SO happy to be staying with TWCS. Now, I have to find some part time work! I am looking into some tutoring opportunities with the school district for next year. I'll let you know how that goes.

So, everything is still good, right? The offer still stands? **It can work until at least next August?**

SO excited!!!!

Amanda Hayward
Wed, Mar 4, 2013 at 8:26 PM
To: Christa Beebe

Absolutely I will guarantee it until next August.. so from August this year it will go down to $4000 or when ever we said I think it was the September pay it goes down..

I'm glad it is working out.. I want to add more to our work load but I think we can pull it off with some clever organizing which should mean we make more money and there fore it might not be long till you don't have to tutor anymore if that happens..
I just have to make a lot more than we are now.. but it is possible..

Christa Beebe
Wed, Mar 20, 2013 at 4:00 PM
To: Amanda Hayward

Hope you are doing well. Just wanted to check in, one more time, **before I make a major life decision.** *I had a principal contact me asking if I would be interested in a job. Of course, I want to tell her no, but* **once I do, word will get around that I'm no longer looking for a job. I just want to make sure before I close that door, my job is secure until next August.** *Please know I am not doubting you or your word, I just want to be sure that the company still needs me before I tell principals that I'm no longer looking.*

Thanks for understanding.

Amanda Hayward
Wed, Mar 20, 2013 at 4:31 PM
To: Christa Beebe

No problem..... tell them no... unless you want to take it of course... I don't want to assume you don't want to go back to teaching.. and no I am not being funny I am generally asking..

But on my side I guarantee your job until next September.

These email strings made up the basis of Christa's claims against Amanda. Amanda guaranteed her job through the end of the following school year, plus the summer break, but barely more than seven months later, she terminated Christa under the termination clause in the service agreement.

You can see how Kantner might have been desperate to keep this from a jury, particularly when you broke it all down. Christa made it clear that she was willing to make sacrifices for the company, including taking a pay cut, so long as she could be guaranteed employment for one more school year.

As a teacher, if she wanted a job for the fall semester, the time to apply and interview was spring, so once she took herself off the teaching market in the spring of 2013, it would affect her for the entire 2013-2014 school year.

Amanda understood this, telling Christa that "I just know that March is a time you need to apply" for a teaching position. Christa also emphasized to Amanda that losing her job would "devastate" her and put her family in "serious trouble," and that choosing not to take an offered teaching position was a "major life decision."

Knowing all that, Amanda guaranteed her job, not once but twice, in writing, only to fire her in the middle of the fall school semester.

Kantner asked Christa about the termination clause in her service agreement with TWCS Operations, and Christa said Jenny told her that, when she asked Amanda about it, Amanda said "this was just something that had to be done on paper, and that Amanda swore on her daughter's life that she would never terminate her."

Christa went on to say, based upon assurances from Amanda, "I had no reason to believe that my job was in jeopardy from signing this."

It's important to note, regardless of the fact that Christa signed the agreement knowing the termination clause was in it, it was several months after she signed that Amanda guaranteed her job. No way did Kantner want Christa's claim presented to the jury.

I left the deposition knowing it was just a matter of time before this part of the case would be settled.

Jenny's Story

I was relieved that Mike and Brent believed Mr. Kantner would settle quickly with Christa. That hope helped alleviate my guilt at having brought her to Coffee Shop, sacrificing her teaching job in the process. She never wavered in her belief that I was a partner and she was secure because I co-owned the company, but neither of us knew of Amanda's hidden agenda.

A company meeting in Las Vegas in late 2012 was the beginning of the end.

We met in a hotel room, with Lea Dimovski appearing by Skype, and listened to Amanda lay out her plans to fire most of the editing staff, claiming that their salaries ate into profits. She also insisted that the first money due from Random House was delayed. Our primary question was how to stay afloat until that money came through.

Amanda wanted to get rid of the editors. I mean, why would a publishing house need editors, right? That should have been a massive clue something was afoul.

Lea agreed to absorb most of the editing responsibilities and oversee the few editors we kept. Cutting the editors was a huge mistake. We had some fantastic authors in our line-up, and it was the editing team that had brought our most significant names.

I expressed my concern, but I was outvoted. I realized later Amanda had already made up her mind to get rid of them before we even met. Less than a year later, Amanda played out this same scenario at another meeting, but this time I wasn't present, and the heads on the chopping block were Christa's and mine.

I hated that Christa and I were now jobless and, in a lawsuit, being grilled by Amanda's lawyer. But Christa is fierce. As Mr. Kantner asked questions, she didn't back down nor did she get riled up. I was very proud as I watched her. She, too, simply told the truth. In my deposition, I had to admit my naiveté, but Christa relied on cold, hard facts: she had an agreement that guaranteed her a job, with emails to prove it, and Amanda had broken that agreement.

Mr. Kantner tried for over two hours to get her to change her story, but the truth doesn't waver.

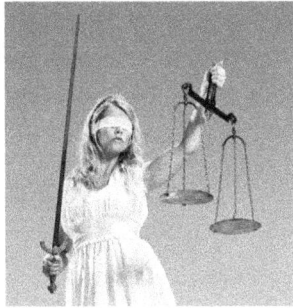

CHAPTER TEN: Amnesia

I can only wait for the final amnesia, the one that can erase an entire life.
              —Luis Bunuel

Mike's Story

JENNY AND CHRISTA met Brent and me at our office on Thursday, then I drove us to Jones Day's office building just north of downtown, close to what was known as the "uptown" area, for Jennifer McGuire's deposition. Brent suggested I play some "battle music" as we drove, so I found "Drums of the Islands," by the Makaha Sons. Not exactly battle music, but one of my favorites from one of my favorite Hawaiian groups. More fitting with my Type B personality than a John Philip Sousa march or Wagner's "Ride of the Valkyries," popularized in the movie *Apocalypse Now*.

After we arrived, we took an elevator to the reception floor, identified ourselves, and were ushered to a conference room, where the court reporter had already set up, along with a videographer. I took my place on one side of the conference table and placed a stack of exhibits in front of me, while Brent, Jenny, and Christa sat to my right. Kantner came in and sat across the table while Jenn McGuire took her place at the end, to my left, directly across from the video camera.

The deposition started at 9:27 AM, and for the next five hours, I participated in one of the most remarkable episodes of amnesia and ignorance I have ever witnessed in over 30 years as a lawyer. McGuire answered very few questions outright, hedged on others, and, as her most popular response, defaulted to "I don't know," "I honestly don't know," "I don't remember," "I honestly don't remember," "I don't recall," and "I have no idea," or some variation of those. When I later received the typed transcript from the reporter, I made an attempt to count how many times she had given an answer from that family of responses. I ended up losing count, but I can safely say it numbered north of 200 times in 177 pages.

It became clear McGuire had been coached to deny the existence of a partnership, but she had the disadvantage of having authored numerous emails that admitted its existence. She also slipped a few times and admitted it even without a document in front of her. For example, one of my earliest questions was:

"Am I correct that it was in July of 2011 that you first accepted an invitation to be a partner in The Writer's Coffee Shop."
"Reluctantly, yes, I did," she answered.

Then I handed her an email exchange with Amanda and Jenny that confirmed this. On July 17, 2011, Amanda wrote:

Do you have any receipts for the last year at all to post to me?

Just thinking about budget and tax season here :)

Also Jenny brought up the partnership thing with me again tonight.

It means your [SIC] responsible for 33.3% of the tax on profits which for now means nothing as there will be no profits but later I have no idea.

We need to know soon if you want to be a partner or not.

McGuire answered:

I do have receipts. I'll get them all together tonight and get them to the post office tomorrow.

Thinking about the whole partnership thing scares the fuck out of me. How the hell have you dealt with this shit for about a year now? *sigh* I'm all in this with you girls so lets' go for it.

Amanda replied:

he he he.. yeah Just don't think about it.. that is how I get through it.. :)
thanks for the receipts :)

Jenny then wrote:

Yeah jenn. It's scary. But we got each others backs. I have a very good accountant if you want to use him when the time comes. But let's face it. 33.3% of nothing won't be so hard to swing. Lol. Love y'all. Let's do it.

That, to me, sure looked like an acknowledgment from Amanda that she and Jenny were already partners in a pre-existing partnership, that they were inviting McGuire to become a partner with them, and that McGuire accepted the invitation. I followed up with McGuire on the emails, trying to nail it down.

"When you answered my question, you said 'reluctantly, yes.' Why do you mean 'reluctantly'?"

"The idea of partnership scared me, so I—I really—didn't want to do it. And you can tell from the email they really talked me into it."

"Why did the idea of a partnership scare you?"

"Because I—My job, I work paycheck to paycheck. Sometimes by the time I got my paycheck, I might have had five dollars in my bank account, so I had no money to contribute. And the liability if—you know, if something happened and I'm—I'm responsible to take care of a portion, I just—that's what scared me."

Clearly, she understood exactly what she was committing to: partner status with responsibility for partnership liabilities. It appeared that she soon started having second thoughts, realizing she had strayed from the "there-was-no-partnership-Amanda-was-a-sole-trader" talking point.

"Was it your understanding that at this point, July of 2011, that Jenny Pedroza and Amanda Hayward were partners in a partnership?" I asked.

"As far as I knew—as far as I understood, there was no partnership at the time."

"Then what was it that you were invited to join in July of 2011 in this email?"

The look on her face told me the realization set in that her earlier answer had veered off course from the party line. She responded with a remarkable bit of double-talk as she struggled to fix the problem.

"When—It was in order to get a setup for banking properly in the U.S. We needed a partnership, because that's the way the business had— When the EIN [employer identification number from the IRS] number

was set up, it was set up as a partnership instead of a corporation like it was supposed to have been set up. So, at this point, they were trying to get things fixed so taxes could be filed and then bank—bank—U.S. bank accounts could be taken care of, and then we were going to fix it back to a corporation once we got it all settled right."

"When you say 'fix it back to a corporation,' had it been a corporation at one time before?"

"It was a sole trader, from my understanding, from the beginning."

"What is that understanding based on?"

"My conversations with Amanda."

"So, when Amanda Hayward sent you this e-mail and said, 'Jenny brought up the partnership thing with me again tonight,' what did you think she was talking about?"

"I thought she was talking about the fact that we had to get the partnership set up because that's the way it was—she had set it up with the EIN number."

My head was spinning. Her answers made absolutely no sense. I had seen this before—it was the behavior of someone who either didn't know what they were talking about or they were trying to be evasive, so they rambled, double-spoke, and contradicted themselves. In February, 2011, Jenny had, with Amanda's blessing, obtained an EIN for Coffee Shop as a partnership. She passed along the number to Amanda, who promptly emailed another Coffee Shop staffer that "we are now a company in the United States." All this talk of "fixing it back to a corporation" was absurd.

"It also says in that e-mail, Ms. Hayward says to you, 'It means you're responsible for thirty-three-point three percent of the tax on profits which for now means nothing as there will be no profits but later I have no idea.' Do you see that language?" I asked.

"Yes."

"What did you understand that to mean?"

"To me, it was saying that—You know, I—I was scared about, you know, being partly responsible for—of taxes, of course, like it says. And like I said, at that point, you know, there were no profits because that account was a zero—basically a zero account. Money came in, and then that money went right back out to pay U.S. contractors."

"So, it was your concern, then, that if you became a member of a partnership, you would have liability?"

"Yes."

"And that was why you were reluctant to accept?"

"Yes."

"On page one of that exhibit, in response to Ms. Hayward, the last line, you say, 'I'm all in this with you girls so let's go for it.'"

"Yes."

"Does that mean your response to Ms. Hayward was, 'Yes, I'll be a partner?"

"Yes."

She seemed relieved when I left the email exchange, but her relief was short-lived. It wasn't as if this was the only writing with her name on it with which she could hang herself.

After a few lead-in questions, I handed her a contract between Coffee Shop and a company called KOBO, Inc., which was an online retailer of e-books. After she identified it, I asked her to turn to the last page, which bore her signature, large as life, as a "partner" on behalf of "The Writer's Coffee Shop (partnership)."

"Why were you signing the KOBO contract as a partner in The Writer's Coffee Shop partnership in May of 2011?" I asked.

"Honestly, I don't even remember seeing the title down there, so I—And that's several years ago. I honestly can't remember what I was thinking or was happening at the time."

"But you didn't object to signing this, did you?"

"No."

"Did you raise any questions with anybody about why it had the word 'partnership' in there?"

"No. I didn't even think about it."

She then admitted she used the partnership EIN on various contracts she signed on behalf of Coffee Shop. And, in August of 2011, when Amanda conducted a staff meeting on Skype of Coffee Shop contractors and employees worldwide and said, "I have three other partners in this business," and identified those partners as Jenny, McGuire, and Lea Dimovski, then posted the transcript on Coffee Shop's blog site, McGuire didn't have a problem with that.

"Did you ever object to Ms. Hayward about having this language in the blog?" I asked.

"I don't remember."

"Were you concerned about being viewed by the people who had access to this blog as a partner?"

"I'm going to assume—I—I honestly don't remember but I—I—I guess no."

Additionally, when Jenny was tasked with setting up a bank account for Coffee Shop, as opposed to continuing to use a personal account in her own name for company business, McGuire signed documents, which were delivered to financial institutions, that identified her either as a partner or as an owner of Coffee Shop. Those included a Certificate of Authority for Wells Fargo bank, a draft partnership agreement Jenny had prepared, and an Assumed Name Certificate to be filed in Tarrant County, Texas.

She signed the partnership agreement, she said, because:

"I thought it's what we needed to do to get the bank accounts up and running."

"Did you have a problem signing this document as a partner to give to a bank?" I asked.

"I did not really think about it when I did it."

"And you certainly weren't intending to defraud the bank, were you?"

"No."

"But you wouldn't want to present a document to the bank with your signature on it that wasn't an accurate and correct document, would you?"

"No."

She tried to hedge when I asked her about the Certificate of Authority for Wells Fargo, but eventually backed down.

"It says 'full legal name of owner, partner, officer, or member,' correct?" I asked.

"Yes, it does."

"Which were you signing as?"

"I honestly couldn't tell you."

"Did you believe you were a partner of the company?"

"I honestly don't know if I would have believed I was a partner."

"Okay. Well, you responded to Ms. Hayward's email in July of 2011 and she asked you to be a partner, your answer was, 'I'm all in with you girls, let's go for it.' So, aren't you accepting the offer of partnership then?"

"Yes, I did accept at that time."

"And you signed a contract with KOBO as a partner?"

"I signed the contract with KOBO," she said, then claimed she didn't remember whether she saw the words "partner" or "partnership" when she signed the contract.

"You certainly weren't intending to defraud KOBO, were you?" I asked.

"No."

"You weren't trying to make KOBO think that there was a partnership when there wasn't?"

"No."

"And you weren't trying to make KOBO think that you were a partner when you weren't?"

"No."

I asked that same series of "you weren't intending to defraud, were you?" questions about all of the documents that she had signed for presentation to banks or other companies. It might seem sneaky, but it pretty much ensured that she could answer only one way unless she wanted to admit that she had committed fraud. I didn't believe that she was trying to defraud anyone; I believed that she *knew* that Coffee Shop was a partnership and she was a partner. My goal was to get her to state the truth and not simply toe the party line.

Perhaps more serious, though, was the fact that she received a K-1 for the tax year 2011 from Coffee Shop, and she claimed a partnership loss on her income tax return.

"Did you understand when you filed your tax returns with this K-1," I said, *"that you were informing the recipient of the filing that you were a partner in The Writer's Coffee Shop?"*

"Yes."

In other words, she knew that she was telling the IRS that she was a partner in that partnership, something she surely would not have done had she thought otherwise. She also acknowledged that, when the decision was made to sell *Fifty Shades* publishing rights to Random House, she knew that she would be responsible for her portion of the tax on profits.

"I knew," she said, "but I did not think this partnership would last into 2012."

Intriguing! If there was no partnership, then what wouldn't last into 2012?

"Why didn't you think it would last into 2012?" I asked.

"I thought we were going to dissolve it in 2012 to get the company properly set up as a company——as a corporation."

"You thought it was going to be dissolved in 2012, or before 2012?"

"In 2012."

"So, when you said you didn't think it would last into 2012, how far into 2012 did you think it was going to be dissolved?"

"I figured——I thought by tax time."

"Which would be, for most people, April 15th?"

"I didn't think that far ahead, but, yes."

I handed her an email she had written to Jenny on March 6, 2012, in which she said:

"Can you ask the accountant a few questions? Number one, bonus income

is subject to 25 percent Federal Withholding tax. Is that the rate no matter the amount of the bonus? Is bonus income subject to FICA?"

She acknowledged that the "bonus" she referred to was her part of the $500,000 advance payment to be made by Random House.

I continued reading the email to her.

"Number two, you say, 'If we receive the bonus before we dissolve the partnership how does this affect the taxes we pay on the bonus? If we receive it after the partnership is dissolved and it is part of 1099 miscellaneous income does that affect the taxes we pay?' Did I read that correctly?"

"Yes."

"Would it be fair to say that, as of March 6, 2012, you did not believe the partnership had been dissolved?"

"Yes."

"Does Exhibit 19 [the March 6 email] refresh your recollection, at least as of March 6, 2012, you didn't believe the partnership had been dissolved, yet, correct?" I asked.

"Yes."

And, unless it was dissolved in that intervening three days, which it wasn't, then Jenny's rights as a partner in the Random House contract were locked in when Random House signed the contract on March 9.

By the time the deposition ended, I was able to reach several concrete conclusions. One was Jenn McGuire either had the worst memory of anyone I had ever met or it was intentionally selective. Here is a remarkable example of her rampant amnesia when I questioned her about a meeting in the summer of 2013, which she attended, but Jenny did not, in which Amanda first discussed the idea of terminating Jenny and Christa.

Q: Who first brought up the idea of letting Ms. Pedroza and Ms. Beebe go?

A: I don't remember.

Q: What was the conversation about whether to let them go? Was it about whether to let them go or when to let them go?

A: I don't remember.

Q: What was the discussion about?

A: I honestly don't remember.

Q: Were you in favor of letting them go?

A: I don't remember. I'm trying—I'm trying to remember the conversations. I don't remember them.

Q: So, you can't remember whether or not, less than a year ago or about a year ago, you were in favor of letting them go from the company?

A: I don't remember. I—I can't remember the flow of the conversation, what—how it was discussed. I don't remember any of it.

. . .

Q: Was there any discussion about changing their job responsibilities?

A: I don't remember.

Q: Moving them to another department?

A: I don't remember.

Q: Giving them a cut in pay as opposed to letting them go?

A: I don't remember.

Q: You said you weren't provided any financial documents. Were others in the meeting provided financial documents?

A: I don't remember.

Q: As of this time, July of 2013, do you know how much money had been paid by Random House under that deal?

A: No.

Q: Do you know if it was more than $10 million?

A: I don't know any figures.

Q: Do you if it was in the millions?

A: I have no idea.

Q: You were aware, weren't you, that the original deal—the original advance was seven figures?

A: I don't know any figures.

Q: Did you not see any media reports about it being a seven-figure deal?

A: Yes, there were media reports, but I don't know any solid figures.

Q: In that meeting where letting Ms. Beebe and Ms. Pedroza go was discussed, did Ms. Hayward make any mention of the fact that she had guaranteed Ms. Beebe her job through the 2013-2014 school year?

A: I don't remember.

Q: You don't remember her saying that one way or the other?

A: No, I don't.

Q: Do you remember whether Ms. Hayward mentioned the fact that she had told Ms. Pedroza in an email that she would never terminate her, she swore on her daughters' lives?

A: I don't remember.

Q: Have you ever seen that e-mail?

A: I've seen it.

Q: You've seen the one where she says, 'I swear on my daughters' lives I would never do that'?"

A: I saw the e-mail.

Q: Did you ever discuss that with Ms. Hayward?

A: No.

Q: Do you know what different had happened between that e-mail and July of 2013?

A: I do not know.

Q: Do you know when they were notified they were actually being let go?

A: I don't remember.

Q: That meeting, you said, was in July of 2013, correct?

A: Yes.

Q: Did y'all put a timetable on when to effectuate letting them go?

A: I don't remember.

But for all that, between memory lapses, McGuire confirmed what Jenny had told me, including the fact that Coffee Shop was a partnership—with Jenny, Amanda, and McGuire, at a minimum, as partners—and continued to exist as a partnership beyond execution of the contract with Random House.

That meant that Jenny's right to Coffee Shop's profits extended to all payments made to Coffee Shop by Random House.

Jenny's Story

Jenn McGuire's deposition was hard to witness. Her struggle to remember was frightening. Unless there was evidence in front of her, she pretty much denied everything.

By the end, I think we all felt a bit of pity for her. It appeared that she had been coached to deny, deny, deny, but in doing so, she looked guilty. How can you "not recall" or "have no recollection" of details that made a significant impact on your life for over three years?

She might not have been able to remember anything, but I remembered *everything*.

I also knew that she, like me, had placed considerable trust in Amanda. I understood that she wanted to be loyal to her friend, but I kept hoping that she would just admit the truth. On occasion, when she felt her back was against a wall, such as when Mike asked about defrauding a company, a bank, or the government, she admitted the obvious.

In those moments, I knew that she knew what I knew: that we were partners in a partnership.

It seemed as if Mr. Kantner did little to help her during Mike's questioning. He occasionally objected but not often. There were times when he didn't appear to be listening. I knew he must have been, but his demeanor was different from the vigilance that Mike displayed during Christa's and my depositions.

Mike and Brent had watched me carefully, asked for breaks when it seemed like I needed them, and took notes. We appeared united as a team. With Jenn, it looked more like she was on her own, thrown to the sharks without a life jacket and left holding the chum bucket. It was painful to watch.

During Mike's questions about the Chicago meeting in 2013, during which there was discussion about terminating Christa and me, I hoped to gain some insight into why Amanda felt the need. She claimed that the company wasn't making money, but having seen what happened with the editors, I thought there was more to it.

I intended to be present for that meeting, but I broke my arm in early July—a straight break that couldn't be placed in a cast due to swelling—and my doctor wouldn't clear me to fly. Instead, Amanda, Cindy, Lea, and Jenn met to decide Christa's and my fate.

I didn't know, at the time, what had been discussed at that meeting but afterward, based upon hints from Amanda, I knew that the clock had started ticking on our demise; I just didn't know why.

Neither Christa nor I knew that, no matter how hard we worked or how many hours we gave to the company, nothing would save our positions. Cindy started to take on a more active role in marketing, displacing the two of us, which was troublesome. But we both believed that I was a partner and that, although Amanda could let Christa go, she couldn't just fire me. I even told Christa that I would give her half my salary if she was terminated, which would help keep her and her family afloat until she found another job.

I'll never forget how easy it was for Amanda to discard me.

Jenn's amnesia didn't surprise me; I just didn't expect it to hurt as much as it did.

CHAPTER ELEVEN: Alternative Facts

Respect for truth is an acquired taste.
    —Mark Van Doren, *Liberal Education*

Mike's Story

BRENT, JENNY, CHRISTA, and I drove to Jones Day's offices again the morning of August 7, the Thursday before the scheduled temporary injunction hearing the following Monday, this time for Amanda Hayward's deposition. I had been looking forward to it if for no other reason than to lay eyes on the woman who had sowed so much confusion from Australia. I didn't know what to expect from her when she testified, whether she would be an amnesiac, evasive, or straightforward when she answered questions. As it turned out, she was a mixture of all three, although the straightforward part was remarkable for its twisting of common usages of English words into meanings that defied logic.

I started by taking her through the complicated business structure she set up in the latter part of 2012 (diagrammed in Chapter 9). Remarkably, but maybe not surprising, she couldn't give me a straight answer as to the purpose of the structure nor did she even know what the bulk of those companies did. A number of them didn't have bank accounts or assets, nor did they engage in any actual business. The only two of any real significance were TWCS Operations, with whom Jenny and Christa had contracted as independent contractors, and another called SpoiltOne Investments Proprietary, Ltd., which Amanda identified as her "family investment company." I later learned the purpose of this company, solely owned by James Hayward, was to acquire real estate and make investments with Random House royalty payments, and to ensure they were out of reach of Amanda's creditors.

I asked Amanda about the service agreements she had coerced Jenny and Christa into signing.

"Why was it to be with TWCS Operations Proprietary instead of one of the other companies?"

"Because that's what that company particularly did. It was set up to do operations. I operate how the company would run."

"Now, when you presented that to Jenny Pedroza, she had questions for you about it, didn't she?"

"Yes."

"And one of her concerns was that there was a termination clause. Do you remember that?"

"I do."

I handed her a copy of an email string with Jenny in November 2012 then asked:

"Jenny expressed concern to you about the termination without cause provision. Look at the page that's numbered, in the bottom right, 650, and read to me, if you would, your response on that page to Jenny."

"'I would never do that to you even if we had a falling out or some huge fight. Out of respect to you and our friendship I swear on my daughters' lives.'"

"What did you mean by that?" I asked.

"I felt very comfortable stating that I—There's actually been—been cut out here."

"What's been cut out?"

"That I would not fire her without cause."

"Well," I said, *"on the next page, 651, you also say, 'If and I mean if we have to shut the company down I'll work around you and Christa going back to work.' Do you see that, as well?"*

"Yes."

"Where in there is language that is missing?"

"I just remember reading something different. That's all. So, I'm just assuming that there is something different."

It was a remarkable bit of revisionist history. She wanted to take the position, and would do so at trial, that what she actually said was she would never terminate Jenny *without cause*, although the clear intent was she would never terminate Jenny at all. She had told Jenny the clause was meaningless, but her lawyers insisted on including it. In the latter part of the email, she offered this bit of nonsense:

"The reason for the clauses about firing is because your [SIC] a contractor if you want security of being more then you have to be staff

etc. that's the problem I guess I spoke to the lawyers and they said you can't have it both ways :("

Keep in mind that, at the time she sent the agreements to Jenny and Christa to sign, Amanda had already received a royalty payment from Random House of $16.5 million. As a partner, Jenny was entitled to her share—either $4.125 million, if there were four partners, or $5.5 million, if there were three partners.

But Amanda had not told Jenny she received that payment from Random House. Instead, she told Jenny she was having difficulty getting Random House to pay, and, earlier that month, had even allowed Jenny to spend approximately $14,000 of her own money to pay Coffee Shop debts, even though she was sitting on that first huge payment. Then she convinced Jenny to sign a contract that gave her the unfettered right to terminate Jenny from the business.

Still selling, now she was trying to convince me part of this email's language had been "cut out."

"Did you produce a copy of this e-mail to your counsel to produce to me?" I asked.

"I believe so."

"And you think it has something different in it, or additional in it, than is contained here?"

"Yes, either that or I'm remembering a different email."

"What did you mean, though, when you said, 'I swear on my daughters' lives'?"

"That I felt very comfortable in what I was saying."

137

"Do you often say things and swear on your daughters' lives?"

"Yes."

Unbelievable!

She also testified she terminated Jenny and Christa less than a year later because "we were losing more and more money as the months went on. And the company just couldn't sustain— keep sustaining all of those losses." Yet, by the time Amanda terminated them, she had received roughly thirty-five million dollars from Random House. It was a shame the company couldn't sustain "losses" like that.

Amanda also testified she couldn't tell Jenny the terms of the Random House contract because she signed a non-disclosure agreement with Random House. I didn't believe her.

"When did you sign a non-disclosure agreement with Random House?"

"I don't recall."

"Was it at the time the Random House contract was signed?"

"I don't recall."

"Was it subsequent to that?"

"I don't recall."

"Was it a separate document from the publishing contract with Random House?"

"I don't recall."

Now she was starting to sound like Jennifer McGuire.

"Is there a reason why you haven't produced it to your counsel to produce to me?"

"I thought we had," Kantner said.

"No," I said.

And if he had, he would have known it.

"Then I don't have it," Kantner said. *"We would have produced that, I think. So, I don't have an answer for you on that right now, but there is a non-disclosure agreement. You can check with Random House if you don't want to—"*

"I have."

I had gotten documents directly from Random House when Kantner failed to produce complete royalty statements, and I reviewed the contract between Random House and Coffee Shop, and all of the royalty statements, and there was no NDA. Why Kantner insisted that there was based on nothing more than his client's statement intrigued me. If he hadn't seen it for himself, how could he know for sure? Then Amanda pulled the credibility rug right out from under her own lawyer.

"Did you sign a non-disclosure agreement with Random House?" I asked again.
And this time, Amanda said, *"I don't recall."*

After we had been going about an hour, we took a break, during which time Kantner was going to search for the NDA, but when we resumed a few minutes later, he still hadn't found it among the documents his client had given him. Hadn't found it, because it didn't exist. Now Amanda sang a different tune—the

139

NDA she signed was with Erika Mitchell, the author of the *Fifty Shades* trilogy, and not with Random House. When I asked her again about Random House, her memory failed her:

"I don't remember anything."

Those of you old enough to remember the television show *Hogan's Heroes* will understand why I could almost hear the voice of German guard Sergeant Schultz in my mind as the Allied POWs carried out their shenanigans right under his nose: "I see nothing!"

Turning to her treatment of Christa, I tried to impress upon Amanda how bad her actions looked. She admitted she knew that, when Christa quit her teaching job to work full-time for Coffee Shop, Christa was concerned about her ability to pay her home mortgage.

"I took that under consideration in what she was earning that year," Amanda said.

"Do you remember Christa telling you, in the spring of 2013, that she had been approached by a principal with a teaching position, but she didn't want to take it if she could continue to work for The Writer's Coffee Shop full-time?" I asked.

"I don't particularly remember about a principal coming forward, but I do remember something along those lines, yes."

"Do you remember telling her that you had guaranteed her job through the following school year?"

"Yes."

"In that e-mail, Christa says, 'Just wanted to check in, one more time,

before I make a major life decision.' Did you have an understanding of what she meant by 'major life decision'?"

"Yes."

"What did she mean by that?"

"She wanted to make sure she had a job."

"And you guaranteed her a job through the following school year, correct?"

"I did."

"And did you terminate her before the following school year was over?"

"I did."

I tied it up a few minutes later, drawing the inescapable conclusion.

"But you do agree that you guaranteed her job through the school year?"

"Yes."

"And you didn't keep that guarantee?"

"No."

If that didn't convince Kantner he needed to settle at least Christa's claims, nothing would.

What was particularly interesting about Amanda's deposition were her efforts to explain away black-and-white emails and words with common meanings. She denied the plain language in a number of those emails, such as the invitation to McGuire to become a partner in Coffee Shop. Instead, Amanda came up with a convoluted explanation that she had merely invited McGuire to share tax liability on "profits" in a bank account—an account in Jenny's name but not Amanda's.

She argued that she would ensure there would never be any profits on the account—I'm not sure how one has profits on a bank account; there's either a balance or not, but not profits—because she would make sure all money flowed through the account, leaving it without any "profits." So why would Amanda need McGuire to assume liability for taxes on those non-existent "profits"?

As a reminder, this is the particular sentence in Amanda's email to McGuire in question:

"Also Jenny brought up the partnership thing with me again tonight. It means you're responsible for 33.3 percent of the tax on profits which for now means nothing as there will be no profits but later I have no idea. We need to know soon if you want to be a partner or not."

Here's how my exchange went with Amanda as we discussed this sentence:

Q: When you said to Jenn McGuire, "We need to know soon if you want to be a partner or not," what did you mean?
A: Who would basically be on those tax returns for that one account in 2011.
Q: I don't see anything in there about a tax return. Did you advise Jenn McGuire that the whole question you were asking is whether or not she wanted to be responsible for tax on profits, but not be a partner?
A: For that one account that needed to be a tax return filed for 2011.
...

Q: In your e-mail to Jenn McGuire, I don't see any reference to a bank account.

A: But that is what we were talking about.

Q: Why would you tell her that she would be responsible for 33.3 percent of the tax on profits if all you were talking about was a bank account?

A: That is—that didn't even happen, actually, on the bank account. In the end, I wasn't even included on that tax return at the end of the year, so this was just an idea that Jenny had brought to my attention after I had asked some questions about how we were going to deal with the wrong tax number.

Q: Objection, non-responsive. [Court reporter read back the previous question.] *And so that's the question I'm asking you.*

A: I understand that. I just don't understand why my answer wasn't clear, so I'm just trying to see if I can rephrase it myself. The profits on that bank account was not going to be any profits because it was a trading account that only accepted Amazon money through the company. And we were paying U.S. employees and office through that account, so there was not going to be any profits within that account. And that's what I meant by that sentence.

Q: So, you were referring to a bank account having profits?

A: Yes.

Q: You're not referring to a company having profits?

A: No.

Q: Why would you be asking Jenn McGuire to be responsible for 33.3 percent of the tax on the profits on a bank account?

A: Because Jenny was worried, with her bankruptcy, that she couldn't have actually put it through on her own.

Q: When you say, "We need to know soon if you want to be a partner or not," what did you mean?

A: Whether she wanted to go on the tax return for 2011 to help.

Q: To help what?

A: To help with the tax that we had worked on—that had been filed wrong.

Q: Did Jenn have to pay 33.3 percent of the tax on profits in 2011?

A: There wasn't going to be any tax left on profits. I made sure that there was going to be a—close to nil on the end of that account because that's what it was there for, to have money come in and then money go out.

I felt as if I had been trapped in a bad Abbott and Costello "Who's on First" parody. Her answers spun circles that defied logic. As best I could interpret it, her story was this: I wasn't asking Jenn McGuire to be a partner in a partnership—even though those are the words I used. Instead, I was asking her to go on a tax return for a business bank account, even though I never used the words "tax return" or "bank account." I did it because I wanted her to be responsible for one-third of the taxes on the profits in that account, even though bank accounts don't have "profits." It really didn't matter, anyway, because I was going to make sure there wouldn't be any profits, so the liability I was asking her to assume would never exist. Nevertheless, I still wanted her to assume that non-existent liability on a bank account that was not in my name and to "go on the tax return" for the bank account's non-existent profits.

The 2011 tax return that Coffee Shop filed was a Form 1065 "U.S. Return of Partnership Income" and was signed, with Amanda's knowledge and blessing, by Jenny as a "general partner." Coffee Shop also issued Schedule K-1s, reflecting "Partner's Share of Income, Deductions, Credits, etc.," utilizing the "partnership employer identification number," to Jenny and to Jennifer McGuire. Again, with Amanda's knowledge and blessing.

But Amanda Hayward wasn't about to let facts get in the way of her story.

She also acknowledged that, in April 2011, Jenn McGuire signed a contract with e-retailer KOBO, Inc. on behalf of "The Writer's Coffee Shop (Partnership)" as a "partner," and Amanda knew it at the time. She said that "needed to be changed because it was in error," but she was forced to admit sales summaries sent by KOBO from April 2011 to August 2013 continued to identify Coffee Shop as a partnership.

Amanda tried to spin other documentary evidence by theorizing the word "partner" didn't have legal significance but was merely a "friendship thing." She told the worldwide staff of Coffee Shop, in a meeting conducted via Skype in August, 2011, "I have three other partners in this business," and then named Jenny, Jennifer McGuire, and Lea Dimovski as those partners. She even had the transcript of that meeting posted on Coffee Shop's blog spot, while the company website identified the four women as "co-founders" of Coffee Shop.

Her explanation for why she called them "partners"?

"As a friendship thing and also to show that who was actually—I was in charge and having a hard time at that point nobody was listening to anybody below me. And it was a way of showing that they were above their roles. Their roles that they were having as director, nobody was listening to them. They all had to come and talk to me, and I just could not manage all the e-mails and everything that I was getting because nobody would listen to those three people."

"Is there a reason why you used the word 'partners' instead of 'colleagues,' 'co-workers,' something else?" I asked.

"'Partners' is just an endearment term that we used."

"What is your understanding of the term 'co-founder'?"

"They were there from the beginning."

"Was there anybody else there from the start of The Writer's Coffee Shop besides you, Jenn McGuire, Jenny Pedroza, and Lea Dimovski?"

"There were, but they were very minor roles."

"So 'co-founder,' or 'founder' means something more than just they were there at the start, correct?"

"Well, yeah, it's a friendship thing, that they were there from the beginning with me."

Amanda continued to redefine words throughout her deposition. When major publishers came knocking, Amanda sought the agreement of her partners in the decision whether to let Erika Mitchell out of her contract with Coffee Shop and which publisher to sell the rights to. This was "probably one of the biggest decisions I actually had to make, ever," she said. She emailed Jenny and McGuire about a proposed response she had drafted to Valerie Hoskins, the author's agent, and told them, "Of course, it also needs to be discussed if we all agree with this decision."

"Why did they need to agree," I asked, *"if they were not partners?"*

"Oh, they weren't partners. It was just advice."

"Well, it doesn't say 'advice.' It says 'if we all agree,' doesn't it?"

"That's exactly what I meant, though, and I've—I've used that sort of phrasing before."

"Okay, so when you say 'agree,' you mean 'advise'?"

"Yes."

Of course! How stupid of me to think otherwise. She utilized the same definition to explain her February 12, 2012, email to author Erika Mitchell, in which she wrote, "I spoke to the girls this morning, and we are all in agreement that we are willing to let you go but for a price." "Agreement," she said, merely meant she had solicited their opinions.

By the time I was finished with the deposition, I was able to put together what I came to call the "Amanda Hayward Lexicon," with her alternative meanings for commonly understood words.

We set it up on a demonstrative exhibit for use at trial:

The Amanda Hayward Lexicon

What Amanda Said Then	What Amanda Now Says She Meant
"We need to know soon if you want to be a partner or not..."	Do you want to be on tax returns to help?
"Profits"	Interest on a bank account
"Partner"	It's a friendship thing Or it's an endearment term Or just a term of affection Except when talking to Jenn McGuire about being a partner – "That was to do with the bank account." Or unless it's on the KOBO contract
"Co-founder"	"It's a friendship thing" and simply refers to people who were there at the beginning with her.
"Founder"	People who were around at the beginning. But not everybody who was around at the beginning
"Name change"	Not a name change but instead a brand new company that didn't exist before
"We" and "Our"	"I" and "my"
"Our new venture"	A friendship thing
"Agree"	Advise; give an opinion
"Come on board"	She has no idea what she means
"Company"	Not a company
"We are now a company in the U.S."	We're not a company but "... we actually can trade and kept a bank account in America"
"Agreement," as in "we are all in agreement"	Advice; opinion
"I swear on my daughters' lives"	Absolutely nothing
"Guarantee"	Absolutely nothing

13839-501-021.1

When Amanda signed the contract with Random House, she wrote her personal Australian tax file number on the line that called for "Federal Identification Number."

"Why didn't you use the EIN for The Writer's Coffee Shop?" I asked.

"Because it wasn't valid then."

"Why wasn't it valid in March of 2012?"

"Because we had gotten rid of it and changed it over for the beginning of January 2012."

"You had gotten rid of the EIN at the beginning of January of 2012?"

"Yes."

"And changed it over to what?"

"Amanda Hayward, trading as The Writer's Coffee Shop. I opened a bank account in 2012 with Chase in New York."

While it's true Amanda opened a Chase account in early 2012, the EIN was still valid as of March 9, and Coffee Shop used it on other contracts well after the Random House contract was signed, as well as on tax documents Coffee Shop provided to authors. I suspected then, and am convinced now, the reason why she told Jenny she had been forced to sign a non-disclosure agreement with Random House was because she needed an excuse to prevent Jenny from seeing the contract, which would have raised red flags when she saw a different number than the Coffee Shop EIN on the line for "Federal Identification Number."

I wrapped up my questioning by asking about an email that

had given Kantner a red face at Jennifer McGuire's deposition. When I had handed him a copy of it at that deposition, he read through it as I asked questions. According to Brent, it appeared from the way in which Kantner's face turned beet red, that he was seeing it for the first time. If that was true, then it meant Amanda had not given it to him as part of her document production. That seemed entirely possible to me, since it was clear from the meager number of pages Kantner produced that either he, himself, withheld a lot of documents or Amanda hadn't given him everything.

Amanda sent this particular email, dated June 21, 2012, after the Random House contract was signed, and also following a period of a month or two during which, according to Jenny, Amanda had gone silent, not responding to emails or returning phone calls. I believed it was during this period that Amanda was working with her Australian lawyers and accountants to restructure the business to exclude her partners. This email, in my opinion, confirmed that.

The email, addressed to Jenny and McGuire, was lengthy, so I won't include all of it, but here are pertinent excerpts, complete with typos and grammatical errors, and with my highlighting to emphasize certain passages:

I've copied Jenn in on this so she knows what is going on... I sort of want you to both understand what I'm doing and how much work I have to do.... and probably why I'm getting headaches.. I keep telling myself it will be set up properly soon but the thing is... it won't be.. I probably have 6 months of fucking work here to get the company acting the way it should operational wise.. which is why I need you both to help me here....

can you both talk to Janine? Get shay and Kathie in on it.. explain.... This is what HAS to happen EROTICA or TWCS won't be around like this in a few years time... honestly the lectures I have had from the accountant won't help..

can you and Jenn have a meeting with them? I think having that meeting will also show **you two are also in charge not just me**... *you can also tell them yes I'm not well but I'm also setting the company structure up right.. which is really long freaking winded.. BUT it will be better in the long run.. so they know I am actually still working my arse off.. just in a different capacity*

Cindy is being great she is making sure everything is done my end and helping me get through the fucking tax shit that I HAVE to do by the end of the month **so I don't get audited from the government... I've been told to stop doing press on me.. or I'll def. get them sniffing around which we don't want as a lot of what we did earlier is not brilliant tax wise..**
...
...the accountants say we should be giving higher salaries and no bonus' for the next 2 years so we can settle the finances down.. so as of October I'll be giving you and Jenn 5000 a month.

I've decided not to take a salary and just wait until things happen with the finances.. I don't need it.. James is earning a fortune and I think it would be better to be rewarded later. . . I just want TWCS a success so you girls don't go back to your jobs and are enjoying life too

Tax wise... the accountants say we need to change a few things on our website... 1. no mention of Staff... say our TEAM.... and we have to dump the words co-founders as I'm a sole trader.. or we could be up for more tax... can you get annalise and Jonas to do this for us immediately? I don't know what to say to that and change it to.... but we have to show I'm the owner somehow, which pisses me off royally but I get it.. I understand why we so don't want to have to pay more tax.. I hope you girls understand... I'll

tell Lea... after I hear back from you.. could be another way to push her out a little more.

...

okay rambled on enough I have to get going as I need to get to the accountants for freaking hours.. god I HATE this stuff... REALLY HATE IT... but someone has to do it.. and be responsible and good..... *THAT IS SO NOT ME!!!!!! I like being naughty...*

love you both.. **hope you understand all of the above..** *please write to me and talk to me about your thoughts.. always worried how you'll react as I'm making decisions that effect all of us.. just know I am doing the best I can....*

Jenny's response?

"We are also 100% behind you. Whatever you need from us we are here for ya. Don't worry. The three of us know that we are a team. We are partners. Whatever the rest of the world sees is fine. We trust you completely."

There were a number of things about Amanda's email that troubled me, so I started with her line about showing "you two are also in charge not just me."

"Nobody was listening to anybody but me," Amanda said, parroting her answers to my prior questions about the Skype meeting in which she said she had "three other partners in this business." She continued, "And I just didn't have the time to actually answer every single e-mail and answer every single thing and it was driving me crazy, so I was trying to show that they could actually go to other people that spoke to me regularly and I would get them so in the end—if the—if they wanted—the author or contractor wanted to know what was going on, it cc'd me, but at least I was made aware of it instead of them actually coming to me all the time and just solely me."

Silly me, and there I thought it meant what it said—that Jenny and McGuire were also in charge. I also took note of what I considered an "over-explanation," which usually signaled to me not to put too much stock in the answer.

I moved on to a line that particularly intrigued me.

"We have to show that I'm the owner somehow."

Her position in the lawsuit was Coffee Shop was her company, and always had been, and she had been a sole trader, or sole proprietor, since Coffee Shop's inception.

"If you were always the owner, why didn't you always show that you were the owner on the website?" I asked.

"Because I didn't want to be the owner at the time. I wanted it to be shared around. I wanted the job shared around. I didn't want to basically have to always deal with everything that came through the door."

"But were you the owner?"

"Yes."

"You just didn't want the world to know?"

"I was—I was very, very, very, very busy."

"Did you not want other people to know that you were the sole owner?"

"No."

"Why not?"

"No. I mean, that's not the reason."

"Then I'll get back to my original question: Why didn't it always show that you were the owner?"

"It did. As CEO, I was in charge. I didn't like the word 'owner.'"

"Well, does 'CEO' mean that you are the owner?"

"It just means I was in charge."

I could see I was getting nowhere, but recognizing nonsense for what it was, I moved on.

"And then you say, 'I hope you girls understand.' What did you mean by that?"

"That I was changing all the names that we had been calling everybody for years as a sign of affection and friendship, and I was being told that that wasn't the way we should be running the business. It was beyond friendship. We were building the company as a company. We had to show that we were trying to behave like a company."

"But what was there for the girls to have to understand?"

"That we were changing all their roles, the names that we had been calling."

"But again, if you were always the sole owner, didn't they know that?"

"It wasn't that, that I was cranky about it. It was that I had to change everything on the website."

Shortly after that, I ended the deposition, letting her answers speak for themselves.

Jenny's Story

Hearing Amanda's answers infuriated me. She wanted to change the facts, but fortunately, I out-emailed her. Perhaps there was always a part of me that questioned her motives, but I never deleted an email from our conversations. At the very least, the email chains and other documents that Mike presented forced her to take a hard look at what we built together. She could change the wordage all she wanted, but she clearly held us out to the world as partners. Yes, she put up money at the start, but Jenn and I poured our sweat equity into the company. We worked long hours, often after having already put in a long day at work and taking care of our families.

I bristled as she sat at Jones Day's super edgy and modern conference table and tried to rewrite the narrative. I looked right at her. I wanted her to know I was listening. I wanted her to look me in the eye and tell me we didn't build this company together, but she never did. She looked at Mike; she looked at James, her husband; or she looked at Mr. Kantner. She couldn't look at me and tell me I wasn't a partner because the evidence and the facts proved that both Jenn and I were partners from the very beginning. We worked together to build an international online company, but when money started coming in, she wanted it all for herself. She felt she was more deserving and, unfortunately, we allowed this to happen.

One of the hardest moments for me was hearing about the timing of Random House payments. Amanda's mantra had always been that she was having trouble getting Random House to pay and that she couldn't tell the rest of us anything about it because she had signed a non-disclosure agreement. There were several occasions when I used my own money to pay authors' royalties and staff salaries because Amanda said that Random

House had not paid. I knew they counted on their money, and I knew that withholding payments for days or weeks might damage a family's financial condition. The way the process worked was that Amanda typically sent me statements, and I sent out the checks but, sometimes, when we were short, I covered the payments until she could wire funds to reimburse me.

Once, I spent over $14,000 of my personal money on Coffee Shop bills. If I hadn't been a partner, and if Coffee Shop had been solely Amanda's, do you think I would have used my own money to pay *her* bills? What I didn't find out until later was that, on the occasion of the $14,000 payment, Amanda had received a payment of over sixteen million dollars from Random House just a few days earlier. From there, the money apparently took flight to several different companies and investment accounts, but very little, if any, came back to Coffee Shop. I was devastated when I learned this. We could have continued to be a front-runner in the new publishing world but, instead, Coffee Shop died.

She now assumed that she could make others believe that "partners" meant "friends," "we" meant "I," and "us" meant "me." I didn't put my career on hold because I wanted my "friend's" company to prosper. I put my family, career, and livelihood on the line because I wanted *our*—a plural pronoun that included me—company to prosper.

We were partners and nothing Amanda now said could change the paper trail that led to that obvious conclusion.

CHAPTER TWELVE: Temporarily Enjoined

Justice is the great interest of man on earth. It is the ligament which holds civilized beings and civilized nations together."

—Daniel Webster

Mike's Story

TEMPORARY INJUNCTION HEARINGS are an interesting creation in procedural law. The idea of the injunction is to maintain the status quo while a lawsuit is pending, so it temporarily stays a defendant from taking certain actions, and often freezes assets, until the lawsuit is over.

We had to prove several things in order to get a temporary injunction:

(1) Jenny had pled a proper cause of action against the defendants;

(2) unless injunctive relief was granted, Jenny would suffer "probable injury," which was both imminent and irreparable, and for which she had no adequate remedy at law; and

(3) she would likely prevail at trial on her cause of action. Under Texas law, we didn't have to prove we would definitely

156

succeed at trial[18], but merely a "probable right of recovery," which is shown "by alleging a cause of action and presenting evidence tending to sustain it." [19]

The hearing is like a sneak preview of coming attractions—you give the judge a taste of what the evidence will be at trial. It's abbreviated, and you don't have to put on your full case. In fact, since you haven't yet completed discovery, and sometimes haven't conducted any discovery, you couldn't put on your full case even if you wanted to.

The make-or-break issues for us were whether Coffee Shop was a partnership and, if so, whether Jenny was a partner. If Coffee Shop wasn't a partnership, or even if it was, if Jenny wasn't a partner, we would simply pick our chins up off the floor, pack our bags, and go home with nothing.

Although the detailed story of what had happened at Coffee Shop, from inception to deception to expulsion to oppression to litigation, was compelling, and portions of it were necessary to frame the partnership issue, this particular hearing was neither the time nor the place to tell it in full.

I would save that for trial.

The hearing started on the morning of August 11, with Amanda and James Hayward sitting at the defendant's table with Kantner, while Jenny and Christa sat directly behind Brent and me at the plaintiff's table. Also present, but sitting in the gallery, was an attorney representing Random House. Although Random House was not a party to the lawsuit, it obviously had a keen interest in the proceeding since it needed to know what to do with any unpaid royalties that had been frozen by the TRO.

---

[18] *Walling v. Metcalfe*, 863 S.W.2d 56, 58 (Tex. 1993).

[19] *IAC, Ltd. v. Bell Helicopter Textron, Inc.*, 160 S.W.3d 191, 197 (Tex. App. – Fort Worth 2005, no petition).

This was the first time I ever saw Judge Susan McCoy, who presided over the hearing—and would preside over countless more hearings, and the trial, over the next nearly two years. I think I ended up spending more time in her courtroom in that relatively brief period than in any other judge's courtroom in my 30+ years as a lawyer. She was one of the smartest and most hard-working judges I ever practiced in front of.

The first question Judge McCoy asked was "Is any press here?"

Not an unreasonable question, given the media attention that had been garnered by filing the lawsuit. I wasn't surprised no reporters were present, though, since I hadn't contacted them, and I seriously doubted if Kantner had. I thought the last thing he or his client wanted was to be under the media spotlight when we introduced evidence of Amanda's conduct.

In my opening statement, I tried to frame the key issue for Judge McCoy, who would be getting her introduction to the case. "The issue is: Was The Writer's Coffee Shop a partnership? If it was a partnership, has it been dissolved, wound up, and terminated? And if not, if it still exists, what are the partnership assets, and what are the rights of the respective partners in the partnership to those assets?"

I cursorily walked through the history of Coffee Shop and Jenny's involvement in it, and highlighted facts that supported the five factors Texas courts consider in determining whether a partnership exists:

(1) receipt or right to receive a share of profits of the business;

(2) expression of intent to be partners;

(3) participation or right to participate in control of the business;

(4) agreement to share or sharing losses of the business or liability for claims of third parties; and

(5) agreement to contribute or contribution of money or property to the business.

I learned over the course of this case that Judge McCoy was one of those rare judges who read everything the lawyers filed, did her own research, and always came to court fully prepared and knowledgeable about the facts, the law, and the issues. I didn't know that at the time, though, so I had filed a brief that outlined the five factors and listed some of the evidence supporting each.

In my opening statement, I zeroed in on the key point I intended to later argue to a jury. "The real issue for this Court is, as of the time that the Random House contract was signed, was there a partnership? Because if there was a partnership, that Random House contract was a partnership asset."

In his opening, Kantner claimed, of the four people Jenny said were partners, "only one of the four partners is going to tell this Court that there was a general partnership." He attributed all of Jennifer McGuire's admissions in emails and signatures on contracts as "mistakes," and even brought up Jenny's bankruptcy again, as if it mattered.

Then, referencing the de Fontgalland letters, he attacked the very act of our filing suit as some sort of tactic. "There's an old saying in litigation," he said, "the best defense is a good offense. In fact, that saying crosses a number of boundaries. And I think what they decided was the fact, the fact of fear of being sued, and candidly, the increasing knowledge that *Fifty Shades of Grey* was a big hit, is what has brought about this lawsuit."

What actually "brought about this lawsuit" was Amanda Hayward had taken for herself about ten million dollars belonging to her business partner. And she nearly got away with it, too. That was where the cease-and-desist letters came in: a bullying act that brought Amanda's conduct to my attention and cried out for justice.

I called Jenny as my first witness, and she told her story in a straightforward fashion, entirely consistent with everything she had told me before. When you're telling the truth, consistency follows.

On cross-examination, Kantner started in immediately on Jenny's bankruptcy. After confirming Jenny and Amanda started Coffee Shop in 2009, he asked:

"At that time, you and your husband were still in a bankruptcy proceeding in the bankruptcy court here in Fort Worth, is that correct?"

"Yes."

"That bankruptcy proceeding did not conclude. You were not discharged until June of 2012, is that correct?"

I needed to head this off before it even got started. Clearly, his intent was to remind Jenny of de Fontgalland's criminal threats.

I stood and said:

"Your Honor, at this point I have to object that this is irrelevant."

Judge McCoy, who seemed puzzled by the questioning, asked Kantner, "How are you going to tie this in?"

In other words, it wasn't obvious on its face that there was any tie-in whatsoever to the issues in the lawsuit, so an explanation was in order.

"Your Honor," he said, then went on to misstate the law, "simply that if she truly believed she was a partner, she was obligated, under the bankruptcy law, to have reported the partnership and its assets and income to the bankruptcy court, to supplement her schedules at all times up to and including the discharge date."

"All right," Judge McCoy said. "So noted. Let's tie that in quickly."

"I will." Kantner then immediately moved to a different line of questioning, likely knowing full well he couldn't tie it in, no matter how much time he had.

After Jenny testified, Brent questioned Christa, who corroborated Jenny's testimony. Kantner asked very few questions of her, then I called Amanda Hayward as my next witness. It seemed as if she was surprised, though I didn't bother to look at Kantner for his reaction. He probably assumed that I would wait and cross examine her after he questioned her, but I can't be sure of that. I certainly got the sense that Amanda thought that, which would explain the look of surprise on her face.

Normally I might have waited, but I saw what a terrible witness she made for her own case when I deposed her. I didn't want to allow Kantner to first lob softball questions to elicit rehearsed answers before I got my shot. Instead, I wanted Judge McCoy's first impression to be the same as mine had been at the deposition. I hoped Amanda would be the same disaster in the courtroom as she had been in the conference room.

She was.

I started with an exhibit showing the complex company structure she set up in 2012. She admitted that those companies had not existed in any form prior to that, which was important for interpreting the "release and bar" clause in the service agreements. I also wanted Judge McCoy to see the shell game this structure represented.

"Did you explain to Jenny Pedroza that you were setting up all these companies?"

"Yes."

"And you explained that you were setting up eight or nine or ten different companies?"

"I did tell her it was complicated, yes."

"But other than saying it's complicated, did you tell her there were multiple companies that were set up?"

"Yes."

"How many companies did you tell her were set up?"

"I didn't specify."

"Did you tell her what the companies do?"

"No."

"You don't even know what the companies do, do you?"

"No."

So, there you had it. A simple online publishing company had now expanded to include a plethora of new companies, but Amanda didn't know why or what they did.

I then asked about concealing the Random House contract from Jenny. Amanda claimed she used her personal tax file number on the contract because the EIN "was a mistake that Jenny Pedroza made in 2011." A "mistake" made with Amanda's full knowledge and blessing.

"I did tell her that I had to—I had signed a nondisclosure agreement, which I did believe I had," she said.

"Who did you sign a nondisclosure agreement with?"

"Erika. I'm sorry. E.L. James."

"But E.L. James is not Random House, is she?"

"No. But she also signed on the document."

"But there was no document you signed that said you couldn't show Jenny Pedroza the Random House contract, was there?"

"No."

Hmmm. Remember Kantner's insistence at Amanda's deposition that she had signed an NDA with Random House and he thought he had produced it? Yeah, I remember that, too.

I drove my point home with one final question:

"Isn't the real reason why you didn't want her to see [the Random House contract] is you didn't want her to see that you had not used the EIN number on your signature?"

She answered in the negative, but I doubted if anyone in the courtroom believed her. Sometimes lawyers ask questions, not for the answers, but simply so the judge or jury will think about the question, not the answer.

From there, I moved to another absurdity in her position: that she had terminated Jenny and Christa because of supposed financial problems. I walked her through each royalty payment that had been made prior to that termination: $16.5 million, $15.7 million, and $2.8 million.

"And you just took all the money yourself?" I asked.

"Correct."

"If you add up all the royalty payments to date, do you know what that number totals?"

"No."

"Something in the neighborhood of thirty-six million dollars?"
"Okay."

"Does that sound right to you?"

"Approximately, yes."

I figured Judge McCoy could draw her own conclusions about the existence of supposed financial concerns. I then went through Amanda's twisting of the English language to explain away certain emails. As we neared the end of the day, it became clear I wouldn't finish my questioning and would have to continue the next morning. I had one final set of questions for the day, though, when she volunteered how much she "absolutely" trusted Jenny.

"Do you think she trusted you?" I asked.

"I thought she did."

"Do you understand now why she doesn't?'

In a thoroughly disgusted, and condescending, tone, Kantner said, "Objection, Your Honor. Argumentative."

Judge McCoy looked at me over her reading glasses, which she had pushed down on her nose, smiled, and said, "All right, this sounds like a good place to stop and take up again in the morning." She never ruled on the objection.

Because I was seeking an injunction to freeze funds, I needed to show that, unless an injunction was entered, there was a real threat she would spend or conceal the Random House payments she had already received. That's where I started the next morning.

"Do you know how much of that thirty-seven million dollars you have spent?" I asked.

"Not off the top of my head, no."

"Do you have a rough estimate?"

"No."

"Would it be fair to say that you have spent or paid taxes on thirty-seven-plus million dollars?"

"Yes."

"What kinds of things did you spend the money on?"

"I bought properties. I've also invested in shares and stocks."

"When you say you bought properties, have bought houses?"

"I have."

"You've bought commercial property?"

"I have."

"You've invested in businesses?"

"I have."

"Have you bought personal property?"

"I have."

I thought I had made my point. Unless Amanda was stopped, she'd keep spending, and pretty soon all the money would be gone, or at least converted into something else that we'd never be able to reach even if we got a judgment.

The rest of the day was fairly uneventful. Kantner put Cindy Bidwell and Lea Dimovski on the stand, as well as Jennifer McGuire. Bidwell and Dimovski added very little for either side, but Jennifer McGuire was the same mess she had been at her deposition. On cross-examination, I questioned her about the troublesome email in which Amanda invited her to be a partner.

"You testified in response to some questions from Mr. Kantner," I said, *"that you were very concerned about the possibility of having liability if you became a partner, correct?"*

"Yes."

"And it is expressed in your e-mail, right?"

"Yes."

"Because you understood what it meant to be a partner and share liability, right?"

"Yes."

"And so, knowing that, you said, 'I'm all in this with you girls so let's go for it,' didn't you?"

"Yes."

"So, you understood that you were accepting an invitation to be a partner in a partnership with Amanda and Jenny?"

"Yes."

Then I directed her to look at the March 6, 2012, email she wrote to Jenny in which she asked about tax treatment of the "bonus" from Random House, and how her taxes would be affected if the bonus was not received until "after the partnership was dissolved."

"Would it be fair to say that, as of March 6, 2012, you believed the partnership that you had accepted the invitation to join still existed?" I asked.

"Yes."

"And it had not yet been dissolved?"

"Yes."

"In fact, are you aware of it ever being dissolved?"

"I thought it had been."

"Did you ever send a notice to any of your other partners saying that you wanted to dissolve the partnership?"

"Not an official notice."

"What kind of notice did you send?"

"We talked about it."

"You talked about it. But did anybody ever send an official notice, 'We are going to dissolve the partnership'?"

"Not that I'm aware of."

"Were the assets of the partnership ever liquidated, liabilities paid, and the remainder distributed to the partners?"

"I do not know."

"Did you ever receive a distribution of assets with the partnership being wound up?"

"No."

When the hearing ended around mid-day, Judge McCoy took the matter under advisement. Now came the waiting game.

Jenny's Story

The courtroom was a beautiful, yet intimidating, room full of church-like seats for spectators and a podium facing the elevated judge's bench. On either side of the podium were two tables for counsel and clients.

It was an almost exact match to my television-induced imagination. Judge Judy did not whisk in and demand justice with harsh criticism but, rather, Judge McCoy entered, seeming larger than life. She appeared to be absolutely no nonsense, very interested, and driven by fairness and impartiality. I was scared to death of her. However, as scared as I was, I felt she would handle this case reasonably.

In what I was becoming to understand as true Bob Kantner fashion, he led with questions to me about my bankruptcy. Mike quickly objected, and the Judge was just as quick to move Mr.

Kantner along. This was a relief because I honestly had no idea what my bankruptcy had to do with this case. Mike explained later that this was a tactic to make me nervous.

After that confusing beginning, the rest of the questions at least seemed relevant. He again over-asked and repeated, but this time my strategy was to wait for him to talk out his question, listen to the last thing he said, repeat it back to him if I needed, and then answer. That worked for most of my testimony that day.

I had used the time between my deposition and the hearing to mentally prepare for my questioning, but it didn't appear that Amanda and Jenn did the same. I might have been wrong, because I knew nothing about lawsuits, but the whole "I don't recall" patter didn't seem particularly sound.

Neither Jenn nor Amanda could recall even minor details about Coffee Shop, much less about where over thirty-six million dollars went. How can you not know where all that money went? And how did this become their first line of defense?

Seriously, it began to feel like a *Twilight Zone* moment. It was like asking a child what happened to the broken vase, and his answer is, "What vase? I don't see a vase." Clearly, there is a broken vase right next to the ball lying on the ground. Clearly, the child knows something about the ball as he is holding a baseball glove.

Even more clear is that the child doesn't want to be responsible for breaking the vase, so his defense is to pretend the vase doesn't exist. That might work for a four-year-old but sitting on a witness stand in a courtroom under the watchful eye of a fierce, no-nonsense judge didn't seem like the time to regress to childhood. As I watched Judge McCoy listening to the proceedings, I imagined that she thought Amanda's lack of memory was a bit crazy.

Or maybe just convenient.

Mike's Story

The lawyers gathered again in the courtroom on September 25, and Judge McCoy issued an oral ruling on our application for temporary injunction.

"I think that, according to the elements required, after hearing the evidence which I received and the arguments of counsel, I find and conclude that the plaintiff will probably prevail on the trial in this cause. That the plaintiff has met her burden. By that I want—I want to divide that out, specifically Jennifer Lynn Pedroza—plaintiff Jennifer Lynn Pedroza has met her burden to demonstrate entitlement to a temporary injunction. Unless the defendants are deterred from carrying out or destroying—I'm going to call it the Random House funds, and we'll be more specific in a minute—at issue in this matter, Plaintiff will suffer irreparable harm, and it will be without any adequate remedy at law."

There were other issues that still had to be hashed out, though, before an order could be signed. I had asked for funds to be placed in the court's registry, including a $1.3 million payment that Random House had been holding since it was frozen by the TRO, but Kantner complained that if TWCS Operations, an ongoing business, couldn't receive the payment, then "as of the end of October, certain people are not going to get paid."

Huh? Amanda had already received more than $35 million from Random House, yet she couldn't make payroll unless she got the next payment?

At a subsequent hearing, on November 7, before a temporary injunction order had yet been signed, Kantner reiterated this argument. I responded, "Ms. Hayward has received thirty-seven million dollars. She testified that she has an investment account with seven-and-a-half million dollars sitting in it. I'm not sure why the money she's already received is not enough to cover any ongoing expenses."

Then Kantner raised an issue that I'm sure was dear to his heart.

"We are nearing a point, Your Honor, where it will be impossible for my clients to pay my bills...as we expand the scope of this order, I'm getting real concerned about whether they can pay me and my firm without violating the Court's order. If that's the case, I'll have to withdraw and cause her to be pro se and they can then enforce their judgment in Australia."

I didn't have a problem with Kantner and his firm getting paid,[20] but Amanda already had plenty of money with which to pay him. If we could get the formerly-frozen Random House payment in the court's registry, then we could at least preserve that amount in Texas, and it could be used to either satisfy an ultimate judgment or perhaps to contribute to a settlement. Unfortunately, Judge McCoy declined to grant my request and, instead, permitted Random House to make the payment to Amanda, with language in the order "that explicitly allows for payments of attorney's fees and experts" and "ongoing business expenses," as well as a requirement for a "strict accounting" of all Random House payments.

Amanda later used that last Random House payment as the first funds to pay ongoing business expenses and attorney's fees, before resorting to the prior payments she had received. I subsequently got monthly accountings from Kantner showing how Amanda drained every single dollar of that payment while the tens of millions she had already received were spent on real estate or personally invested by her husband. I'm not sure which would have been worse: simply not knowing where the money

---

[20] In hindsight, maybe I should have had a problem with it.

went or knowing where it went but that there wasn't a damn thing I could do about it.

But I'm getting ahead of myself.

On November 19, 2014, Judge McCoy signed the "Order Granting Application for Temporary Injunction." By then, as I expected, Kantner and I were in serious settlement discussions of Christa's claims and, in fact, we reached an agreement the following day.

The injunction order began by reciting a preamble of facts, including the judge's findings that "Pedroza will probably prevail on the merits of her partnership claim at the trial in this cause," and that, without an injunction, "Pedroza will suffer irreparable harm for which she has no adequate remedy at law."

It then said:

IT IS THEREFORE ORDERED, ADJUDGED AND DECREED that Defendants Hayward and TWCS, and their officers, directors, agents, employees, successors, assigns, representatives, affiliated entities, and any other person or entity acting in concert or participation with them who receives notice of this Order Granting Application for Temporary Injunction (the "Order") by personal service or otherwise, be temporarily restrained from:

(a) Enforcing, or attempting to enforce, the [Service] Agreements in any other jurisdiction or court.

(b) Dissipating funds they receive in the future and any funds they have already received from retailers of books published by Coffee Shop, including without limitation Random House, Amazon, and Barnes & Noble, that were paid to Coffee Shop, Hayward, and/or TWCS arising out of the Random House Deal and any publishing contract to which Coffee Shop is or was a party, that still remain in the WestPac account or any other TWCS account, except those monies used to pay ongoing business expenses.[21]

(c) Transferring, moving, disposing of, alienating, destroying, or concealing any cash, certificates of deposit, and bank accounts, including all savings and checking accounts, stocks and bonds, mutual funds, and any other intangible assets traceable to the Random House Deal, except those monies used to pay ongoing business expenses.

(d) Transferring, moving, disposing of, alienating, destroying, or concealing any tangible assets traceable to the Random House Deal, including real and personal property,[22] except those monies used to pay ongoing business expenses.

(e) Destroying, altering, concealing, or moving any books, records, accounting records, tax returns, invoices, contracts, and ledgers of Coffee Shop and/or

---

[21] This "ongoing business expenses" phrase, repeated throughout, along with subsection (f), which permitted Amanda to pay her attorney's fees from Random House money, allowed Amanda to spend the entirety of the Random House payment that had, up until then, been frozen by the TRO.

[22] I'll discuss this more later, but this is the clause that I believe Amanda's husband, James, violated when he sold real estate that had been purchased with royalty payments, but owned in the name of a company that he solely controlled. The injunction order extended to not only Amanda, but also to "any other person or entity acting in concert or participation" with her, which included James.

TWCS.

(f) Nothing in this order shall prohibit or enjoin the Defendants from paying their litigation expenses in connection with this matter, including attorney's fees, expert's fees, and costs of court, which shall be deemed ongoing business expenses.

IT IS FURTHER ORDERED, ADJUDGED AND DECREED that the Defendants shall provide an accounting, for the period commencing with the end of the business day on August 12, 2014,[23] and continuing on a monthly basis through the conclusion of this case, of every dollar received from the Random House Deal and spent, invested, or otherwise disposed of, including an accounting of every dollar in and every dollar out of the accounts (whether bank accounts, brokerage accounts, investment accounts, or any other repository of funds) of either or both of the Defendants or their related entities, including without limitation those entities identified on the chart admitted as Exhibit 71[24] at the hearing in this matter on Plaintiffs' application for temporary injunction. Such accounting shall be treated as highly confidential, pursuant to the Protective Order entered by the Court in this matter on July 18, 2014.

The order also set the case for trial for February 9, 2015, less than eight-and-a-half months after we filed the lawsuit. To make sure there was no uncertainty as to whether the case would

---

[23] This made the accounting retroactive to the date of the temporary injunction hearing.

[24] This is the chart, in Chapter 9, that I created based on public records from Australia.

actually be tried then, particularly since Kantner's clients and witnesses would be traveling from Australia, Judge McCoy cleared her docket for the two-week period starting that date. We knew we were going to trial in less than three months. Time to buckle down for the stretch run.

Jenny's Story

This would be when the music got deep and loud as the screen faded to black for a commercial. In another three months, I would have my day in court in front of a jury of my peers. My story would be told publicly, and I would no longer have to live in the shadows of doubt. That was a fantastic feeling. Amanda had done more than deprive me of my share of partnership profits. She had made me doubt myself. It was hard to explain to someone who hadn't been in that situation, but she used my insecurities to her advantage and got me to believe that I was not worth what I knew I was.

Having my day in court meant that I would get to stand in front of Amanda, Jenn, Lea, Cindy, and anyone else who refused to believe in the partnership and speak up for myself. My contributions had been invaluable to the success of our company and, just because they chose to turn their backs on me and rewrite the narrative, didn't mean that I had to sit and take it anymore. I knew that I was in for the fight of my life. Although I didn't know what the outcome would be, I was proud to stand up and let my voice be heard.

CHAPTER THIRTEEN: Countdown

Time was meaningless, except each moment was a countdown to the end.
　　　　—Lisa Henry, *Dark Space*

Mike's Story

TRIAL WAS NOW less than three months away. That might seem like a long time—and it is, if you're counting down the days to a Hawaiian vacation—but it passes frightfully fast when you're facing a jury trial at the end of it. It's particularly fast when you lose time due to the year-end holidays. There was still a lot to be done before I would be ready, including additional discovery to be completed, such as the deposition of Paul Varga (Jenny's accountant) and a trip to Sydney, Australia, for depositions of four members of Amanda's entourage: James Hayward, Lea Dimovski, Cindy Bidwell, and Amanda's accountant David Wayling.

Varga's deposition took place on December 1, then, on December 4, I boarded Quantas Airlines flight #7375, for the roughly 17-hour non-stop flight to Sydney, carrying one small bag onboard after checking my suitcase and two briefcases stuffed chock-full of documents, legal pads, deposition transcripts, and whatever else I needed. Several partners in the firm had encouraged me to fly first-class, which was actually called Business Select, but when I looked into the fares, I decided I couldn't justify the price difference. My Business Economy seat cost plenty—$4,027.60—but the higher-class ticket was $13,037.60. Sure, the firm was advancing expenses but, if we succeeded in the lawsuit, it would recoup those expenses off the top of any recovery. That meant the $9,000 difference would come out of Jenny's pocket. I refused to charge her for my personal comfort—especially since, as it turned out, I slept for about half of each leg of the round-trip flight.

I left Dallas at 8:10 PM on a Thursday, crossed the International Date Line somewhere in the middle of the Pacific Ocean, and landed in Sydney at 6:05 AM on Saturday morning, December 6, jet-lagged and wondering what the hell happened to Friday. After grabbing my luggage and passing through Customs, I jumped in a cab, which delivered me to the Intercontinental Sydney hotel, on Macquarie Street, near the Sydney Opera House and Sydney Harbor. Fortunately, my room was ready, so I checked in, took a short nap, then set out on foot to explore the city. I had exchanged U.S. dollars for Australian currency before I left Texas, so I had money in my pocket to spend, and shock to register at the high prices, even with the mental conversion back to U.S. dollars.

I walked to the Royal Botanic Gardens and Hyde Park, scouted out the nearby location of Jones Day's Sydney office in Governor Phillip Tower, and then crashed that evening, still fighting jetlag. I woke early Sunday morning and again set out to explore. I took a ferry across Sydney Harbor to the town of Manley, where I explored Manley Beach and ate a nice lunch. By evening, I was exhausted, so I ate dinner in my room—take-out from Burger King, which I found close to the Harbor—then spent about two hours preparing for the next day's depositions before dropping off to sleep.

Monday morning, I sought out a small breakfast place I had spotted during my wanderings the day before, then returned to the hotel to gather my briefcases for the deposition. Fortunately, I had a rolling case, so I stacked the second one on top of it and wheeled them to Jones Day's offices, located on "level 36" of the office tower, with a spectacular view of Sydney Harbor. A receptionist led me to a conference room where the court reporter and videographer had already arrived, and they established a connection via the magic of...well, something, to Brent's laptop computer back in Dallas, where he waited in the firm's main conference room with Jenny to watch and listen. David Wayling's deposition was scheduled for 9:00 AM Sydney time, which made it late afternoon in Dallas. If they sat through both depositions scheduled for that day—Cindy Bidwell was to begin at 2:30 PM Australia time—it would make for a late day back in Texas.

I was struck by Wayling's snarky belligerence in answering my questions. It was as if he felt personally affronted by my mere presence in his city. On the other hand, I called into question his conduct in setting up the "shell game" of companies, so maybe he had a right to be a bit snarky. Over the next nearly four hours, I listened to him growl, evade, condescend, and lecture, often with a sarcasm that dripped venom. However, I gained valuable answers from him, the value of which I doubted he understood. For instance, he testified you can't be a sole trader and a company at the same time, because a sole trader is a single individual.

I asked him, *"What is your understanding of what the word 'company' means?"*

"A company is a registered body with the Australian Securities Commission. Has shareholders and directors. Is governed by corporations law."

"So, a company can't be a sole trader, correct?"

"Correct."

Later, he said, "As a sole trader, you can't be a company...you can be one or the other. You can't be both."

He also testified a sole trader can't have co-founders. "...because a sole trader is a single person."

Yet Amanda, who now claimed to have always been a sole trader, had repeatedly held Coffee Shop out to the public as a "company" and having co-founders.

Wayling also testified the purpose behind the multiple company structure he set up was "asset protection...to isolate risk." I read "asset protection" to mean hiding assets from creditors, something I could use later, if need be.

During Wayling's deposition, I also had a chance to see the unbridled Bob Kantner in action. Remember that Agreed Protective Order I talked about in an earlier chapter? The one that allowed him to designate virtually every document he produced as either "confidential" or "highly confidential"? Yeah, that one.

The order said:

"The parties expressly agree that all persons not [qualified to receive confidential or highly confidential information] ***may be excluded*** *from any portion of any deposition in which Confidential Information or Highly Confidential Information is disclosed."*

I emphasized the words "may be excluded" to point out it wasn't mandatory but was simply permissive. Kantner had first invoked that provision at Jennifer McGuire's deposition, then again at Amanda's, and asked that Jenny and Christa leave the conference room until the questioning moved on from what he considered confidential information. On both occasions, and at his request, they did just that.

Which was how it was supposed to work. If he wanted to invoke the provision, it was up to him to do so.

I had multiple copies of all exhibits I used at the deposition, and I gave a copy of each to Kantner at the same time that I showed it to the witness, so he knew if an exhibit was marked "confidential" or "highly confidential," and he could act accordingly before I asked any questions about the document. After I had questioned Wayling extensively about several highly confidential documents without a peep from Kantner, he suddenly erupted when I got to exhibit number 142.

"Let me cut in here," he said, his voice rising. "You have Jennifer Pedroza listening in to this deposition?"

"Yes," I said.

Yeah, something he had known from the get-go, and had obviously forgotten. I didn't know if Kantner suddenly realized it on his own, or if perhaps Amanda had nudged him and reminded him, but he decided to go on a tirade as if I was the only one responsible for ensuring that confidential information wasn't disclosed to Jenny. I suspected his outrage was for his client's benefit.

"You are giving highly confidential—and you're asking this witness to comment on highly confidential information your client is not allowed to see while she is listening?"

"Then we will ask her to step out of the room," I said.

"I don't understand why you didn't do that in the first place," he said.

Nor I, him.

Keeping up the volume of his voice, he defaulted to condescension, not for the first time in this case.

"You know what the protective order requires. I would ask, yes, if you are going to be showing him a bunch of highly confidential information—you know under the protective order she is not entitled to see. She has got to be excused until you finish that examination. I'm disappointed that I had to tell you of your responsibilities."

Well, damn! I sure was sorry I had disappointed him. After all, I lived to make him proud of me.

I was a little disappointed in him, too. After all, he knew the provisions of the order just as well as I did, probably better, since he had drafted it. He had seen the words "highly confidential" on the exhibits before I asked questions about any of them, yet he hadn't expressed any concerns about Jenny listening in. In fact, on exhibit 138, I asked (according to my count in the transcript) 14 questions without a word of complaint or objection from him. It took three more exhibits for him to speak up.

We took a break, and Kantner left with his clients, red-faced. While he was out of the room, I called Brent on my cell and suggested that, rather than simply sending her out of the room, Jenny might as well go home because it would be in-and-out for the rest of the day. When Kantner returned a few minutes later, I tried to speak, but he was having none of it.

"You fucked up," he said. Then he added, "The clients think you did it on purpose."

I decided not to engage with him, because he was obviously embarrassed he had failed, in front of his clients, to protect the information.

The vehemence of his reaction, particularly when we went back on the record a few moments later, suggested he hadn't been the one to figure it out, but his client had told him.

Now let's examine his accusation that I had done this on purpose.

If I wanted to reveal these confidential documents to Jenny, would I show the documents to her privately so that neither Kantner nor Amanda would ever know or wait until I was in a conference room with both Kantner and Amanda, with Jenny watching and listening in from the other side of the world; tell both of them that Jenny was watching and listening; hand Kantner copies of documents marked "highly confidential" so that he knew exactly what they were and could invoke the protections of the protective order; and then, with both of them looking on, ask questions about the documents so that Jenny could hear and they could know she heard?

When we resumed the deposition, Kantner announced that he wanted to make a "short statement on the record." He said "short statement," but he apparently meant "condescending lecture."

"Mr. Farris has handed the witness this morning a series of documents designated highly confidential. On one of them he asked the witness particular questions about the amount of money referenced on the exhibit."

That was the document I had asked 14 questions about while he was asleep at the switch, and I had even moved off of it onto other exhibits before he woke up.

After a few words about the particular nature of that document, he said, "Notwithstanding the designation as highly confidential, and notwithstanding the clear terms of the protective order, Mr. Farris has this morning examined this witness on numerous documents including that one designated highly confidential with Jennifer Pedroza listening in via some kind of satellite link or other communication link. Clearly under the terms of the protective order, she is not entitled to see or hear about this information. Therefore, it is the defendant's position that the protective order has been breached. I have made this clear to Mr. Farris off the record."

As I said before, Kantner had undertaken the burden at prior depositions of invoking this permissive, not mandatory, clause of the protective order, but now he acted as if it was solely my responsibility to protect *his* confidential information. His voice began to rise to what I considered a shout, and he sermonized with the zeal of a televangelist. I was reminded of the words of author Cathy Burnham Martin in her book *The Bimbo Has Brains: And Other Freaky Facts:* "Some people believe that if they yell and scream, others will get the point of just how serious they are. For me, all I get is the point of just how out of control that someone is."

"I make it clear to him now on the record, should there be any additional happenstance where highly confidential information is discussed and we find out Ms. Pedroza is listening in any way, shape, or form, or otherwise receives the information, we will address it with the Court with a motion for personal sanctions against Mr. Farris—" He punctuated these words by jabbing his index finger toward me. "—whom we feel is responsible for the breach that has already occurred." He paused, then concluded, "That's it."

Rather than respond and point out his own failure to speak up timely, or to become indignant that he had chosen to yell at me, I simply said, without looking at him, "For the record, I will state that Ms. Pedroza has gone home. She is no longer listening in on the deposition. The only person at the other end is Brent Turman, an attorney at my firm."

With the sideshow over, we continued the depositions without further incident.

Two days later, I returned to Dallas on a flight that left Sydney at 3:25 PM on December 11 and arrived at Dallas Fort Worth Airport at 1:45 PM, also on December 11. Man, that sucker was fast. I wish I could have seen it take off.[25]

---

[25] That's the punchline, of course, to an old joke.

Jenny's Story

A few years ago, I was doing a writing assignment with my class about idioms. I asked the students to think of other ways to say, "All bark, no bite." In light of Mike's story about the Wayling deposition, I thought that reviewing some of those would be apropos.

Here were a few that the students came up with:

All sting, no bee.
All sizzle, no steak.
All talk, no action.

And my personal favorite, being a Texan, might easily apply to Mr. Kantner's conduct in Australia: *"All hat, no cattle."*

His reaction at the deposition didn't surprise me. In the few times I had seen him, he appeared quick-tempered and easily riled. I couldn't imagine going to a baseball game with him, sitting in the hot sun, eating a bag of peanuts, and having a good time. He impressed me as someone who worked 60-80 hours a week, took his phone and briefcase along on dinner dates, and missed Little League games. I could have been wrong, and I hoped I was. In the end, I left Brent and Mike to take care of the depositions, and I went home to bed. I had a classroom to run first thing in the morning, and it looked like idioms were back on the menu.

The whole "highly confidential" documents stratagem seemed, to me, like just another way for Amanda to conceal information. I never saw those secretive documents of hers, other than those that were introduced as exhibits at trial or that I already possessed. A few of the confidential, highly confidential, or really, really, really, highly confidential (I didn't even care at this point) documents were actually emails that I had sent to

Amanda, and I had my own copies. Emails that I had already given to Mike and Brent to produce to Mr. Kantner. As for the others, Mike simply said that he and Brent would review them for useful information for trial.

At any rate, Mr. Wayling didn't tell me anything that I hadn't already figured out. Amanda worked diligently to hide what she didn't want us to find. I would never know the extent of where she spent, invested, and tucked away money and, truthfully, I didn't care. Money makes people do crazy things.

So, why was I suing her?

Because she should have shared Coffee Shop's profits with her partners, in the first place. I had walked away from my career to build the company, which turned out to be very profitable. Forty million dollars split four ways was ten million dollars per partner. That would have set all of us up for life. Was it greedy for me to ask for my rightful share? Mike, Brent, Christa and I believed it wasn't.

Hopefully, a jury would agree.

PART III: TRIAL BY FIRE

CHAPTER FOURTEEN: First Impressions

We are lonesome animals. We spend all our life trying to be less lonesome. One of our ancient methods is to tell a story begging the listener to say—and to feel—'Yes, that's the way it is, or at least that's the way I feel it. You're not as alone as you thought.'
—John Steinbeck

Mike's Story

BETWEEN THE DEPOSITIONS in Australia and the beginning of trial, Brent and I immersed ourselves in final preparations, reading and re-reading documents and deposition transcripts, preparing exhibit lists and copies of exhibits, marking portions of deposition transcripts, and working with the good folks at Courtroom Sciences, Inc., to create demonstrative exhibits to show the jury and to edit video deposition excerpts. Jackie Arguijo was assigned to work with us in the courtroom as part of CSI's "presentation technology," projecting exhibits, highlighting and magnifying excerpts on the fly, and presenting the edited deposition transcripts to the jury. She proved to be an invaluable part of our team. To say she was fantastic would be an understatement.

It had been only ten months since Jenny gave me the go-ahead to file suit, and eight-and-a-half months since I actually filed it, when we gathered at the Tarrant County courthouse on the morning of Monday, February 9, 2015, to start jury selection. That Friday, the movie *Fifty Shades of Grey* was scheduled to open in theaters nationwide.

Lawyers for both sides had actually been summoned to the central jury room the previous Friday, when a jury panel of 85 was called and assigned to our case. Working together, the lawyers had created a jury questionnaire we passed out to the panel, then we waited until they had each answered the questions. Copies were made and given to us, to assist in preparing for Monday's *voir dire*.

Technically, *voir dire* should be given its French pronunciation—vwar deer—but in Texas, we say vore dyer, with a long o, long i. The term literally means "to speak the truth" [26] and refers to the jury selection process. The questionnaire was designed to speed that process along, giving us an advance look at answers from each potential juror. Some of the questions were generic, designed to communicate general information about the person and their interests, while others went to the heart of what the case was about.

These were the 21 questions asked:

1. Name and place of birth.
2. Please list your occupation and employers for the past ten (10) years.
3. Please list your spouse's name, employer, job title or description, length at current job, and employers and job titles for the past 10 years.

---

[26] www.merriam-webster.com

4. Have you or an immediate family member ever felt like you were wrongfully terminated from a job? Answer Yes or No. If yes, please explain.

5. List your favorite TV shows.

6. What are your hobbies?

7. What are your parents' occupations?

8. List the newspapers, magazines, journals, websites you regularly read.

9. Please give your educational background. Please include how far you went in school; the names of any technical or trade schools attended; any college and graduate schools you have attended, together with major subject and degrees received, if any.

10. Have you ever read any newspaper article or any online article, blog, or comment about any of the following? Answer "yes" or "no." Jennifer Pedroza: ___; Christa Beebe: ___; Amanda Hayward: ___; Fifty Shades of Grey: ___; This case – Pedroza v. Hayward: ___.

11. Have you heard about any of the following persons or topics? Answer "yes" or "no." Jennifer Pedroza: ___; Christa Beebe: ___; Amanda Hayward: ___; Fifty Shades of Grey: ___; This case – Pedroza v. Hayward: ___.

12. If you answered "yes" to any sub-part of question 10 or question 11, please state what opinions you formed as a result of what you read or heard.

13. If you or a family member have any relationship to the legal field, please describe.

14. Have you seen any advertisements for the movie Fifty Shades of Grey? 14a. Have you read Fifty Shades of Grey, Fifty Shades Darker, or Fifty Shades Freed? Answer "yes" or "no."

15. Have you ever written or read any fan fiction, that is a fictional story involving characters from a preexisting

work? Answer "yes" or "no."

16.   Have you or any member of your immediate family ever been a partner in a partnership? Answer "yes" or "no." If you answered "yes," please explain the circumstances.

17.   Do you believe that a business partnership can only be formed by a written agreement? Answer "yes" or "no." If you answered "yes," what is the basis for your belief? If you answered yes: If the judge instructs you at the end of trial that a formal written agreement is not required, will you be able to follow that instruction?

18.   Have you or a family member ever been cheated in a business deal? Answer "yes" or "no." If yes, please explain.

19.   Have you or a family member ever owned a business? Answer "yes" or "no." If you answered yes, please explain.

20.   Have you ever been a party to a lawsuit? Answer "yes" or "no." If you answered yes, please state generally what type of lawsuit it was and whether you were plaintiff or defendant.

21.   Given that some of these questions related to *Fifty Shades of Grey*, are there any comments you wish to make? (you can write on the back page).

These questions and answers offered a jumping off place when we started *voir dire* on Monday morning. On Sunday afternoon, Brent and I had checked into a downtown Fort Worth hotel for the duration of the trial, so we arrived early to the courtroom. The chairs at the lawyers' tables had been turned around on the bench side, so that we sat facing the gallery as the panel of 85 citizens of Tarrant County filed in and filled the courtroom. Jenny sat between Brent and me at the plaintiff's table, located closest to the jury box, while Kantner sat at the other table along with Amanda and James Hayward, and Caroline Harrison from the Fort Worth law firm of Cantey Hanger LLP. Kantner had also hired a jury consultant to assist him with the process.

Caroline Harrison had been added to the defense team about a month prior, presumably because Kantner wanted a Fort Worth firm attached to the defense, I suppose to curry favor with a Fort Worth jury. He made a good choice, as Caroline was a very skilled and accomplished litigator. I enjoyed working with her.

The one answer to the questionnaire that stood out in everybody's mind was an answer given by one male panel member to the question that asked if they had ever been wrongfully terminated from a job.

His answer was: "I didn't kill the racoon but because it happened on my shift." He had apparently lost his job at a restaurant when a dead, or dying, raccoon had been found in the kitchen. He didn't make the final jury, but he certainly provided some good comic relief.

Voir dire lasted the better part of a day, but by late afternoon we had seated a jury of 12, plus one alternate. Several of the potential jurors had to be questioned separately, in front of Judge McCoy but outside of the presence of the other panel members, because of issues they had with the erotic subject matter of *Fifty Shades of Grey*.

They were all excused for cause.

The final jury consisted of eight men and four women, while the alternate was also male. Four of those were high school graduates, five had at least some college, two had bachelor's degrees, and two had master's degrees.

I liked the jury we selected and felt confident that they would be able to fairly decide the case.

Who knew if I would still feel that way after it was over?

Jenny's Story

Jury selection was nuts! I had never seen anything like it on any courtroom drama. When we first got back the questionnaires, it was interesting to see what people wrote. Most had heard of the book, and a few found the subject matter deeply disturbing. From those questionnaires, we were able to get an initial idea of who might be a good juror. When the jury pool was brought in, the lawyers for each side asked a series of questions to help narrow down who we wanted to serve. Mike went first, then Caroline Harrison took over for the defense team.

At the end of the questioning, the jury pool was dismissed from the courtroom. A few of them had expressed objections to serving on a case about *Fifty Shades of Grey*, because they were offended by the subject matter. The bailiff brought those in one at a time, and the lawyers asked additional questions at the judge's bench. All of those were dismissed "for cause," then the two sides went to their respective tables to consider those remaining. Each side got six strikes, and I huddled with Mike and Brent to decide whom to strike. I learned that picking a jury wasn't necessarily about who you wanted, but rather deciding who you didn't want and then striking them.

After both sides made their strikes, a final jury of twelve, plus one alternate, was selected. The pool was brought back in, then the lucky winners' names were called, and they filed into the jury box. Based solely on my very limited ability to read body language and respond with my own smile to theirs, I was happy with the outcome. They all appeared level-headed and friendly, and seemed ready to take on this trial.

When those who hadn't made the cut were dismissed, one leaned in toward me and whispered, "Good luck. I'll be praying for you. Keep your head up."

How amazing was that? This lady didn't know me outside

of the few facts she had gleaned from questions asked during selection, yet she offered me support and comfort. I, of course, thanked her and then burst into tears. What can I say? It had been a very emotional few months.

Mike's Story

The actual trial started at 9:15 on Tuesday morning, February 10. All last-minute preparations had been done, and now months of hard work were about to culminate in a process in which we would ultimately place Jenny's fate in the hands of twelve perfect strangers. Brent and I sat at the plaintiff's table, with Jenny seated directly behind us. At the table just on the other side of the lectern, Bob Kantner and Caroline Harrison sat, with James and Amanda Hayward behind them. At the instruction of the bailiff, we all stood as Judge McCoy entered the courtroom and took her place on the bench, motioning us to be seated.

The defense had asked that the courtroom be sealed, taking the position Amanda's finances were of such a sensitive and confidential nature that no one other than the parties and their lawyers should be allowed to hear the evidence. Their biggest concern, I gathered, was the media. After all, it was an article in *Fort Worth Weekly* that reached the shores of Amanda's home country that triggered the lawsuit. I could only surmise they were afraid of something becoming public "down under," perhaps tax issues they wanted to conceal from the Australian taxing authority.

Their motion to seal the courtroom flew in the face of the American tradition of open courts. As a country, we pride ourselves on justice playing out in public, not behind the secrecy of locked doors. If any wrongdoing occurred, it should be exposed to the sunlight. If none occurred, that fact, too, should be brought into the open. Apparently Judge McCoy agreed with me.

"Before we bring the jury in for opening statements, we have a few items that we discussed," she said. "Number one pertains to sealing of the courtroom or clearing of the courtroom. It is my opinion, after reviewing the case law, that the issue of the amount of royalty payments paid to Ms. Hayward or to a TWCS entity or entities is not something that rises to the level of needing such protection as to violate the First Amendment rights of the press or others. So, in that regard, I am going to deny any motions to seal or to clear the courtroom for those purposes."

She then addressed the issue of documents that Kantner had decided to mark "confidential" or "highly confidential" under the protective order in the case. I had not raised any objections, although I felt it was ridiculous for him to so label in excess of 90 percent of the documents he produced, including documents Jenny already possessed, as well as some public records. During discovery, I had largely skirted the problem—other than that blip in Australia at David Wayling's deposition—by simply utilizing Jenny's documents, and not those produced by Amanda. When Jenny was either a recipient or sender of supposedly confidential emails, she already had her own copies, and those were the ones we used as exhibits, not the versions produced by Kantner.

There were a few documents, though, like Amanda's personal financial records, that we had only because they had been produced by Kantner. Amanda was still, even at this late stage, trying to prevent Jenny from knowing what she had done with the Random House money. Since our position was at least twenty-five percent of that money rightfully belonged to Jenny, then she was entitled to know what happened to it.

Again, Judge McCoy seemed to agree. "There has been an issue with regards to the documents that have been through the case designated as highly confidential and whether or not those can be used at trial. And in particular, the question was that Ms. Pedroza was not to have seen any documents that were designated as 'highly confidential.' Obviously, as the trial progresses and she's in the courtroom, she will not have to leave for that information. Looking at the Agreed Protective Order signed on July eighteenth of 2014, if you look at Section Six-F, it does state that at the trial or in a court hearing in this action, the parties may freely use 'highly confidential information produced in this action, subject to the rights of any party or third party to pursue further protection as provided in this protective order and the Texas Rules of Civil Procedure.'" [27]

She admonished everyone that, even though the documents could come in at trial, "the parties are under the obligations of the protective order, meaning they cannot go and speak to the press about these issues even if they have been disclosed in court."

Then, after going through a few other minor issues, Judge McCoy instructed the bailiff to bring in the jury. My heart rate ticked up a notch as they filed in and took their seats.

The judge confirmed that no members of the press were present, then turned the floor over to me for my opening statement. I stood and walked around the table to the well—the area between the judge's bench and the jury box. My heart pounded, but I took pains to hide my nervousness. As the old saying goes, "Never let them see you sweat."

I was keenly aware of the importance of my statement. Up until then, the jury knew only that the case involved a business dispute behind the publication of *Fifty Shades of Grey*. At best, that wasn't even a skeleton of a story. It was my job in opening

---

[27] This just further emphasized how unnecessary Kantner's outburst at the Wayling deposition had been because, ultimately, Jenny would have been exposed to "highly confidential" documents at trial, anyway.

statement to build the rest of the skeleton for the jury, especially the spine. During the presentation of evidence, we would flesh out the bones, but the jury first needed to know the foundation of the story. Only then could they gauge our success in the fleshing-out process.

"What this case is about," I said, "is a group of hardworking women who created a publishing company called The Writer's Coffee Shop. And when The Writer's Coffee Shop was right on the verge of true financial success, one of the people in that group, the defendant Amanda Hayward, decided to take the position that this was not a partnership, this was not a company, this was simply hers. It was her business. She was a sole trader. It was always her business. The other women worked for her out of the goodness of their hearts, and so she decided to make off with all the money. That's what the case is about."

And there you had it—my "elevator pitch." The question I had always heard at writer's conferences was, if you got on an elevator with a book publisher or film producer and you had only the time it took to ride up or down on an elevator from one floor to the next to pitch your story, what would you say to make sure they got the gist?

Continuing with the pitch—we could now assume the elevator got temporarily stuck between floors—I said, "You're going to hear two different stories today. One of the stories is a group of women got together and created a partnership, worked hard, got financially successful with a big hit book, *Fifty Shades of Grey*. Ms. Hayward took off with the money, kicked Jenny Pedroza to the curb, and she has all the money.

"The other story you're going to hear is the one I alluded to a moment ago: Ms. Hayward was a sole trader all along. Always her business, start to finish. The other women worked hard for her out of the goodness of their hearts. Worked for no pay for a couple of years out of the goodness of their hearts. And then when financial success hit, she took the money, kicked Jenny

Pedroza to the curb and went off with all the money. Y'all get to decide, after you hear the evidence, which of the first parts of those stories is true. And then you get to decide whether or not you want to rewrite the ending. That's what this case is about."

To put a button on my elevator pitch—the elevator started moving again—I added, "There are several themes that are going to run through this. And I want you to listen to these things as you hear the evidence. From our point of view, this is a case about betrayal and breach of trust. Ultimately, it's about misplaced trust. You're going to hear those undercurrents that flow through all the evidence."

The elevator reached the ground floor. Had I been successful with my pitch or not? While a publisher or producer would be getting off the elevator at that point, fortunately I had a captive audience in the jury box. The real question was whether I had hooked them yet. If I had, and if the evidence supported what I told them, then I liked my chances.

For the next half hour, I retold the story in more detail, from Amanda's "we have joined forces" email, to the partnership EIN, to Jenn McGuire's acceptance of a partnership offer, to Amanda's "I have three partners" statement, to the documents used to try to set up a bank account, including a written partnership agreement. I told the jury that, contrary to what Bob Kantner would later say, Amanda Hayward agreed to sign that partnership agreement. She simply put off signing it each time Jenny followed up, with one excuse or another.

And then the sea change occurred, the moment that I believed, and still believe, triggered Amanda Hayward to wrest control of the company from Jenny and her other partners. Money loomed on the horizon, and she wanted it all.

"And this is—if this were a movie, this is where the ominous music would be queued," I said. The last time Jenny followed up with Amanda about the written agreement, "...the response she gets from Ms. Hayward is, 'I've got a big problem.

Two film companies are talking to E.L. James. We might lose her as an author.' This is a significant event, because at that point, the first two books have been published. It's starting to make some money. Starting to generate some buzz. And everybody knows that if film companies want to buy the film rights to the book, then Ms. James is probably going to want to go to a bigger publisher at some point.

"She's got a contract with The Writer's Coffee Shop, but whoever takes over the rights is going to have to buy out The Writer's Coffee Shop. In other words, there's money down the road. If this thing pans out, there's money to be had. This is the financial success that The Writer's Coffee Shop has been looking for."

I wanted the jury to understand the significance of what it meant for film companies to want to buy the film rights. The author, Erika Mitchell a/k/a E.L. James, kept those rights when she signed the publishing agreement with Coffee Shop, so Coffee Shop wouldn't share in any movie money. But Coffee Shop had leverage when it came to whether it would let James out of that contract so she could move to a larger publisher. I pointed out Amanda needed the "agreement" of her partners in order to let the author out of the publishing contract, something she wouldn't have needed if it had been solely her company. Her partners agreed and a deal was made with Random House.

Amanda signed the contract first, on behalf of Coffee Shop, and then Random House signed it on March 9, 2012. If I succeeded in making but one point to the jury, it had to be driving home the importance of that date.

"That's a significant date, because that's the date the Random House contract has been signed by both parties," I said. "At that point, the deal is locked into place."

Not only was the deal locked into place, but so were the partners' rights in that deal. As of March 9, if Coffee Shop was a partnership and if Jenny was a partner, then she was entitled to her share of Coffee Shop's profits, including any profits attributable to that deal with Random House. I needed the jurors to understand that. I also needed them to understand that *Amanda knew that* and, after March 9, she embarked on her takeover scheme.

"Four days later, Christa Beebe receives an e-mail from the *Wall Street Journal*, and she forwards it on to Ms. Hayward and says, 'Is there anything I shouldn't say in responding to this?' Because this is the *Wall Street Journal*. I mean, you want to be right. And Ms. Hayward tells her, and I think it's very significant not so much what she tells her, but what she doesn't tell her. She tells her, 'The only thing not to say is that Jenn and Jenny are partners, because for tax reasons, we have to say we're business associates.'

"Not 'don't say they're partners because they're not.' But 'don't say it for tax reasons.' In all the evidence we'll see, March 13th is the first time anybody ever said 'don't say we're partners.' But that's four days after the contract is signed."

I continued to roll forward. There were a lot of facts, and a lot of emails, but it was ultimately a fairly simple story. I discussed Amanda's June email in which she told her partners that her lawyers and accountants needed to change the company structure to make it appear that she was the only owner. Tantamount to "the devil made me do it." Then came the sleight of hand, the service agreement with TWCS Operations Amanda claimed she was going to use to funnel partnership profits to Jenny. The agreement with the termination clause that worried Jenny—the clause Amanda swore on her daughter's lives she would never exercise.

At about this point in the story came another key moment. Sometimes, if the facts, alone, aren't enough, a lawyer will appeal to a jury's sense of justice. And sometimes to a sense of outrage. I wanted to appeal to all three: facts, justice, and outrage.

In the final meeting Brent and I had with Jenny and Christa on Sunday afternoon before we started trial, two facts came together that highlighted the injustice of what Amanda had done, and it outraged me. I already knew Jenny had fronted personal funds to pay some Coffee Shop debts, because the company supposedly, according to Amanda, didn't have the money to pay those debts. But it wasn't until Christa pointed it out that I realized the significance of the timing. I had not raised this at the temporary injunction hearing, nor in any depositions, but I planned to hammer on it now.

"There's an e-mail, November fifth, where Jenny is communicating with Ms. Hayward about roughly fourteen-thousand-plus dollars in expenses for various things that have to be paid, and there's no money in the account. And Ms. Hayward's response is, 'What are we going to do?' So, Jenny agrees to transfer personal funds into the account to pay those expenses. And she knows she'll get reimbursed. She transfers personal funds over to pay it. This is November 5, 2012."

Then I connected the dots. "What Jenny doesn't know, and what Ms. Hayward didn't tell her, is that four days earlier, Random House wire transferred the first royalty payment of the *Fifty Shades* trilogy in excess of sixteen-and-a-half million dollars."

I paused to let that soak in. With millions of dollars sitting in her personal bank account, Amanda pleaded poverty so Jenny would dip into her personal funds to pay fourteen-thousand dollars in Coffee House debts—debts that, if you bought into Amanda's theory that she was always the sole owner of the company, belonged to Amanda. In other words, Amanda sat on sixteen-plus million dollars while Jenny paid her debts. If that didn't strike a chord of outrage, nothing would.

Then, I told the jury that, in the fall of 2013, Amanda did the thing she swore on her daughters' lives she would never do: she terminated Jenny and Christa from the business. Her reason?

Things were not going well financially with the company. To borrow a good Texas word, bullshit!

Now it was time to tie it together, sit down, and shut up. "At this point, we had a royalty payment on November first of 2012 of roughly sixteen-and-a-half million dollars. Had another royalty payment in the spring of 2013, fifteen point seven million dollars. The day before Jenny and Christa are terminated for 'financial reasons,' another royalty payment comes in of two point nine million dollars. To date, just so you'll know, the total amount that has come in from Random House is just under thirty-nine million dollars."

I paused and surveyed the jury. The shocked looks on faces told me they had no idea the level of money this case was about.

"What happened to the partnership?" I asked. "Well, nothing happened to the partnership. Everybody is going to testify, 'I never withdrew from the partnership. I never gave notice I wanted to dissolve the partnership.' Assets of the partnership were never distributed to people."

So, what did that mean? "The partnership is still there. The fact that Jenny signed a contract with a different company doesn't mean she's not a partner. In fact, she's told over and over again by Ms. Hayward, this is just a way to get the money to you.

"What happened to the money? Well, Ms. Hayward spent most of it. She bought millions of dollars of homes. I mean, multiple homes in Australia that were more than a million dollars. A gymnasium. Out of the just under thirty-nine million dollars that has come in, Jenny has received one-hundred-fifty thousand dollars.

"We're going to ask you to find that there was a partnership. Because if there is a partnership, the Random House contract was a partnership asset that was locked into place. And then we're going to ask you to decide, if there was a partnership, did Ms. Hayward breach some duties that she owed to her partners?"

I paused again and then moved to my final point, foreshadowing the Hayward lexicon. "Listen very carefully to what people say, and then what they now say it meant at the time and see if that makes sense to you. Because, quite frankly, a lot of the things that you're going to hear from the defense simply do not make sense. They do not stack up."

Jenny's Story

At this moment, I couldn't have loved Mike Farris more if I tried. He hooked the jurors from the moment he looked them in their eyes. Shakespeare said, "All the world's a stage, and all the men and women merely players." Mike claimed ownership of the stage, and his words flowed with an ease that made him appear ten feet tall. I was blown away by his telling of the story...and I had lived it!

Several times during the trial, I almost felt the mood of the jury like something tangible. One of those times was when Mike told how I floated money for Coffee Shop bills while Amanda sat on over sixteen million dollars. An electrical buzz hummed in the air as the jurors took in those words. I doubt if any made up their minds right then, but I'd bet my life they remembered that bit of treachery.

While Mike spoke, I watched the jurors. Some took notes but all appeared engrossed in the story. This was something I came to understand about my lawyer. Anything Mike wrote or said in this case was written or spoken in plain English. There was very little "lawyer speak" in his words. That wasn't to say that he didn't throw out legalese when it was called for, but he always spoke from the heart. He was a down to earth guy, with his feet planted firmly on the ground. I thought the jurors would appreciate this and, from the way they looked at him, I believed they did.

Mike's Story

After a brief break, during which Bob Kantner and his team set up an easel and visual aids, court was called back into session. I sat on the edge of my chair, notepad in front of me, ready to take notes of anything Kantner said that might require rebuttal, at least in the presentation of evidence, and also during my closing argument. I was particularly interested to hear how he was going to spin the story in Amanda Hayward's favor, because I didn't see how he could.

But I never underestimated the creativity of lawyers.

"There are several points I'd like to make for you right up front with regard to his issue of whether there's a partnership," he said. "Number one, there was no partnership. This was a hobby for these ladies until such time as they sold enough books to begin to make some money off of it, and then it became a job."

Nothing new there. Kantner had been slinging the "it started as just a hobby" shtick from the start. In fact, I agreed with that. Where our paths diverged, though, was the point at which it became a business. I believed that happened when they obtained an EIN from the Internal Revenue Service as a partnership and began signing legally binding contracts with authors. Even Amanda, as soon as she learned of the EIN, emailed a Coffee Shop staffer, to tell her "we are also now a company in the U.S." And there was Lea Dimovski's email with Jenny and Amanda on October 18, 2011, in which they discussed "cutting loose" an author. Lea wrote, "This is a business. Businesses need to make money." Kantner would have to do better if he wanted to trouble me.

"Number two, Amanda Hayward took the risk, 2009, 2010, well into 2011," he said. "She paid for everything. Everything. She paid for the domain name The Writer's Coffee

Shop. She paid for software. She paid for service—access to a server and maintenance of a server and use of a server, storage of information on a server. She paid to ship the original books. They had them printed and shipped. She took the risk; Ms. Pedroza did not."

Jenny took no risk, that is, if you discount the fact she quit her teaching job she had held for more than a decade to dedicate herself full time to Coffee Shop. There is risk, and then there is *risk*.

"When it became a business, while Amanda certainly consulted with others, she consulted with Mrs. Pedroza, she consulted with Mrs. McGuire, she consulted with Mrs. Dimovski, and she consulted with other people. In the end she made the decisions, for the most part, what books to print to try to sell, what to spend money on. We have emails where Mrs. Pedroza asks Mrs. Hayward for permission to spend as little as one hundred dollars. That reflects the fact that she was paying all the expenses, of course, and it reflects that she was making the decisions."

That didn't worry me too much, either. Those emails he referred to were written long after March 9, 2012, and they reflected Jenny's role as an independent contractor for TWCS Operations, a different company. Other emails made it painfully clear that, when it came to the biggest decision Coffee Shop ever made, selling publishing rights to the *Fifty Shades* trilogy, Amanda didn't "consult" with the others, but actually sought their *agreement*. If you were the sole owner of a company, why did you need non-owners to agree before you could take action? That didn't make sense. I had warned the jury to pay attention to those things that didn't make sense. I hoped they were listening.

"Number four," Kantner continued, "Amanda Hayward never signed a partnership agreement that Ms. Pedroza sent to her. That's not disputed. Never signed it. Mrs. Pedroza did go to the trouble of drafting one. And she sent it to Amanda. She sent it to Mrs. McGuire. And she sent it to Lea Dimovski."

At that point, he digressed to a discussion of Lea Dimovski, whom he said would testify she was never a partner. "Under their theory, Mrs. Dimovski would be entitled to ten million dollars nearly. She's not claiming it. And she'll tell you why. It was Amanda's company."

Again, nothing I couldn't live with, because Dimovski didn't say there wasn't a partnership; she said that, once the partnership was put together, she decided not to be part of it. Big difference.

"Jennifer McGuire. Now, Jennifer McGuire did sign the partnership agreement, and she'll come and tell you why. She thought it was necessary to get a bank account, and she signed it. But in the end, she'll say, 'My understanding was getting that EIN was a mistake and was going to be fixed, and the whole partnership agreement was not going to be implemented. But I thought if we needed it for a bank account, I would sign it.' But Mrs. McGuire, under their theory of the case, would be entitled to nearly ten million dollars. Mrs. McGuire is going to take the stand, I anticipate, and she's going to tell you, 'I'm not asking for a penny of that money because it's not my company. It's Amanda's company.'"

I found that to be interesting. For one thing, McGuire had already testified twice, once at her deposition and once during the temporary injunction hearing, that she had been offered a partnership and she took it, that she thought the partnership was still intact as of the spring of 2012, and that was never dissolved.

But what was really interesting was Kantner telling the jury McGuire had knowingly signed the written partnership agreement in order to help the company get a bank account even though, according to Kantner, she knew it "was not going to be implemented." He failed to mention she had also signed other documents as a partner to submit to banks, and she had even signed a binding contract with the e-retailer KOBO as a "partner" in "The Writer's Coffee Shop (Partnership)." Was he saying she committed fraud?

"So, in the end," Kantner said, "we've got four alleged partners. Only one of them is going to tell you there's a partnership. And what's interesting is the one who's going to tell you there was a partnership, Mrs. Pedroza, she signed a service agreement."

Yeah, with a completely different company. In fact, the only one who was actually going to say there *wasn't* a partnership was Amanda Hayward. Dimovski would simply say she wasn't a partner in the partnership. And McGuire? Well, bless her heart, she would say there was and there wasn't and there was and there wasn't. And, in order to believe Amanda, the jury would have to ignore her own words in dozens of documents and emails, and they would have to accept new definitions of commonly understood words, including personal pronouns.

Kantner also addressed the use of the term "partner," which, it's true, doesn't always mean a business partner in the legal sense. Trying to emphasize that truism, he made a statement I tucked away in my mind to revisit later during closing arguments.

"I can't tell you how many times, particularly in small towns in Texas, I've heard the phrase, 'Howdy, partner,' especially among people, like me, who have some gray hair. They don't mean we're partners in a business sense. It's a way of saying 'Hey,' in Texas. It's a way of—a friendly way of saying 'Hey' in Texas."

That was an interesting thing to say by a guy who had objected to my use of the fine Texas term "y'all" at Lea

Dimovski's deposition in Australia.[28] I've actually heard more Texans say "Howdy, y'all" than "Howdy, partner." And I've never heard an Australian say either.

By this point in Kantner's statement, I was ready to get started with the evidence. I had promised the jury what the evidence would show, and I was convinced I was right. Kantner, on the other hand, was writing checks I didn't think he could cash.

In closing, Kantner relied on a cliché often employed by defense lawyers in civil cases: he attacked Jenny as greedy. It was a tried-and-true technique, and Kantner poured it on.

"What is she asking for in this case? We thought, initially, based on the papers that were filed initially, she was asking for twenty-five percent. Based upon papers filed more recently, we understanding she's asking for a third. I take it the position now is Mrs. Dimovski is not partner. She said in her deposition Dimovski was. Now she's saying, well, maybe she's not."

Actually, we were asking the *jury to decide* who was and wasn't a partner. It was the defense saying Dimovski wasn't a partner, not us. If there were four partners, so be it; but if there were three, we would be just as happy. That's not greed, although Kantner wanted to paint it that way. That's simply following the evidence. And if Jenny's share turned out to be one-third instead of one-fourth, he'd have no one to blame but

---

[28] After I referenced "discussions with Ms. Hayward, Ms. Pedroza, Ms. McGuire," that exchange at Dimovski's deposition had had gone like this: Farris: Did y'all discuss what genres you would publish?

Kantner: Could we get who "y'all" is? I'll object to the form. I'll object to the form. It's your call. If you want the clarity you will get it. If you don't, you don't.

Farris: A Texan jury will understand, but I will clarify. Did you and Ms. Hayward and Ms. McGuire and Ms. Pedroza discuss such things...."

his own witnesses.

"In addition, she's asking for punitive damages. Based on disclosures served on me, I understand she's asking for two times actuals. So actual damages are one-third, they want punitive damages, two-thirds. One-third plus two-thirds. They want it all. She wants it all."

Then he shifted into sarcasm—the last resort of desperation, as far as I was concerned. "Thank you very much, Mrs. Dimovski, for your contributions. Glad you're not saying you're a partner. Thank you very much, Jenn McGuire, for saying, yeah, you signed an agreement and you signed a contract, but you're saying there's not partnership. Thank you very much. I'll take your share."

In other words, greedy old Jenny Pedroza wanted to take Lea Dimovski's and Jenn McGuire's shares for herself. It may have sounded bad, but the reality was Amanda Hayward didn't just *want* to take everyone's shares for herself, *she had actually done it*. She had taken Jenny's share, as well as Dimovski's (if she was a partner) and McGuire's. I didn't think anyone in that courtroom believed that, if Jenny hadn't filed this lawsuit, Amanda was going to voluntarily give ten million dollars each to Dimovski and McGuire. In fact, she had already spent or invested nearly all of it, buying real estate and setting up family companies. To act as if Jenny was now trying to deprive others of their fair share was ludicrous.

The truth was, Jenny didn't care about punitive damages. They were available under Texas law, so it would be foolish not to plead for them, but I wouldn't argue for them at the end of the trial, and Jenny wouldn't get on the stand and ask for them. All I wanted, and all Jenny wanted, was her share of the partnership's profits, which Amanda had taken from her.

Kantner closed by painting his client as a poor hapless victim of greedy old Jenny Pedroza. "And Amanda Hayward, having paid all of the expenses, and I mean every dollar for years, thank you very much for setting this business up. I'll take your share, too. Give it all to me. Give it all to me."

Yes, the poor hapless victim who had allowed Jenny to spend her personal money to pay company debts while she sat on over sixteen million dollars, and who had made off scot-free with forty million dollars, the bulk of which didn't belong to her. Yes, poor victim, indeed.

With that bit of ridiculous sarcasm, Kantner was through.

Jenny's Story

If I told you how I really felt about Mr. Kantner's opening statements, I might get in trouble. So, instead, I'll explain what I *didn't* feel. I never wanted all the money to myself, because I never felt that I should take what didn't belong to me and hide it away in secret companies and investments. I never wanted more than what was rightfully mine. If Mr. Kantner wanted a model to fit his description of someone who wanted it all, he needed to look no farther than the woman sitting next to him.

During my deposition, he asked me if I had been repaid for the expenses I paid for the company. I told him I had, and he then asked if I felt that Amanda had been reimbursed for the amount of money she put into the company. That baffled me. It was true that she put in most of the start-up money. Lea Dimovski helped with financial support when she came on as a partner, but in the beginning, it was Amanda. I often reminded her to keep a list of her costs so that, when we started making a profit, she would be repaid first.

But that wasn't to say that Jenn and I hadn't made contributions. Maybe not monetary, at first, but we put in a significant amount of "sweat equity," for which we weren't paid a dime. So, when Mr. Kantner asked if I thought Amanda had been repaid, I replied with an unequivocal, "*Yes!*" Forty million dollars more than repaid her.

After the judge released us around noon, the Pedroza Party began what I called our standard lunch. Downtown Fort Worth is known for great restaurants, but there were very few around the courthouse, and only a couple of sandwich shops within walking distance. With less than an hour for lunch most days, my parents started getting sandwiches and chips for us and bringing them back to a small cafeteria in the courthouse, where we ate and talked about the morning's proceedings. It's now hard for me to look at a sub sandwich without being transported back there in my mind.

Mom and Dad made sure everyone in our camp ate lunch every day. It was their way of taking care of us when they didn't know how else to help. Everyone appreciated it, even if there were days when I didn't feel like eating. I learned that every second in a trial is stressful, even if you're not physically on the stand. My family and friends, who merely watched, were stressed. Mike and Brent were always anxious about the afternoon's proceedings, and Christa and I held it together minute by minute. So, being able to come together for a few moments, relieve some anxiety, and laugh over a cold sandwich created great memories.

People bond in traumatic situations, and we all came together during these times away from the madness.

CHAPTER FIFTEEN: Telling the Story

[S]tories matter…stories are the most obvious way that humans organize, communicate, receive and digest facts."

—G. Christopher Ritter, *Powerful Deliberations*

Mike's Story

CREDIBILITY IS VITAL for a litigator. It didn't matter how much a jury liked a lawyer if he didn't prove what he said he was going to prove and if he didn't introduce evidence he said he would. That failure breeds distrust for whatever else the lawyer says. To quote Friedrich Nietzsche, "I'm not upset that you lied to me. I'm upset that from now on I can't believe you."

So, it was "put up or shut up" time. In my opening statement, I had told the jury a story that I now needed to prove. And I had given them an ending I now needed them to change. My story had to lay out so compellingly, so irresistibly, that it demanded a new ending. Not necessarily a fairy tale "they all lived happily ever after" ending, but a just ending. Trials and courts and lawsuits were, after all, supposed to be about justice. An injustice had been committed here and cried out to be corrected. My job was to lead the jury to that new ending, to convince them my new ending was not only just but also

210

inevitable. To do that, I called on my experience, and knowledge, as a storyteller.

Classic storytelling structure follows three acts. In Act One, the "set-up," you introduce your protagonist, or hero (in this case, Jenny), and identify her goal—what she wants to accomplish. You also introduce other characters, including the antagonist. Antagonists are not always villains, in the traditional sense—though they often are—but are simply characters who stand in the way of the protagonist accomplishing her goal. Here, the antagonist was Amanda—also, arguably, a villain.

In Act Two, the "complications," the hero starts on her journey toward her goal, but complications arise. Typically, a significant event occurs at the mid-point of Act Two, sometimes referred to as the "point of no return." The complications continue, the stakes rise, and a crisis point is reached that propels the story into Act Three, the "pay-off," which resolves the crisis and leads to the climax.

This case followed that structure perfectly.

I called Jenny to the stand as the first witness. That's generally a good idea in storytelling—introduce the hero as early as possible so the reader (or jury) can identify with her from the start. It was, after all, Jenny's story we were telling, so her voice needed to be the first that the jury heard.

As Jenny approached the stand, Kantner rose and said, "Your Honor, for the record, the defendants invoke the rule."

Judge McCoy explained "the rule" to the jury: "Ladies and gentlemen of the jury and those who are sitting out in the gallery, what the rule means—because we do have more than one rule, books of them—but what we call 'the rule,' that means either side has the right to request that anybody who is going to be, or who might be, a witness in this case—obviously not the jurors—please leave the room while the others are testifying."

The concern was that later witnesses might, if they were

allowed to hear earlier testimony, artificially adapt their testimony to conform to it. In order to ensure that didn't happen, witnesses were required to wait outside the courtroom until it was their turn to testify. Parties, or their representatives were exempted from the rule, so Jenny and Amanda were allowed to stay, as was James Hayward as the duly designated representative of TWCS Operations. Because we had settled Christa's claim, she was no longer a party and was among those leaving the courtroom, along with Jennifer McGuire, Cindy Bidwell, and Lea Dimovski.

Once Jenny was seated and sworn in, we began with Act One, which followed the timeline in this exhibit that we displayed to the jury:

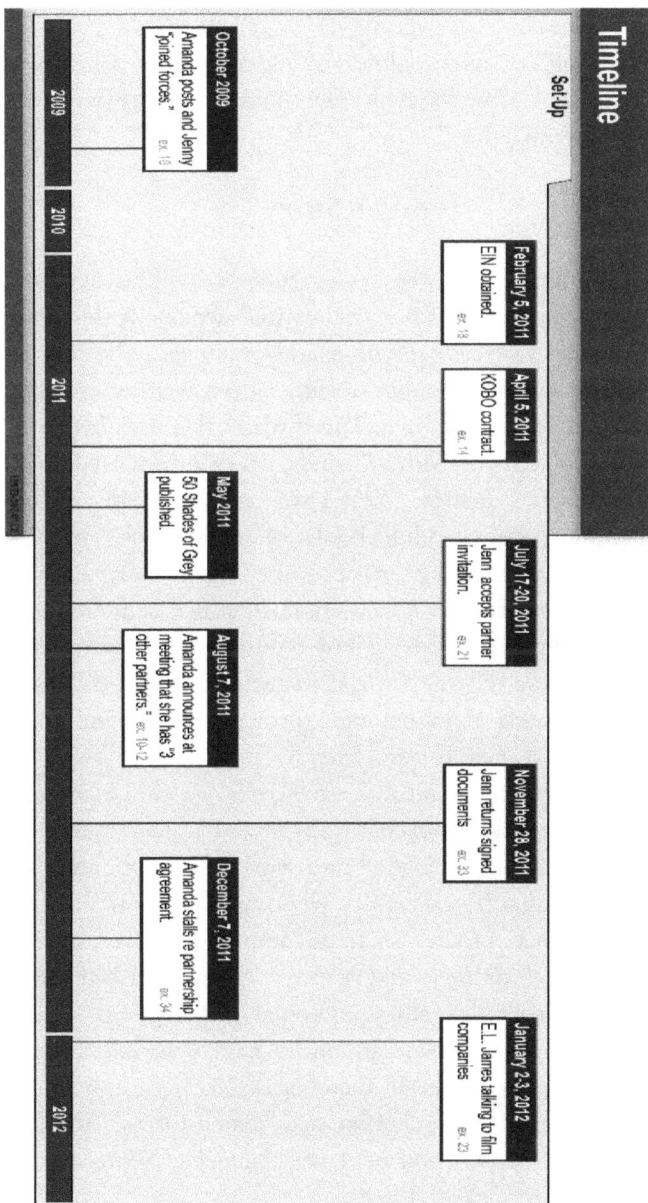

Timeline

Set-Up

October 2009
Amanda posts and Jenny "joined forces." ex. 10

2009

2010

February 5, 2011
EIN obtained. ex. 18

April 5, 2011
KOBO contract. ex. 14

2011

May 2011
50 Shades of Grey published.

July 17-20, 2011
Jenn accepts partner invitation. ex. 21

August 7, 2011
Amanda announces at meeting that she has "3 other partners." ex. 10-12

November 28, 2011
Jenn returns signed documents ex. 33

December 7, 2011
Amanda stalls re partnership agreement. ex. 34

January 2-3, 2012
E.L. James talking to film companies ex. 23

2012

"When did you first meet, or come in contact with, Amanda Hayward?" I asked.

"It was online, in an online writing community which was fanfiction.net. And we started communicating via reviews and different things like that."

Jenny's Story

Once upon a time, there was an elementary school teacher from Mansfield, Texas. One of her friends told her about this crazy book everyone was reading with sparkly vampires. She read it, loved it, and found an online forum where writers used the characters in tales of their own. That's where this story began.

My involvement with Amanda Hayward started with Stephenie Meyer's *Twilight*. Yes, I was an almost 40-year-old woman reading young adult books about vampires in high school. While researching an upcoming movie adaptation, I came across a reference to a fan fiction site called fanfiction.net, on which I found hundreds, if not thousands, of stories from unknown authors using the *Twilight* characters. One of them was written by Amanda Hayward and, through the site and other online forums, we soon became friends.

At first, we communicated exclusively via online postings and email but quickly moved to Skype and instant messaging programs. Technology made the world smaller, and we communicated almost constantly, while making allowances for the time difference. I found her to be funny and creative, and we connected as both mothers and readers. When she asked me to help her finish her online story, I jumped at the chance. I loved to write, and it thrilled me to finally have a forum through which to express my ideas. In October of 2009, we announced on her fanfiction.net page that we had "joined forces." Readers loved our new chapters and next we planned to write a book together called, ironically, *Mistakes*.

During this same time, Amanda, Jenn McGuire (a fan of Amanda's story, whom I also met online), and I worked to establish our own fan fiction library. We envisioned a site that would allow authors free creative range. With the help of an amazing programmer living in Belgium, Jenn learned to program code and create a large data base website, and she researched servers to get the library up and running. When Amanda directed fan fiction authors to our site, Jenn created graphics for their stories. We knew we needed to attract popular authors, with large audiences, so we used the story Amanda and I were writing, which had developed a sizeable fan base, to prime the pump.

On January 24, 2010, The Writer's Coffee Shop Library went live and, within an hour, we had 130 members. By the end of the night, we had reached nearly 3,000. Every time I wrote a new chapter and posted it, membership soared. When other popular stories arrived, the site nearly exploded, and it was all we could do to keep the servers from crashing.

We learned a lot in those first months about running an online business but our greatest challenge came when we started publishing books. In addition to signing authors to contracts and working out the details of publishing, we still had to promote the library, which we viewed as a marketing tool, and navigate the waters of e-retailing. We published our first books in late 2010 and, by March 2011, had almost 20,000 members on the library, with an average of 50,000 views a day.

We needed a way to monetize the library, to help pay for the publishing business, and marketing the website fell on my shoulders. I researched the best ways to advertise, including reading *Google AdSense For Dummies*, which, in turn, led to our utilizing that Google service, and we began accepting paid advertising on the site. For the first time, we actually had revenues, so I opened an online USAA bank account in my name for the business.

With the advent of The Writer's Coffee Shop Publishing House, we also began to receive money from Amazon Kindle from preorders, but that money went straight to a PayPal account. Amanda had put up the initial capital to get the company started, and we discussed repeatedly that, as soon as we could, the company would pay her back. A benefit to using PayPal was that Amanda was able to access the account from Australia, which cut down how much she needed to continue to spend of her own money.

In May 2011, ironically the same day that the book Amanda and I co-authored, *Mistakes*, was published, we introduced the world to *Fifty Shades of Grey*. Preorders immediately deluged us. With the sudden influx of funds, for some reason PayPal put a 60-day hold on our account, but then we had a new problem. How do you pay for printing and shipping books if the purchase money is tied up for two months? We were afraid we would lose customers if we couldn't cover the book orders, so enter Lea Dimovski. Lea had been a pre-reader of our fan fiction chapters and also did odd editing jobs, so I already knew who she was. When Amanda approached Jenn and me about bringing Lea on as a partner to help with the financial side of the company we both agreed, and Lea "came aboard."

From that point forward, all four of us participated in all major decisions for Coffee Shop, holding quarterly meetings, hiring and firing staff, and publishing books. We were still in the honeymoon stage, and we relied on each other while we struggled to keep up with a company that was growing faster than any of us ever imagined.

Mike's Story

By the end of 2010, Coffee Shop was fully operational as a publishing house, and Jenny and Amanda decided the time had come to make their business venture more formal.

"At some point, did you obtain an employer identification number from the IRS for The Writer's Coffee Shop?" I asked.

"Yes."

"Do you recall when that happened?"

"I believe it was in early February 2011."

"What was the purpose of getting the EIN?"

"Well, when we started working with Amazon and KOBO and getting the bank account, and all those kinds of things, it became apparent that we needed to have a tax identification number. And so that's why we got it."

"Was there a discussion about whether or not this should be for a corporation or for a partnership?"

"Yes."

"What discussion did you have with anybody about that?"

"Amanda and I spoke specifically about this, because I told her, you know, if we go—how do we want to word this? Do we want to be a corporation, which would cost a lot of money, take a lot of time? And we wanted to get up on these sites now. And I said we could be a partnership corporation that way, or we can just be a general partnership. And to get it done, we went to the general partnership."

"Did Ms. Hayward agree with that decision?"

"Yes."

Jenny's Story

We had been using an online USAA bank account for all United States money and PayPal, then later Commonwealth Bank in Australia, for money that came primarily from orders on our website. Most of our sales were on Amazon, iTunes, and Barnes & Noble online stores, and that money went to my USAA account. As Amazon orders began to build, it looked like 2012 was gearing up to be a fantastic year with the upcoming final book in the *Fifty Shades* trilogy. Going forward, I knew we needed a formal business account for the company.

With Amanda's blessing, in February of 2011, I had obtained an employer identification number from the U.S. Internal Revenue Service for Coffee Shop as a partnership, and in November, we started researching the steps to set up a new account for that partnership. Wells Fargo Bank offered a business solution that allowed Amanda to access the account from Australia, plus online banking that we would use for website sales. We already had the partnership EIN, but the bank told me they also needed an assumed name certificate and a copy of our partnership agreement in order to set up the account.

Jenn, Amanda, and I all agreed this was the direction we needed to go. I was tasked with getting the necessary documents for the bank, including drafting a partnership agreement, which I did using a form I found online. Jenn signed the documents immediately. Amanda agreed to sign but, when I didn't receive the signed documents back from her, I followed up a couple of times. Each time, she promised she would take care of it, but the last time I followed up, on January 2, 2012, she didn't immediately reply, which wasn't like her.

I got nervous, so I emailed again and, teasing, asked if she was dumping me. Her reply a day later was, "I've got a big problem." My mind immediately went to health or family issues, but her response to my inquiry was, "Erika [Mitchell] is talking to 2 film companies for fifty shades…which means we will probably lose her as an author; on the upside we have her books for 3 years."

In hindsight, I find it disheartening that she initially said, "I have a problem." Before, it was always *"we"* have a problem. At least her response to my follow-up was that "we" might lose Erika as an author, but from then on, she stiff-armed any discussion of a U.S. bank account and the partnership agreement. I now wonder if the prior email, using the personal pronoun "I," had been a slip, inadvertently revealing her intent to take over the company

Mike's Story

"Do you recall when *Fifty Shades of Grey* was first published?"

"I believe it was May of 2011," Jenny said.

"What were sales like initially?"

"They were good compared to our other books. Nothing like what it became, but it was definitely our top seller. Very quickly, the preorders went—were selling very well."

Fifty Shades Darker and *Fifty Shades Freed* were published over the next few months, and by early 2012, Coffee Shop had sold a combined approximately 250,000 copies of the trilogy in e-book and print-on-demand, and *Fifty Shades of Grey* ended up on the *New York Times* bestseller list.

Yes, books were selling very well, indeed.

Jenny's Story

January 2012 was a remarkable, once-in-a-lifetime period of my life. Around January 5th, Diva Moms in New York contacted us. They billed themselves as "New York City's premier socializing network for moms (and moms-to-be) and their totally adorable babies," [29] and regularly got together to talk about family, books, movies, and life. Lyss Stern, the group's leader, had heard about the upcoming publication of the final book in the trilogy, *Fifty Shades Freed*, and offered to host a book launch party. We all agreed it would be a great way to showcase the book.

Amanda and I flew to New York, along with one of Coffee Shop's employees who would help sell the books during the launch, and Erika Mitchell met us there with her agent, Valerie Hoskins. Getting 300 books to New York in less than two weeks wasn't easy, but we managed to do it, along with *Fifty Shades of Grey* bags and bookmarks that Amanda, Jenn, and I created, using beads and ribbons.

Neither Amanda nor I had been to New York before, so the excitement was electric. The party was a huge success, we met some amazing women, and Erika read parts of her book to a group of awestruck fans. The media covered the event and, later in the week, we were featured on ABC's *20/20*. Back at the hotel after the party, we watched as e-book sales for the entire trilogy shot up like a rocket. Each time we hit refresh on the Kindle site, the numbers climbed by the thousands. It was a crazy night, one I wouldn't soon forget.

With the success of the evening, Amanda and I began to think about the future of Coffee Shop. We envisioned using the success of *Fifty Shades* to pave the way for new marketing efforts, but we weren't equipped for it. Amanda asked how I felt about leaving my teaching job and heading up marketing, handling the press for *Fifty Shades* as well finding new avenues to market our other authors. Knowing we needed to strike while the fire was hot, I agreed.

I knew this was going to be more than a one-person job, given the interest from book stores, other publishers, and worldwide media outlets, so I told Amanda that Christa Beebe

---

[29] Divamoms.com

would be a great addition to the marketing team. I felt confident that, between the two of us, Christa and I could tackle any challenge. Amanda agreed, and we called Christa from New York and extended the offer. She asked for time to think it over and called back later and accepted. We both then tendered our resignations from teaching, effective the end of our contracts for the current school year, and Coffee Shop's full-time marketing team was born.

Larger publishers began making inquiries into the *Fifty Shades* publishing rights. As Amanda had anticipated, Erika and her agent expressed legitimate concerns that Coffee Shop wasn't equipped to handle the magnitude of the phenomenon. I hated to see her go, and was proud of her success, but I knew it was inevitable. With the explosion of book sales, we struggled to handle the orders that flooded in. Coffee Shop sold physical copies of the books through our website, as well as Amazon, and by the time we returned from New York, we had a backlog of thousands of orders.

The central hub for shipping became my parents' living room. Mom and Dad, along with family and friends, worked around the clock to print and box books, then deliver the packages to the Post Office. It was insane. On a good day, they might finish about 500 books. There were countless stories of shipments getting lost, Amazon complaining about our tracking system, customers in prisons not getting their books (like prisoners really *needed* these books), and bookstores ordering hundreds of copies directly from us because other retailers couldn't keep up.

Barnes & Noble contacted us about printing and distribution, television news companies and newspapers wanted interviews with E.L James (a/k/a Erika Mitchell), and several of the Big Six[30] publishing houses made offers to buy the publishing rights. So, in addition to my full-time teaching job (which would continue to the end of the school year), I fielded calls from news reporters, media outlets, and other publishing companies. Christa and I wrote a press release that was picked up worldwide and, in March, *Fifty Shades of Grey* sat atop the *The New York Times* bestseller list at Number One.

Like Charles Dickens, I felt that it truly was the best of times and the worst of times because, although we were riding high at the moment, trouble was brewing. While I was turning in my resignation to move into a full-time marketing role, Amanda was secretly making a move of her own.

Mike's Story

At the end of 2011, fame and fortune came a'knockin' on Coffee Shop's door and, when film companies began talking to Erika Mitchell about movie rights to *Fifty Shades of Grey*, the story spun into Act Two with a fury. What had started as a friendly partnership was about to get ugly because, along with film interest, came interest from larger, mainstream publishers, who wanted to acquire the publishing rights to the trilogy. The author was under contract with Coffee Shop, so she needed the partnership's blessing to escape her contract and sign with a larger publisher that could accommodate the public's demand for the books. Coffee Shop could, if it wanted, hold James hostage (in effect) until another publisher offered the right price.

And you know what happens when money is involved. See the Act Two timeline.

---

[30] The Big Six were Random House, Penguin, Simon & Schuster, HarperCollins, Hatchette (formerly known as Warner Books), and MacMillan.

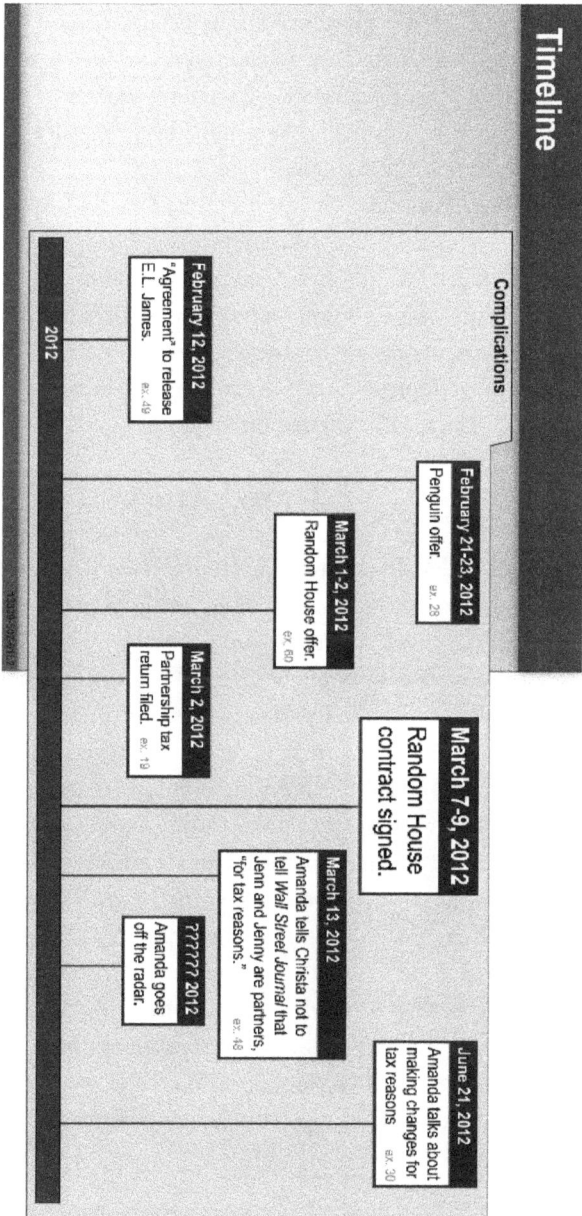

Timeline

Complications

2012

February 12, 2012
"Agreement" to release
E.L. James.   ex. 49

February 21-23, 2012
Penguin offer.   ex. 28

March 1-2, 2012
Random House offer.   ex. 60

March 2, 2012
Partnership tax
return filed.   ex. 19

March 7-9, 2012
Random House
contract signed.

March 13, 2012
Amanda tells Christa not to
tell *Wall Street Journal* that
Jenn and Jenny are partners,
"for tax reasons."   ex. 48

?????? 2012
Amanda goes
off the radar.

June 21, 2012
Amanda talks about
making changes for
tax reasons   ex. 30

In early 2012, the partners discussed options on how to handle E.L. James and her *Fifty Shades* trilogy. They would have loved to keep her in their stable of writers, and even considered, as Jenny put it in an email, "We make her a partner and we all get rich and ride into the night."

"Was there any decision reached as to whether or not to offer [a partnership]?" I asked Jenny.

"I mean, I think—I mean, ultimately there was. She wanted out. And I think things got kind of tense there at the end, so it wasn't even an option. But we did talk about it, if she had an investment in the company she might stay."

But Erika Mitchell had other ideas.

Jenny's Story

Amanda and I desperately wanted to find a way to keep Erika and the *Fifty Shades* books with our company, and I thought inviting her into the partnership might give her a reason to stay. Not only would she benefit from the profits of her own book, but she could potentially earn money on other authors' books. I never mentioned this to her, and I don't know if Amanda ever did, but in hindsight, I know it wouldn't have worked. Erika's priority was getting her books to the public on a massive scale, and she needed a large publisher to accomplish that.

By the end of February, we had two solid offers for *Fifty Shades*. Penguin offered Coffee Shop a deal directly, while Random House[31] went through E.L. James and her agent. Amanda, Lea, Jenn and I had multiple discussions about our options. We knew we had to do something, because, even if we reached a deal with Barnes & Noble to assist with distribution, we still couldn't keep up with demand. I just had to look at my

---

[31] Ironically, Penguin and Random House merged a little over a year after Random House acquired the *Fifty Shades* rights.

parents' weary faces to know that. We were facing what I liked to call "The Cabbage Patch Kids" syndrome. Everyone wanted the book, but only a few people could actually get it. People seemed desperate for the product. I once saw a book selling on eBay for over $1,000.

In the end, we had no choice but to sell. We simply had to decide which buyer to sell to. Both deals were good, but Random House offered future royalties that Penguin did not. Ultimately, we—and by "we," I mean Amanda, Jenn, Lea, and I—decided to accept Random House's offer.

In March of 2012, after Random House signed the contract to acquire the *Fifty Shades* publishing rights, I visited Amanda in Australia during my spring break. I brought the partnership agreement with me, but she stiff-armed me again. She said she feared that, with the success of *Fifty Shades*, we would be taxed too heavily if we banked in America but that, if the company was structured as Australia-based with a woman owner, we could get major tax breaks. It sounded legitimate at the time. I had been concerned about taxes, myself, and wanted the company properly documented for the tax man. She asked for my patience and my trust, both of which I gave her immediately.

Things would never be the same.

Mike's Story

Random House presented an offer directly to Coffee Shop to acquire the publishing rights for an advance plus future royalties, with the advance and royalties for a period of three years to be split 50/50 between Coffee Shop and the author. Amanda presented the offer to her partners, who approved it. Amanda then signed the Random House contract on March 7, 2012, as CEO of Coffee Shop. Instead of using Coffee Shop's EIN, though, she used her personal Australian tax file number and gave Random House her bank account number at

Commonwealth Bank in Australia as the place to make all royalty payments. Random House counter-signed on March 9.

Internet accounts called the sale to Random House both a "million dollar deal" and "more than" a million dollar deal.[32] According to an April 18, 2013, article in the *Huffington Post*, after Random House imprint Vintage Books released the *Fifty Shades* trilogy in late March of 2012, it sold 35,000,000 copies by the end of the year in the United States alone, and foreign rights had been sold in 37 countries.[33] According to *The New York Times* bestseller list, *Fifty Shades of Grey* was number one on March 25 and April 1, 2012; and from April 22, 2012, to February 10, 2013, *Fifty Shades of Grey*, *Fifty Shades Darker*, and *Fifty Shades Freed* ranked one, two and three every single week. As of May 18, 2014, *Fifty Shades of Grey* had spent 112 weeks on *The New York Times* top 20 bestseller list (including 52 weeks at number one), *Fifty Shades Darker* spent 95 weeks, and *Fifty Shades Freed* spent 91 weeks.[34]

It was during the first few months after Random House signed the contract that Amanda initiated her scheme to lock in for herself all of the riches flowing from the deal. She told her partners that her attorneys and accountants had advised her to restructure the company to ensure the most favorable tax treatment on royalty payments from Random House, which

---

[32] "Fifty Shades of a Million Dollars" ("The Writer's Coffee Shop has scored a million dollar deal with Random House. . .")
http://www.abc.net.au/local/stories/2012/03/12/3451060.ht m; "Erotic ebook surges up best seller list," ("[Hayward] is unable to disclose the size of the deal, though Australian press is reporting it is more than $1 million.")
http://www.cnn.com/2012/03/12/world/europe/fifty-shades-of-grey/index.html.

[33] http://www.huffingtonpost.com/bethany-sales/fifty-shades-of-grey-publishing_b_3109547.

[34] www.nytimes.com/best-sellers-books/overview.html

meant, she said, making it look like she was a sole trader.

On June 21, she sent that infamous email to Jenny and Jennifer McGuire that said, in part:

Tax wise...the accountants say we need to change a few things on our website...1. No mention of Staff...say our TEAM...and we have to dump the words co-founders as I'm a sole trader. . or we could be up for more tax...can you two get annalise and jonas to do this for us immediately? I don't know what to say to that and change it to...but we have to show I'm the owner somehow...which pisses me off royally but I get it. I understand why we so don't want to pay more tax. I hope you girls understand.

Jenny's Story

After I returned from my spring break trip to Australia, Amanda became reclusive. For most of April and into May, I found it difficult to reach her, whether by phone, email, or instant messenger. On those occasions when we did talk, she claimed to be busy with family matters and working with her accountants. Meanwhile, Jenn and I took up the reins of the publishing house, fielding questions and interviews, taking care of our authors, and working with a PR firm to promote the company. We kept Amanda updated, but she rarely responded.

In May 2012, Amanda resurfaced, coming to Texas for the start of a multi-city publicity tour. The first stop was the morning television show *Good Morning, Texas* on Dallas's WFAA, Channel 8, where Amanda and I talked about our new books and the future of Coffee Shop. Unfortunately, my teaching job required me to miss the rest of the tour, but Christa and our PR firm set up interviews for Amanda from New York to Los Angeles. In June, Christa and I spent a long weekend in New York for Book Expo America, where I spoke on a panel for the UpublishU event. Coffee Shop's story was a true rags-to-riches fairy tale, and the panel drew a large crowd.

After the media tour, Amanda seemed to disappear again. She didn't return emails, set her Skype to private, and only occasionally communicated, sending cryptic messages about being depressed and overstressed. I panicked, concerned she might be in trouble, and I was thousands of miles away, unable to help her. I finally reached her by phone and told her how worried I was and that, if she didn't talk to me, I was coming to Australia to take care of her. She admitted she was sad over losing Erika Mitchell as an author and she felt like it had been a betrayal.

She also told me her lawyers and accountants were upset with how we had set up the company, and they wanted her to restructure it to minimize the tax burden. I tried to tell her all this was good news, that while Erika leaving was sad, she needed to move on to a bigger publisher. I also explained we needed to move forward, too, and minimizing taxes was a good idea.

Then she told me her accountants wanted to set her up as a sole trader. That was the first time I had ever heard that. She said she told them, initially, that she couldn't cut the rest of us out because we were a team. She also said she felt guilty about what they were asking her to do. I tried to ease her conscience by restating my old mantra: "We are in this together. Whatever the world sees, we know we started this together. If this is what we need to do to move forward, then it's what we do, but I believe in you and know you will always have our backs."

Yes, ladies and gentlemen, I said those words—more than once, placing my blind trust in Amanda. In hindsight, her disappearance now makes sense. She wasn't going to hurt herself; instead, she was going to try to rewrite history.

Mike's Story

While Amanda's June 21 email suggested she was going to somehow convert the business from Coffee Shop-the-partnership to Coffee Shop-the-sole-trader (which, of course, means she knew it wasn't a sole trader), that's not quite what happened, as the story accelerated into Act Three. See the Act Three Timeline.

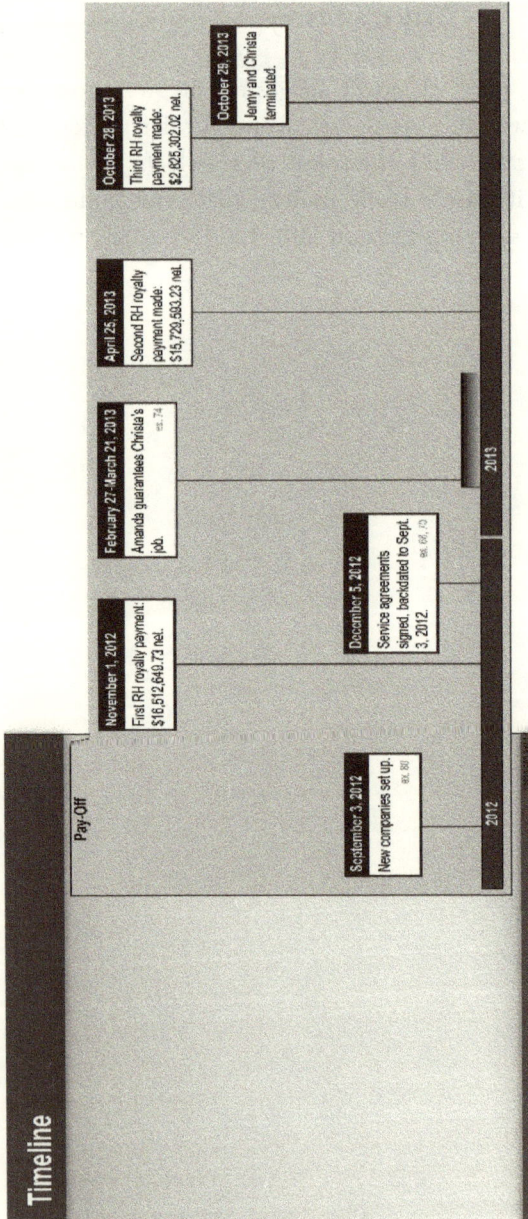

Timeline

Pay-Off

September 3, 2012
New companies set up.

November 1, 2012
First RH royalty payment: $16,512,649.73 net.

December 3, 2012
Service agreements signed, backdated to Sept. 3, 2012.

February 27-March 21, 2013
Amanda guarantees Christa's job.

April 26, 2013
Second RH royalty payment made: $15,729,593.23 net.

October 28, 2013
Third RH royalty payment made: $2,825,302.02 net.

October 29, 2013
Jenny and Christa terminated.

2012

2013

What Amanda failed to reveal to her partners was that she was setting up a complicated scheme of companies (diagramed in Chapter 9) and she had already ensured she, personally, got all of the Random House royalty payments. In late 2012, Amanda began pressuring Jenny and Christa to sign identical service agreements as independent contractors with TWCS Operations, one of the new companies she set up. Those agreements contained a provision that allowed TWCS Operations to terminate either, or both, of them without cause on seven days' notice. That clause greatly concerned Jenny and Christa.

Jenny inquired about it, via email on November 20, 2012, and said, "It's the without cause that is making me a bit worried."

You remember Amanda's response?

I would NEVER do that to you even if we fall out and have a huge fight. Out of respect to you and our friendship. I swear on my daughters lives. . . The reason for the clauses about firing is because your [sic] a contractor if you want security of being more then you have to be staff etc. that's the problem I guess I spoke to the lawyers about this and they said you can't have it both ways. :(

I asked Jenny, *"Did you take this contract to a lawyer to look at?"*

"I did not."

"Did you take it to an accountant to look at?"

"I did not."

"Why not?"

"Because I trusted her. She was a friend, and I trusted her."

231

Jenny was about to learn, the hard way, the true meaning of the Russian proverb made famous by President Ronald Reagan: "Trust but verify."

Jenny's Story

In about July or August of 2012, Amanda first introduced the idea of the service agreement to Jenn and me at a meeting in Dallas. I was stunned. Gone was the friend with whom I had spent countless hours laughing and writing, as she tried to convince us she needed to be seen as the sole owner of the company. After I picked my jaw up off the floor, I reminded her we had been partners from the beginning, and I had given up my teaching career as my way of giving back to the company.

She just nodded somberly, guilt-laden (she said), but protested she was following the advice of her accountants in order to minimize taxes. I thought her motives seemed more nefarious, although I hoped not, because it looked as if she was actually trying to wrest control of the whole venture away from the rest of us. She said that, if we didn't agree to the new company structure, Coffee Shop would go under. That would leave not only me and my family in dire financial straits, but also Christa, who quit her career based upon my co-ownership of Coffee Shop and Amanda's guarantee of her job, and my parents, who closed the doors of their 35-year business in July to work for us in shipping.

Amanda told us we should feel free to talk with a lawyer, and even sent us contact information for *her* attorney—wasn't that sweet of her?—in case we had questions. She implied, though, that if we talked to an attorney, it would hurt her feelings, because surely, we trusted her! In my heart, I wanted to believe her, but my mind urged caution. She was my friend, and I didn't want to accept that she would betray me. In the end, I let my heart overrule my head, and I agreed. As soon as I did, Amanda magically returned to the happy, feisty, and funny friend I remembered.

We spent the rest of the weekend together, but a cloud hung over me.

Mike's Story

"Do you recall when you were terminated from TWCS Operations?" I asked.

"Yes."

"When was that?"

"It was October 2013."

"When you were terminated from TWCS Operations, were you told that you were also no longer a partner in The Writer's Coffee Shop?"

"No."

"Did anybody ever tell you that you were no longer a partner in The Writer's Coffee Shop?"

"No."

"What were the circumstances, if you recall, when you were notified that you were terminated?"

"We had just come back from the Austin Book Festival...."

Jenny's Story

I count October 30, 2013, as one of the five worst days of my life. Christa and I had just returned from the Austin Book Festival, where we had organized Coffee Shop's participation in the event. On top of that, I had recently broken my arm, and my father was in the hospital. Based on doctors' reports, we didn't expect him to live. Amanda knew this, and she knew I was at the hospital with him, yet she insisted she had to meet with Christa to discuss our future with the company. As I came to find out, we had no future.

Christa's perception of these events is clearer than mine, so I'll let her tell it.

Christa's Story

I knew something was up. People acted strange the whole time we were in Austin. People we usually joked around with now suddenly avoided eye contact and kept their distance. When they did talk to us, they said things like, "You two have always been so kind and worked so hard." Or, "I always appreciate how positive and upbeat you guys are, no matter what."

No matter what—huh? It was like they knew something we didn't. Thinking back, I'm pretty sure they did.

When Jenny and I got ready to head home, we went to Amanda's and Cindy's hotel room to say good-bye. They opened the door a crack and peeked out, but didn't invite us in, nor were hugs exchanged. Amanda said she would see us at my house in a couple of days for a meeting. Her face was expressionless and her tone was short, betraying no emotion. We had no clues as to what she was thinking. Cindy, however, gave it all away. She wouldn't look me in the eyes, but she gave me a smile that screamed, "Oh, poor you." My heart dropped, and I knew it was over. I was shocked and upset at first, but when I really thought about it, I got mad. I had given up my entire weekend, and spent months planning this event, and Amanda knew all along she was going to make me work it before she fired me! Really?

The ride home was filled with speculative conversation, angry music, and reflective silence. I knew Jenny had a lot going on in her life, with her broken arm and her dad's health, and now she was concerned about me. She knew how financially devastating this would be for my family, and she felt tremendously guilty. I worried what this would do to her. She said she was going to tell Amanda she didn't have to pay her so I could keep my job, which was so sweet, but something I never would have agreed to. I just kept thinking there had to be another way. If I could just talk with Amanda when she came to my house, maybe we could figure something out.

The next couple days were a whirlwind. Jenny's dad was in the hospital, and he wasn't expected to make it. She worried about him, worried about me, and was still in pain from the surgery on her arm. I was freaking out as well. The thought of losing my job at this point in the school year was terrifying. My wife and I are both teachers, and I knew that being reduced to one salary would be tough. I cried a lot. I felt a ton of guilt for stressing out about my job while Jenny faced the reality of losing her dad. I felt guilty for the situation that I had put my family in. I kept thinking, "If only I had gotten out last year." But why would I? *Fifty Shades* was a mega-hit and kept getting bigger. I had no reason to think this wasn't going to work.

Until now.

A few days later, Amanda met with me at my house. She and Jenny had already talked on the phone, but Amanda didn't tell her much. Even so, I was pretty sure I knew where this was going. Jenny couldn't be there because she was at the hospital with her dad, so it was just me. Alone with her.

Just me and Amanda.

And her designer purse.

That's right. She knocked on my door, came in my house, and placed her, what I believed to be, $20,000 Hermes Birkin bag on my kitchen table. Designer purses have never been my thing, but that orange monstrosity became a symbol to me, a beacon to remind me exactly who I was dealing with. Amanda fired me by stating that the company had no money, and then instructed me to tell Jenny that she was fired, too. She also said a lot of other things, most of which I don't specifically remember, but the gist of it was that she had "to think of the business" and she "wouldn't be doing this if there was another way."

I'm not ashamed to say that I cried. A lot. A very ugly, loud cry. It wasn't a show. It was definitely real, and I made her sit there with me while I cried. If she was going to break her guarantee and fire me, then she was going to have to endure it. I wasn't going to let her off the hook that easy. I told her I couldn't believe this was happening. I told her this was going to ruin my family. I told her I didn't know what I was going to do.

All she could say was, "Well, Jenn (McGuire) told me that there are lots of teaching jobs right now. You just have to look."

Really? She was firing me mid-year because Jenn, the person with zero experience in education, said it was easy to find a job in November? Great!

Amanda told me she knew I worked hard and always did the best I could for the company, and how sorry she was that it ended this way. "This is just business," she said. "It isn't personal."

Then she left without looking back.

Later, in an email, she told me that firing me was one of the hardest things she ever did. She said she was so upset that she vomited shortly after leaving my house. I wonder, now, if she vomited due to the guilt of knowing that, at the same time she was firing me, another multi-million-dollar payment from Random House was being deposited into her account.

I hope so.

Jenny's Story

And just like that, under the guise of money troubles, *my* future in *our* company had ended. When I testified, Mr. Kantner asked me why I didn't shout at her, "Hey, I'm a partner. You can't fire me!" Admittedly, I didn't, but the answer wasn't nearly as simple as the question implied.

By this time, Cindy, Jenn, and Amanda had successfully caused me to doubt everything about myself. Every time Christa and I did what we were asked, they raised the bar.

When we successfully launched book after book, found advertisements and interviews for all our authors, and worked 12-hour days, they wanted more. During a particularly hard time, Cindy and Amanda flew to Texas to "check up" on us. I thought we passed this pop quiz with flying colors. All of our new books were on Net Galley, a service that obtained reviews on commercial websites. We knew how to work the Amazon rating system to elevate our books, and we had a rotating schedule of events for our authors.

Marketing wasn't an overnight success, but what we were doing was working, and we had Coffee Shop on the cutting promotional edge in the explosion of independent publishers and self-published authors. In fact, when the dust settled after Amanda terminated Christa and me, a number of publishers approached us to take over their marketing departments.

Prior to the "check-up" meeting, Cindy and Amanda had complained about the workload of dealing with payroll and accounts payable. I offered to help them, despite my own workload, which Cindy later testified meant that we must have been lying about how hard we were working.

She said that authors had complained about a lack of marketing for their books by the company so, if we didn't have enough time to do our own jobs, how could I find time to help them with theirs? The answer was simple: Christa and I were doing our jobs, but I was desperate for Coffee Shop to flourish, and I was willing to do *whatever else* was necessary to make our dreams for the company a reality.

Amanda claimed that Random House was not paying correctly and that lagging royalty payments hurt the company's profitability.

I believed her so, even with a broken arm and a dying father, I rolled up my sleeves and dug in to save our "unprofitable" company. What I didn't know was that, by the time Amanda terminated me, she had already received about *thirty-five million dollars* in royalties from Random House, and *not a single one of those payments had been late*.

Not profitable, indeed!

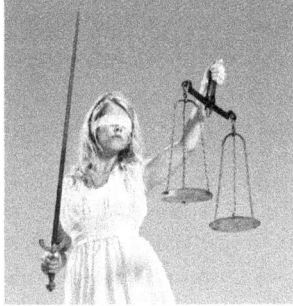

CHAPTER SIXTEEN: Amnesia, Alternative Facts, and the Hayward Lexicon *Redux*[35]

Right now, I'm having amnesia and déjà vu at the same time—I think I've forgotten this before.
　　　　　　　—Steven Wright

Mike's Story

IN BETWEEN JENNY'S testimony and Christa's, I sandwiched excerpts from Jennifer McGuire's video deposition. Even though she was at the courthouse, and I knew Kantner would call her as part of his case, I didn't want him to question her, coached and rehearsed, before I took my shot. So, I played key parts of her testimony that undercut the defense that Coffee Shop was merely Amanda acting as a sole trader.

Panic time arose at 1:30 PM on the second day of trial, when I planned to show excerpts of Amanda's video deposition, for the same reasons I showed McGuire's. The process Judge McCoy followed was for the lawyers to exchange designations, by page and line number, of the portions of depositions they

---

[35] "In Latin, *redux* (from the verb *reducere*, meaning 'to lead back') can mean 'brought back' or 'bringing back'." Merriam-webster.com.

intended to play. Each side could then annotate on the pages any substantive objections, which would then go to Judge McCoy to rule on before the video clips were played.

But Kantner had not gotten his objections to my designated portions of Amanda's deposition in time for Judge McCoy to make rulings before I was ready to play the video. I didn't know if this was deliberate, but I had given him the designations the week before, and he had gotten angry with me when I wouldn't agree to call Amanda live, rather than by video, even though she would physically be present in the courtroom.

This problem at trial was compounded by the fact that I had already called all of the "live" witnesses that I had. As the lawyers stood at the judge's bench for a sidebar conference, Judge McCoy said to me, "I'm not going to say that you have to put a live witness on now, but I'm not going to have the jury just wait around until we get all the objections made and ruled on, and I'm certainly not going to send them home this early."

I said, "If you'll give me a short break, I'll call Ms. Hayward live."

Judge McCoy looked at the clock on the wall at the back of the courtroom. It was nearly 1:30. "How long do you need?" she asked.

"Twenty minutes."

"Why don't we break until 2:00?"

And so that's what we did. Although I knew I would later cross-examine Amanda after Kantner called her as part of his case, I hadn't expected to do so until the following day at the earliest. But direct examination was different from cross-examination and required a more organized approach than simply taking potshots at a witness's prior testimony, and I had not prepared for that. So, I had 30 minutes to pull together a coherent outline for direct.

Fortunately, weeks earlier, I had created, for my own use, a timeline of key events, from start to finish, of Coffee Shop's history. Then, the week before trial, I supplemented the timeline with the numbers of exhibits that correlated to each event. I decided to simply use that, plus my memory, as my outline for questioning.

It turned out to be even more effective than playing the video clips.

Referencing the complicated company structure that accountant David Wayling set up, I asked, "What was originally The Writer's Coffee Shop, The Writer's Coffee Shop Publishing House, it does exist separate and apart from those entities, correct?"

"Yes, because I can't dissolve myself," Amanda said, clinging to the notion that she operated Coffee Shop as a sole trader.

"The Writer's Coffee Shop has not been dissolved, has it?"

"No, it can't be."

"I understand you say it can't be, but it hasn't been dissolved, has it?"

"No."

So, if I could convince the jury Coffee Shop was a partnership, Amanda had just admitted it still hadn't been dissolved. I moved to the email in which Amanda invited Jennifer McGuire to be a partner. I held my breath, hoping Kantner hadn't coached her into an actual coherent answer to explain that away.

I needn't have worried.

"What was the partnership thing that Jenny brought up with you the night before?" I asked.

"It was the EIN number that she went and got that was a mistake in February. I had, around that time, just been going through my tax return for [husband] James, so it actually got me thinking about how I was going to do mine and it got me asking questions, which is why it was in July." She paused, as if she had lost her train of thought.

Or needed to buy more time to create her answer.

"I'm really sorry," she said, "what was the actual question?"

It was almost as if she objected to the responsiveness of her own answer. "What was the partnership thing that you were talking about in that e-mail?" I asked. "You say, 'Jenny brought up the partnership thing with me again tonight.' What was the 'partnership thing' you were talking about?"

"The EIN. Jenny wanted to know whether Jenn would go on—Jenn McGuire, sorry—would go on with the partnership that was the EIN bank account, because she was worried about having only her name as a partnership or the end-of-year tax returns because she was worried about her bankruptcy, and she wasn't allowed to have so much money going in and out so she wanted to share it."

That answer was just as nonsensical as what she had said in her deposition. First, the IRS had issued the EIN to a partnership called The Writer's Coffee Shop, not to a bank account. Secondly, one does not have a partnership in an "EIN bank account," even if such a thing existed. You can be joint account holders, but that's a different creature from a partnership. Additionally, Amanda contended she was a sole trader, and Coffee Shop was, in fact, her and her, alone. So why did she allow Coffee Shop money, which would have been all hers if she was truly a sole trader, to go through a bank account that was not hers? She told McGuire that, if she accepted the invitation, she would be responsible for one-third of the taxes on profits, which meant three partners. Who was the third, if not Amanda?

And even assuming that bank accounts could have profits, as opposed to balances, if proceeds from the sale of Coffee Shop books belonged to Amanda, as a sole trader, then all the profits were hers, right? Yet she claimed Jenn McGuire agreed to assume responsibility for a third of her taxes. Ridiculous!

"I don't see anything in this e-mail about the EIN bank

account," I said. "Tell me what the EIN bank account is."

"She opened up a bank account and attached the EIN number to it."

"What's the EIN number?"

"The one that she got in February that we've seen this morning."

"Okay. That's the EIN number from February 5, 2011?"

"That's correct."

"And you were aware that she [Jenny] got that number at the time, weren't you?"

"I was, but I don't think I was aware that it was a partnership—general partnership. And I didn't realize what that really meant, either."

"Well, she sent you a copy of it, didn't she?"

"She did."

"And it said that she was receiving it as a general partner?"

"It's one of my failings, but I actually don't often open attachments. I just knew what it was. And I always asked her for the number. I never, ever—there's many, many e-mails of me going, 'What's that EIN number again?'"

I had every confidence the rest of her answers to my questions would be a repeat of her past performances. By calling her live, she sat just feet away from the twelve people who would determine the outcome of this case. They saw every hesitation and heard every flippant or nonsensical answer as if she were speaking directly to them, as opposed to their merely being eavesdroppers to an impersonal video. Several of the jurors, with whom I spoke by phone a month after trial, said the effect was devastating.

Soon enough, she also lapsed into her lexicon of redefined terms. I had feared Kantner would have prepared her better, but the problem was there was no credible way to explain away her own words if you actually applied their common definitions.

According to Amanda, "We need to know soon if you want

to be a partner or not" meant "do you want to be on an EIN bank account to help pay taxes on Amanda's profits?" And "profits" meant balances, or maybe interest, in that bank account.

"Partner"? Well, it might be just a "friendship thing." Or a "term of endearment" or a "term of affection." Unless, of course, you were talking about profits on an "EIN bank account." Or if it was on a contract with KOBO, then it meant…well, that was just a mistake.

"Founder" or "co-founder"? That might also be a "friendship thing," like "partner," but it could also simply refer to people who were around at the beginning. But not all of them; just some of them. Well, just Jenny, Jenn McGuire, and Lea Dimovski.

When communicating about selling the publishing rights to *Fifty Shades*, "we" and "our" meant "I" and "my"; "agree" meant "advise;" "agreement" meant "advice" or "opinion." "We are now a company in the U.S." meant "we're not a company" but simply that "we actually can trade and keep a bank account in America."

I "guarantee" your job until the end of the following school year meant "I'm going to fire you in early in the school year."

And "I swear on my daughters' lives?" Well, that meant . . . not a damn thing!

Caroline Harrison, instead of Kantner, followed my questioning, and the most remarkable transformation occurred in Amanda. Where she had been flippant and offhand with me, sometimes belligerent and sometimes sarcastic, but mostly defensive, and rarely looked at the jury, she seemed to morph into "Rebecca of Sunnybrook Farm,"[36] cheerful and helpful, facing the jury to give her obviously-rehearsed answers. The focus of Caroline's initial questioning was the money Amanda

[36] From the classic children's book of the same name, by Kate Douglas Wiggin.

initially invested in Coffee Shop, including buying computers, software, and other equipment, and paying server fees for the website, as if paying money, alone, made her a sole trader. That conveniently overlooked Jenny's contributions of working full-time for Coffee Shop for a couple of years without pay, even quitting her teaching job, all supposedly for Amanda's sole benefit.

And Amanda blamed Jenny for the "mistake" on the KOBO contract.

"Who told KOBO you were a. partnership?" Caroline asked.

"Jenny Pedroza."

"Did you authorize her to tell them it was a partnership?"

"No."

"And, in fact, did you even know that that had been done when it was signed?"

"No. I didn't even know Jenn McGuire actually had signed it on her behalf until way later, because apparently the fax machine was broken or something and she asked Jenn McGuire to sign it on her behalf."

As with the "EIN bank account" answers, this made no sense. If Coffee Shop was simply Amanda acting as a sole trader, but under an assumed name, then Amanda would have had to sign the KOBO contract. Her answer implied that she expected Jenny to sign it, not Jenn, but neither of them was Amanda.

Amanda also had to deal with that pesky issue of the partnership agreement she promised to sign. "When Ms. Pedroza sent this partnership agreement, had you asked her to—how did this come about?" Caroline asked. "You asked her to do something that eventuated into this partnership agreement being circulated?"

"Yes. I was actually trying to work out how I could actually get a U.S. bank account in my name. She was actually trying to find out different banks to what they actually would need to actually put it in the business' name."

I counted five "actuallys" in those two sentences. One has to wonder if that was a paraverbal[37] indicator of…something.

When Caroline later asked, "Did you intend to sign this partnership agreement when she sent it to you?"

Amanda answered, "No. I was thinking about the whole issue, of course. There was so many different ideas that we were actually trying to float just to get one of them to stick so I could actually get an American bank account so I could actually open my own bank account with my name or hopefully The Writer's Coffee Shop so we could actually get Amazon payments to me."

Four more "actuallys."

Still later, Amanda said, "I said I was going to get to it, meaning I hadn't even opened it yet and had a look at it. I was still looking at other avenues. I was very busy. And it was one of those things that I just hadn't got around to yet. So, I did say that I would get to it. And I knew I had to get it notarized at the police station, because I had been talking about it to somebody else of how I actually can get it notarized because we don't call it that in Australia."

The lady doth protest too much, methinks,[38]

She protested too much again near the end of Caroline's questioning. "Did you think that the money from Random House belonged equally to everyone who was working at The Writer's Coffee Shop?"

"No, I didn't, but I wanted to be able to give back to the people who had actually put so much work and effort in for free, even though they keep telling me that I don't have to pay them, they'll do it for free, anyway. But, you know, you can't keep

---

[37] "Paraverbal communication: The inflection, pacing, pitch, and tone of speech, the emphasis one places on particular words, phrases, or pauses while speaking." *medical-dictionary.thefreedictionary.com*.

[38] From Queen Gertrude's dialogue in *Hamlet*.

not paying any friends forever. You know, eventually it's got to—you've got give back and do your part."

"So, who did you think that that money belonged to?"

"Well, it belonged to me. It's just that I wanted to share it."

If anyone had been listening carefully, they might have heard the clicking of my eyeballs as they rolled all the way back in their sockets. They did more rolling and clicking as Caroline neared the end of her questioning and asked about the *Fort Worth Weekly* article that triggered the cease-and-desist letters.

"Did you, in fact, ever read this article?" Caroline asked.

"No...Because my husband and everybody else had read it."

"Did they tell you what it said?"

"Yes. The reason I don't read any press is because, even if it's good, I still get cranky about little things that have not been reported right. And there was too much going on with the press and everything with how much I was in the press that I just stopped, not even—I just don't look at it because I just get upset and angry about it. And there's nothing I can do about it. It's out there. So, I just stopped doing—reading anything about myself or the company. I just got other people to do it for me. And they let me know what I needed to know in those articles."

Protesting too much, again?

"Did they tell you that in this article you were portrayed as basically outmaneuvering Ms. Pedroza?"

"Yes."

"Did they tell you that Ms. Pedroza was essentially making allegations about partnership?"

"Yes."

I objected that the question called for hearsay and that "the best evidence is the article." In other words, jury, read the article and let it speak for itself. I thought it probably would have gone unnoticed by the jury, but now their curiosity was likely aroused. I intended to pour gasoline on the sparks of that curiosity in just a few minutes.

Judge McCoy sustained my objection, but Caroline kept asking about the article. "Until this moment, have you read this article?"

"No."

When it came time for my re-direct, I was champing at the bit. Earlier, in my direct questioning, she said nothing in the article was untrue, just "wasn't very nice." Now she was saying she hadn't read the article at all. So, the whole exercise of sending cease-and-desist letters apparently was based on something she hadn't read.

"Ms. Hayward, do I understand you correctly, you have not read this *Fort Worth Weekly* article by Jeff Prince?" I asked.

"No, not from start to finish. I've read excerpts and that's it."

"Earlier, you said that the things in the article were not untrue; they just weren't very nice. How do you know that if you didn't read the article?"

"Because my husband and Cindy [Bidwell] had read the article, and they told me."

"And what they told you, you understood not to be untrue, but just simply not very nice, correct?"

"No, I just knew it wasn't right at all, and I needed to do something about it. I was actually more upset about the author and *Fifty Shades of Grey* and everything mentioned when we don't do that. Companywise more than—I didn't really care what she said about me as such."

"As you sit here today, you're not saying there's anything untrue in this article, are you?"

"Yeah, there's a lot of untruths in there. She was never a partner."

Well, that was what the lawsuit was all about, wasn't it?

"But you haven't read it, so you don't know, right?" I

asked.

"I have read excerpts, and I have seen that."

"What excerpts have you read?"

"That she got—in my translation without reading it word for word, she got shoved out because a golden handshake or something by her Australian partner or something."

"When did you read excerpts from it?"

"After, I think, you and I had the deposition."

"So that deposition was back in August. Was the first time you read excerpts from it after August or sometime in August?"

"Yes."

Now to drive home the point that the cease-and-desist letters were simply bullying tactics. "So, when the article was published—posted on January 29, 2014, without reading it, on February first, you sent a threatening letter to Jenny and Christa, right?"

Waffle time. Amanda explained that no, she didn't send the letter, Cindy Bidwell did. She had to admit, though, that she authorized it, and in fact she signed it. But when I asked her if she had read the content of the letter before it was sent, she said, "Vaguely."

"So, you hadn't read the article," I said, "and then you authorized the sending of a letter that you only vaguely read. Have I got that right?"

"Correct."

"By the time you had your attorney in Australia send a threatening letter dated February 10, 2014, you still hadn't read it, had you?"

"No."

And now there we were, in court in the middle of a trial, because of those letters. Karma's a bitch, ain't it?

There were two more points I needed to make with Amanda. The first went back to the KOBO contract and Jenny's "mistake."

"Do you recall that in prior testimony in this case you acknowledged that a copy of [the KOBO contract] was sent to you at the time?"

"Yes. Again, I didn't open. I knew that it was a KOBO contract, and I filed it under KOBO."

Ahhh, but damn those pesky transcripts from depositions and hearings. They can lead to all kinds of tap dancing for explanations.

"Do you also recall in prior testimony, you said that it didn't trouble you to see that it was entered into with The Writer's Coffee Shop Partnership?"

"No, because I had to fix it. It was just an issue that we had."

"Do you recall that you specifically said you were content for it to be in the name of The Writer's Coffee Shop partnership because it was 'what we were trading under in the U.S. at that point'?"

"It was funny, because we actually were never able to cash any of those checks. We had to get them redrawn a year-and-a-half later. So, it did matter."

Let's keep running that play until we get it right. "But my question is, do you recall that in prior testimony you testified that it was 'what we were trading under in the U.S. at that point'?"

I had the page of the prior transcript at the ready, to formally impeach her if she wouldn't admit what she had said. I thought I'd give her just a bit more rope, first. The more she argued, the worse she looked to the jury.

"It was," she said, "because of the EIN that mistakenly got done."

In other words, yes, we were operating as a partnership in April of 2011, when the KOBO contract was signed.

"And you were aware of it at the time?"

"I am not sure if I was or I wasn't."

"Well, again, are you aware that you testified that it didn't bother you at that time?"

"It bothers me now."

"But it didn't bother you at that time, right?"

"No. We were just trying to get everything together. And it was—she was helping us out. And it was just one of those things that happened."

It was also important to note, and Exhibit 15 that had been admitted into evidence showed, KOBO made payments under that contract to "The Writer's Coffee Shop (Partnership)" continuously on a monthly basis for more than two years after the contract was signed, and *no one ever bothered to tell KOBO that Coffee Shop was not a partnership.*

Seems sorta significant, doesn't it?

The other key point, one I debated with myself about, involved the statute of frauds. Jenny had testified there was no set time for the partnership, but it could have been ended at any time. In other words, it was an "at will" entity, and so it was not governed by the statute of frauds. But there was a line of cases in Texas law that says if the term of a partnership is not set by the partners' agreement, but it references some factor or timeline outside of the partnership from which a term can be calculated, then that may mean it's not "at will." Kantner's position was that, since Coffee Shop had contracts with authors with three-year terms, then you had to consider those contracts in deciding whether the purpose of the partnership could be completed in less than a year.

Because the statute of frauds was an affirmative defense, it was Kantner's burden to prove it. He hadn't done it yet, nor had Caroline gotten testimony about it from Amanda. I figured there was no way Amanda would say she and Jenny agreed to be partners for the duration of those author contracts, especially since she denied the existence of a partnership agreement in the first place. I could have left it alone, but I made a calculated decision to ask Amanda about it, figuring the odds were with me. I thought if I framed the question just right, she would have to say "no," because to say otherwise would admit the existence of a partnership.

And to say "no" would be an admission directly by Amanda that, if the jury decided there was a partnership, it was "at will." I wanted that admission.

I chose to bury the single question in the midst of questioning on other topics, almost as a throwaway, hoping it would sneak up on her unnoticed. Toward the end of my re-direct, I asked a few questions about money Lea Dimovski had loaned the company, then about a competitor of Coffee Shop. I dropped this in the middle of it: "Did you have an agreement with Ms. Pedroza that your partnership with her would continue for as long as author contracts were in effect?"

With an almost disgusted tone, which matched her facial expression, she said, "No."

I didn't glance at Kantner to see his reaction, but immediately moved to a different topic. I had the answer I needed, and it had come, not from my client, but from Amanda Hayward. That made it an admission, for all practical purposes etched in stone.

Jenny's Story

The 30 minutes while Mike prepared to question Amanda was the only time I saw him seem nervous. I don't think it was nerves, exactly, as much as simply readjusting his thinking. He told us that, due to a mix-up with the video and some objections, there was a change of plans. I thought that something had happened to the video, but I now know that this might have been a tactic by the defense to prevent the jury from viewing Amanda's deposition. Had I known at the time exactly what was going on, I would have been a nervous wreck. But Mike shielded me from the negative, remained positive, and moved forward with an air of grace and determination. My faith in him had already been cemented long before, but as he faced this new challenge, I felt major pride for my friend.

What I found most interesting about Amanda's testimony, other than her memory lapses, was the difference in her demeanor between when Mike asked questions versus Caroline's questioning. She almost looked like two different people. Her comfort increased dramatically with friendly questioning; her voice softened, her body language relaxed, and she looked directly at the jurors when speaking. Brent had told me to avoid looking at the jury when I testified. He said that sometimes jurors feel that witnesses who talk directly to them are trying too hard, perhaps overcompensating for deficiencies in their substantive testimony. Watching Amanda, I saw what he meant. Some of the jurors smiled politely at her, but most shifted uncomfortably in their chairs and looked at everything and everyone *except* Amanda.

I had another secret weapon at work while Amanda testified. When she had visited me in Texas, sometimes staying in my home for weeks, a number of my family and friends came to know her. They knew how much Coffee Shop meant to me and the sacrifices Christa and I had made. Amanda seemed to crave their acceptance, and many of them became friendly with her. When they perceived that she had betrayed me, it angered them.

My parents, my husband, Christa, and family friend Donna McNeil attended every day of the trial, and my sister and her husband came as their work schedules permitted. But on the day Amanda testified, I had new additions to my cheering section: my nephew Jason Vasquez and friends Missi Crossley, Jody Munoz, Kera Eason Beebe, and Chris Wilkins, who had met Amanda during her Texas visits. They sat shoulder-to-shoulder in the seats behind me, gazes lasered on Amanda as she testified.

Fiercely loyal and protective of me, they wanted Amanda to know that they knew what she had done and that they were there to support me.

I noticed how Amanda avoided their stares.

Mike's Story

After Amanda, I called other witnesses by using excerpts of their videotaped depositions, including Lea Dimovski, David Wayling, and James Hayward. I knew Kantner would probably put Dimovski and James Hayward on the stand, live, as part of his case and I wanted to head off damage they might do, although I didn't think they represented any real threat. The danger was Kantner might shade their testimony to muddy the water, so I felt it best to present them to the jury, myself, first.

For example, Kantner said, in his opening statement, that Lea Dimovski would testify Coffee Shop was not a partnership. However, that was not what she testified to before. At the temporary injunction hearing, I asked her, "Did you want to be a general partner in the Writer's Coffee Shop?"

She answered, "There was a time when I considered it, but when it was all put together and I just—it wasn't something that was for me." In other words, when Coffee Shop had been "put together" as a partnership, Dimovski simply declined to become a partner. She reiterated this at her deposition, and I played that excerpt for the jury. I knew Kantner would default to the "there was no partnership" party line later during his live questioning of her, but at least I had already gotten this in front of the jury.

As for David Wayling, Amanda's accountant, I played excerpts from his deposition with his admissions that a sole trader can't have co-founders and can't be a company. I also wanted to deal with another of the defense's default positions: that Coffee Shop was merely a hobby.

"How is running a hobby different from operating a

business as a sole trader?" Kantner asked Wayling in one of the excerpts I played.

"The same way whittling against a piece of wood is different to running a furniture business."

Did I really have to explain how running a free website as a "library" for writers was different from soliciting paid advertisers; executing legally binding contracts to publish books; executing legally binding contracts with retailers like Amazon and Barnes & Noble to sell those books; executing legally binding contracts as a "partnership"; providing documents to financial institutions representing that your company is a partnership; hiring and paying staff to edit and promote books; telling the world, via website, blogs, and newspaper interviews, that the "company" has co-founders and partners; spending funds to market the books; traveling around the world to promote books at writer's conferences; collecting payments from retailers from the sale of books; providing royalty payments to authors and/or their agents; providing 1099s to authors to account to the IRS for royalties paid; and filing a U.S. Return of Partnership Income with the IRS? One was whittling and the other was running a business.

I also played excerpts from the deposition of Jenny's accountant, Paul Varga, and Amanda's husband, James, with questions asked by Kantner as well as questions I had asked. Varga, who prepared the Coffee Shop partnership tax return as well as Jenny's personal returns, testified that Jenny initiated contact in the fall of 2011, "saying that she and another lady were putting a partnership together called The Writer's Coffee Shop."

"When she called you in the Fall of 2011, did she mention the name of the other lady to which she referred?" Kantner asked.

"She did not. She said there was a—I said, 'How many partners do you have?' And I believe she said three or four, we're not sure yet. She said one of them is in Australia but did not give me the name."

"Okay. Do you know as we sit here today who she claims her partners to be?"

"Amanda Hayward is the woman in Australia. The other partner on the partnership return that I prepared was also a girl named Jennifer, but I can't remember her last name."

"McGuire?"

"Yes, sir."

The last witness I put on, by video deposition, was James Hayward, primarily to get one specific answer in front of the jury—and also in front of Judge McCoy, because I would later ask her to impose the equitable remedy of a constructive trust on Amanda. To broaden the scope of that trust, which I'll discuss later, I needed to show Amanda had commingled Random House payments with other assets to the point that you couldn't distinguish what came from Random House and what came from elsewhere.

I played this Q and A for the jury:

Q: *Is there any way, with records that you have available to you, to distinguish that additional money or that money from other sources in that account from Random House money?*

A: *I would have said, without going to a level of forensic accounting, no. If the moneys end up in a bucket, being the account, and then money goes back out. Once you tip water into a bucket, it's hard to say which glass of water it is when you take it back out again.*

After we rested the plaintiff's case, it was time for the defense to put on their case-in-chief. Their first witness was Jennifer McGuire, questioned by Caroline Harrison. She started with questions that allowed McGuire to contradict her own deposition testimony, which we had already played for the jury.

She led McGuire through her early involvement with Coffee Shop and periodically sprinkled in "partnership" questions, like, "Did Amanda ever tell you that she was a partner with Mrs. Pedroza in The Writer's Coffee Shop?"

McGuire consistently answered those questions in the negative, almost as if oblivious to her prior testimony. It also appeared as if she suffered a relapse of amnesia.

"Was there ever a time that Ms. Hayward—before the *Fifty Shades of Grey*, was there ever any time that Ms. Hayward talked to you about splitting profits from the publishing house?" Caroline asked.

"Not that I remember."

"Did you and Ms. Hayward and Ms. Pedroza have any discussions before *Fifty Shades of Grey* was published about forming a partnership?"

"Not that I remember."

"Do you remember a time in early 2011—February 5, 2011, to be specific—when Ms. Pedroza obtained an EIN number?"

"Yes, I do."

"Did you have a conversation with her about that?"

"Yes, I did. She had jumped on Skype and told me that she had gotten the EIN for The Writer's Coffee Shop. And I had asked her if she set it up as a corporation, and she said, no, I set it up as a partnership."

"Did you have any—other than the Skype conversation, did you have any conversation with her about that?"

"Not that I remember."

"Did you have any conversations with her about fixing that?"

"I don't remember."

"Did you talk to Amanda Hayward about that?"

"I don't remember if we had a specific discussion about it at the time."

Caroline then addressed that infamous July 2011 email exchange. "What was the partnership discussion that came up as far as you recall?" Caroline asked.

"I expressed that I was—I was concerned, because it terrified me knowing, you know, what would be expected of me as a partner. And living the way I did, paycheck to paycheck, there was no way I could take care of any issues that arose. And I knew I would be responsible for a portion of them being a partner. And I was reassured that, you know, we're not making any money. Your main responsibility would be on the taxes. And, you know, thirty-three-and-a-third of nothing is nothing."

"Why did you say that you were all in and that you would agree to be a partner?"

"Because we needed to get business done, and we had to do it for the rest of the year until we could dissolve it and get set up properly like we should have been starting the new year."

"Did you think that you were agreeing to be a partner in The Writer's Coffee Shop?"

"No, I did not."

"Did you think that you were agreeing to be a partner in The Writer's Coffee Shop Publishing House?"

"No, I did not."

"What did you think you were agreeing to be a partner in?"

"The EIN number that was set up just so we could do the bank account so we could do business with Amazon. So, the money would come in, we could then pay our obligations to U.S. people."

That was just as convoluted and nonsensical as any answer she had given before. On cross-examination, there was no need to take anything in chronological order; all I needed to do was to bounce from topic to topic, reminding the jury of her prior admissions.

Addressing her email acceptance of the offer to become a partner—supposedly just in an "EIN bank account"—I asked,

"You did accept the offer, right?"

"Yes, eventually."

"Well, eventually, in—on the first page of this exhibit, you say, 'I'm all in this with you girls, let's go for it.'"

"Yes."

"So, you accepted the offer to be a partner on July 20, 2011, right?"

"Yes."

Then I turned McGuire's attention to the KOBO contract. One of the signs that suggested the jury might be leaning our way occurred on this set of questions. I didn't make it a habit of watching them, because I didn't want jurors to notice me watching them. If any of them ever looked at me, I wanted them to see nothing more than my focus on the witnesses.

McGuire had said she didn't see the words "partnership" and "partner" when she signed the contract. Directing her attention to the signature page, I asked, "That is your signature?"

"Yes, it is."

"And it is immediately beneath the words 'The Writer's Coffee Shop, parenthesis, Partnership,' isn't it?"

"Yes, it is."

"And then your name is handwritten beneath your signature immediately above the line that says 'partner,' right?"

"Yes."

"And then below the line that says 'partner' is the date 5/3/11. Is that your handwriting?"

"Yes, it is."

"So, in order to write your name on this contract and to date it, you had to jump over the word 'partner,' right?"

In my peripheral vision, I caught a glimpse of a male juror on the back row jerk a clenched fist slightly forward, as if acknowledging a good punch had landed.

"Yes," she answered.

"Is it between the printed name and the date?"

"Correct."

"Are you saying you did not see the word 'partner' on there when you signed it?"

"I did not pay attention to it."

"But did you see it?"

"I have no idea. I know I was focused on the signature, the name, and the date."

"And you certainly weren't intending to defraud KOBO, were you?"

"Of course not."

"You wouldn't want KOBO to think this was a partnership when it wasn't, would you?"

"No."

"And you wouldn't want KOBO to think that you're a partner when you're not, would you?"

"No, I would not."

McGuire admitted, again, she had signed a partnership agreement, an assumed name certificate, and a certificate of ownership, all as an owner or partner in Coffee Shop, and she knew these documents were to be submitted to, and relied upon by, financial institutions in order to open a bank account for Coffee Shop. Then I turned to an answer she had given Caroline that I hadn't heard before, which was that she thought the EIN was just going to be used through 2011 and then the partnership—the one she said didn't exist—would be dissolved at year end. I pointed out that, in her deposition, she testified she thought it was going to be dissolved at tax time in 2012, not the end of 2011. This was an important distinction because our case required the jury to believe that, as of the date the Random House contract was signed, March 9, 2012, the partnership still existed.

I directed McGuire's attention to the March 6, 2012, email she sent to Jenny questioning tax treatment on the *Fifty Shades* bonus depending upon whether it was paid before or after

Coffee Shop was dissolved. "Would it be fair to say that, at least as of March 6, 2012, you did not believe the partnership had been dissolved?" I asked.

"I didn't know."

"Well, did you ever receive a notice from any partner in that partnership that it had been dissolved?"

"No, I did not."

"Did you ever receive a notice from any of the partners in that partnership that they were withdrawing from the partnership?"

"No, I did not."

"Has the partnership been liquidated and the assets distributed?"

"No."

Point made, I moved on to the Coffee Shop partnership tax return, which included K-1s for both McGuire and Jenny. "Is that the K-1 that Mr. Varga prepared for you?"

"Yes, it is."

"It shows that you were a partner in the partnership The Writer's Coffee Shop?"

"I see that, yes."

"Did you attach that to your personal income tax return and file it?"

"Yes."

"Did you understand that you were telling the Internal Revenue Service that you were a partner in a partnership by filing that?"

She flashed a deer-in-the-headlights look and then defaulted to ignorance. "I just thought I was doing my taxes like I was supposed to."

Toward the end of my questioning, I finally got what I now believe in hindsight—I'm not sure I recognized it at the time— was one of the most sincere and accurate answers she gave all day. Noting that she claimed she had been told there would be no profits in the "EIN bank account," I asked, "If *Fifty Shades of Grey* was being sold through Amazon, am I not correct that moneys from those sales would go to this account?"

"Right, but then they would go back to pay royalties and pay all the contractors in the U.S."

"And if there's anything left over, that's profits, right?"

"If there's anything left over. *But I had no clue.*"

Can I get an "amen"?

Jenny's Story

"I didn't put any money in it. I was simply helping a friend with a hobby that only much later turned into a job."

Some variation of these words was repeated so often that I began to wonder if the witnesses were following cue cards. It seemed as if Jenn had been carefully coached on how to answer the questions from her lawyer, but you can't coach against cross-examination. We had already seen her deposition, and we had documentary evidence, with her signature on it, of partnership. I was never a hobby enthusiast, but I felt like a hobby wouldn't require a partnership agreement, an assumed name certificate, or a business bank account. And I certainly wouldn't have left my teaching career for someone else's hobby.

When Mike cross-examined her, Jenn admitted, just as she had done during her deposition, that there was a partnership and that it had never been dissolved. It was amazing to watch, but the truth was obvious, and she couldn't legitimately dispute it.

Mike's Story

Sure enough, when Kantner called Lea Dimovski as part of the defense's case, he went to the "hobby" default position. "At this point in time, in the 2009-time period, was this a job for you?" he asked.

"No. It's always been a hobby. There was only a small period of time that it was actually my full-time job. I've always worked externally." She went on to say that it wasn't until July 2013 that her work for Coffee Shop became a "job" instead of a "hobby," because that was when it became her "livelihood."

On cross examination, I said, "Look, if you would, at Defendant's Exhibit 5. Do you see that exhibit?"

"Yes, I do."

"What's the date on that exhibit?"

"Eighteenth of October 2011."

"Do you recall a discussion with Jenny and Ms. Hayward about possibly cutting an author loose? And by 'cutting loose,' I mean letting the author go?"

"Yes."

"In that e-mail, a little below the middle, your initial response is, 'Wow! Sounds like I have a lot to catch up on. This is a business. Businesses need to make money.' Did I read that correctly?"

"Yes."

"Do you recall writing that to Ms. Hayward and Jenny?"

"It's there in black and white that I did," she said, sheepishly, I thought.

"Did you understand that, at least as of October of 2011, this was a business?"

"Yes."

"And that businesses need to make money?"

"Yes."

"Would it be fair to say that there's a difference between a business and a hobby?"

"There is, yes."

By late afternoon on Friday, February 13, both sides rested their cases. Kantner then renewed a motion for directed verdict, which he had made earlier that morning at the close of the plaintiff's case. This kind of motion asks the court to enter a verdict in favor of one side or the other on the grounds that the facts conclusively established their entitlement to it as a matter of law, so there was nothing left for a jury to decide.

That morning, Kantner had focused primarily on the statute of frauds defense, pointing to those author contracts with the three-year terms. Judge McCoy made a few comments that tracked my position that the contracts between Coffee Shop and its authors were not the measure of whether the partnership agreement could be performed within one year.

"I will tell you where my thoughts are going, and you may have other grounds for the directed verdict," she said. "But in considering the statute of frauds, particularly under the *Business and Commerce Code*, I was thinking it sounds like, based on the testimony—there's been some testimony regarding how long some of the writer's contracts were envisioned to be performed. And I was thinking about this, and I think in some ways that's a little instructive, but that's not really the point. The point is, was the oral agreement between the parties—or the oral partnership or understood partnership or allegedly agreed-to partnership, I think that's the issue; could that partnership be performed within one year?"

When my time to respond to the motion rolled around that morning, I was more than happy to validate Judge McCoy's thinking.

"I want to address the threshold issue, which is, I think, what you brought up when you first came in, which is, there are two separate issues," I said. "One is the agreement between Ms. Pedroza and Ms. Hayward. The agreement between the authors and The Writer's Coffee Shop is a completely different issue. You don't even get to it until you first analyze the oral agreement between Ms. Hayward and Ms. Pedroza. The law is pretty clear in Texas that agreements at will are not subject to the statute of frauds. Ms. Pedroza testified on the stand there was no set term, and it could have ended at any day."

"Okay," Judge McCoy said. "Agreements at will are not subject to the statute of frauds. Okay."

"That's correct. And Ms. Pedroza testified that there was no set term, and it could have ended any day. That's almost a textbook definition of a partnership at will. Flash forward to Ms. Hayward sitting on the stand. The only time you even start looking at other contracts or extrinsic evidence is if there is no set term. But if the agreement between Ms. Hayward and Ms. Pedroza prescribes conditions from which its duration can be determined, then you look to the extrinsic evidence.

"And I point blank asked Ms. Hayward, 'Did you have an agreement with Ms. Pedroza that the partnership would last as long as any contracts were in effect with third-party authors?' And she said, 'No.' So, Ms. Pedroza says it's a partnership with no term. Ms. Hayward says there's no agreement that the partnership would last for as long as these contracts. So, you never even look at those contracts."

In rebuttal, Kantner tried to get around Amanda's answer. "Now think about that question to somebody who denies there was a partnership," he said. "Did she have a partnership agreement? Well, of course she's going to say 'no' because she denied the partnership."

"I'm going to deny the Motion for Directed Verdict," Judge McCoy said.

In the afternoon, Kantner re-urged his motion, on the same grounds, and I responded. "Mr. Kantner pointed out this morning that, of course she would say that, because she says there's no agreement," I said. "But you know what? That means that the evidence in the record is that it could have been terminated at any time. They could have walked away at any time. And there was no agreement amongst the parties to look to any extrinsic evidence to determine what the period of time was."

In other words, it didn't matter why Amanda said it; it only mattered that she had said it.

Judge McCoy ruled quickly, just as she had that morning. "All right, I'm going to deny the Motion for Instructed Verdict."

Court recessed at 2:25 PM and we left for the weekend, to spend it frantically worried about closing arguments to be held the following week.

Jenny's Story

I went into the weekend feeling great. I thought that the jury had been with Mike throughout the trial, starting with jury selection. It appeared as if they appreciated his obvious honesty and calm demeanor, and I knew that his closing argument would be no different. When I left the courthouse that afternoon, I looked forward to a glass of wine, relaxing with my family, and a good night's sleep. Unfortunately, Mike wasn't in the same boat.

CHAPTER SEVENTEEN: A Chance to Rewrite the Ending

... the arc of the moral universe is long but it bends toward justice.
        —Dr. Martin Luther King, Jr.

Mike's Story

BRENT AND I spent the weekend finalizing our version of a proposed jury charge, or the "Court's Charge"—the questions and instructions we wanted Judge McCoy to submit to the jury. The statute of frauds defense had come up again on Friday afternoon as the lawyers met with Judge McCoy to discuss the charge. Kantner continued to argue that the partnership agreement, which he denied existed, had to be in writing. I thought that was absurd, but I had to take it seriously because, even if the jury decided Coffee Shop was a partnership, if it believed an agreement between Jenny and Amanda to create that partnership violated the statute of frauds, then Jenny couldn't enforce it. And that meant we lost. It was an all or nothing proposition.

We drove to Fort Worth on Monday afternoon and checked into the Worthington Hotel in Fort Worth's Sundance

Square area downtown. Even though we had an extra day because of the Presidents' Day holiday, it still seemed as if I needed more time. But that was nearly always the case in litigation. No matter how much time you had to prepare, you always wanted more.

Brent and I ate a leisurely dinner at a downtown restaurant then returned to our respective hotel rooms. I'm sure Brent must have felt a little useless at that point because I needed to work on my final argument, and I needed to be alone to prepare. I'm not one of those attorneys who has to practice an argument, either to someone else or even standing in front of a mirror. I don't write it out and memorize it. Instead, I come up with what I think is a coherent outline of how to organize my thoughts, then I review the facts and the evidence until I have it so engrained in my head that I can speak, at least for the most part, without notes.

I worked until about midnight, then finally turned out the lights and went to bed. But not to sleep. As had happened every other night during the trial, I tossed and turned, my mind reeling with thoughts about the next day, as well as the preceding days. Had I made our case convincingly? Had I introduced the necessary evidence and asked the right questions of the witnesses? Had I preserved any errors by timely objecting? If not, it was a little late for regrets, but those are the kinds of thoughts that keep litigators up at night during a trial.

I felt an immense burden of personal responsibility for Jenny. She had entrusted me with, not only her case, but also with the duty to protect her interests. It was my job to speak for her and to allow her a forum to speak for herself, to regain her voice after many bleak months about what happened to her and to Christa, for whom she felt responsible. This wasn't about me. It didn't matter if I knocked it out of the park or performed like a master thespian or a trained monkey. What mattered was how this trial, and its outcome, would affect Jenny and her family.

And so, I slept very little that night. I remember looking at the clock at 1:00 AM, and again at 2:00 and 3:00. I think the last time was 4:00, before I finally drifted off.

I had placed an order the night before for room service breakfast—rather than join Brent as we had done every day during the trial. I needed the time alone, again, to review my notes and make sure I was ready. I had just finished breakfast when I heard a knock at the door. I don't remember exactly what time it was, maybe 7:30 or so. I opened the door to confront Brent. He looked pale, his eyes bleary, looking as if he had not slept a wink.

Before I could stop myself, I blurted out, "You look like shit."

"I was up all night. Food poisoning."

I don't think I've ever had food poisoning, but if that's what it made you look like, boy, was I glad.

"I'm going to try to make it today," he said, "but I don't know how long I'll last."

I was betting it wouldn't be long. It turned out I was right. After we both got dressed and carted our boxes and briefcases to the courthouse, he decided he couldn't sit through closing arguments. I told him to go back to the hotel, and he could join me later to wait on the jury.

Jenny's Story

The weekend before closing arguments was torturous for me. My family and friends walked on eggshells around me, my dog became ill (probably because he felt stress in the air), and the only person able to sleep was my 14-year-old son.

To top it off, when the new week rolled around, Christa and I had to miss work again after being off the week before. I was a bundle of nerves but ready to get this resolved one way or the other. I found myself repeatedly reviewing what had transpired during the trial. I replayed every word Mike or Brent had said, and I visualized how the witnesses played out the drama on the stand.

Christa was so worried about me that she had driven me to the courthouse every day. We listened to a "special" playlist to help us remember why we were fighting this fight and to stay strong in the knowledge that we were standing up for ourselves. It helped most days, but this Tuesday, my nerves were just about shot.

When we arrived at the courthouse, Mike told us Brent was not feeling well and wouldn't be there for closing arguments. Not having him sit next to me would be rough. When things got emotional or overly dramatic during the trial, he was like a balm to my soul. He would turn and give me a sweet look or reach out and touch my hand, and it instantly calmed me. It was as if he sensed what I felt.

I knew Mike would stand in front of the jury for much of it, with me alone at the table, and not having Brent by my side would hurt. I knew Brent must be really sick or he would be there. He had invested just as much time and energy into this case as the rest of us. Well, if you count the thousands of emails I sent him to catalog, probably more.

But even without Brent, I had a room full of family and friends, and I had Mike Farris leading the charge. I know he missed Brent, too, but he didn't show any unease. Christa and I left him alone that morning and forewent the usual polite talk before the jury entered.

I watched as he reviewed his notes. He looked like a lion waiting for the zookeeper to open the door to his cage. He was ready. I had confidence in him, and I knew the day was his. The moment he started talking, he controlled the courtroom.

Mike's Story

After a last conference with Judge McCoy to finalize the jury charge, we adjourned to the courtroom where the respective lawyers made their formal objections to the charge, all of it taken down by the court reporter. You couldn't complain on appeal that a question or instruction shouldn't have been submitted to the jury if you didn't object before the charge went to the jury. Amanda's lawyers objected to virtually every question. I objected to the partnership question, because I believed it had been established as a matter of law, and the judge could rule in my favor on it without submitting it to the jury.

I also objected to the statute of frauds question because I believed the evidence had also established, as a matter of law, that Coffee Shop was a partnership "at will." I think Judge McCoy thought so, too. When we discussed it in her chambers, she said, "I think we can go ahead and submit it to the jury. Then I can always entertain a motion if the jury finds against you." I thought she was telling me she believed the jury would agree with me, but if it didn't, she would be inclined to set aside their answer if I made the appropriate motion. Still, I made a formal objection for the record. If the jury found against us and, for whatever reason, she didn't grant a motion to set the answer aside, I wouldn't be able to raise it on appeal unless I had objected.

After we made our objections, which were recorded by the court reporter, the bailiff brought the jury in. Once they were all seated, Judge McCoy allowed me to proceed. I set up a rickety easel in front of her and propped my chart of "Five Factors of Partnership" on it.

Five Factors of Partnership

1. Receipt or right to receive a share of profits of the business	☐
2. Expression of intent to be partners	☐
3. Participation or right to participate in control of the business	☐
4. Agreement to share or sharing losses of the business or liability for claims of third parties	☐
5. Agreement to contribute or contribution of money or property to the business	☐

I placed my notes on the edge of the court reporter's table. I didn't want to use them if I didn't have to, but I wanted the security blanket of having them close at hand, if need be. Then I moved a bit closer to the jury box, but not too close. This was the first time I really focused on them since opening statements. As I said before, I hadn't studied them during the presentation of evidence to see their reactions, because Brent and Jenny and others in the courtroom did that for me. Instead, I had focused solely on the witnesses as they testified, leaving the jury almost as eavesdroppers. Now I directly faced the twelve people whom I would be asking to rewrite the ending to Jenny's story.

It's funny how, even though I stood alone, I felt even lonelier without the comforting presence of Brent at counsel's table. I didn't know if emotional support was tangible or not, but I could verify the absence of it was. Brent had been with me from the beginning, and I missed having him there.

As was obligatory, I started by thanking the jury for their attentiveness. But where that was usually a rote recitation from trial lawyers, in this case, I spoke from the heart. This jury, unlike any I had seen before, had been riveted from the first moments. I had no illusions that it was due to Brent's and my spellbinding performances, nor those of Bob Kantner and

Caroline Harrison. Instead, the subject matter—a famous book—initially grabbed their attention, but I think the human drama also contributed. Who among them had never been betrayed by a friend or made a bad decision because they relied upon a misplaced trust? They saw this was more than a business deal gone bad; this was a friendship gone bad, and the pain, particularly Jenny's, was evident.

I paused as I prepared to move into my argument. At this stage, you hoped you had honored the promises you made in opening statement and introduced the evidence you said you would, and that the jury appreciated your forthrightness and honesty with them.

"I told you at the start that you're going to hear two stories here this week. And I think you have heard two stories. One of the stories was of a group of hardworking women who formed a partnership, had some success, and then one of them took off with all the money. The other story was that one person had a business, a group of hardworking women worked for her out of the goodness of their hearts, and then the first woman took the money and ran off with it. Two different stories."

Most of the jurors were poker-faced, but a nod or two told me that I was on track. Buried in an avalanche of facts, I sensed they had found the threads of those two stories. They were with me thus far.

Then I issued a challenge: "This is your chance to rewrite the ending."

Another nod or two.

"In order to believe Jenny's story, here is what you have to do: Consider the facts at face value and apply common definitions to ordinary words. To accept Ms. Hayward's version of the story, you have to rewrite history, spin documents, and accept alternative definitions of common, ordinary words."

I felt as if I had the jury leaning my way, but you didn't get to simply ask the jury, "Who wins?" Instead, under the Texas system, the jury has to answer specific questions the judge gives them in the Court's Charge. It was crucial to explain exactly what the questions meant, and even to suggest how I thought they should answer them. Kantner would do the same thing when he made his argument, but he would suggest different answers.

The most important question was the first one: Is the Writer's Coffee Shop a partnership? Each of the remaining nine questions had an instruction at the beginning that said, "If you answered 'Yes' to Question No. 1, then answer Question No. ___. Otherwise, do not answer Question No. ___." So, unless the jury found that Coffee Shop was a partnership, the case was over and Amanda emerged as the victor. And even if the jury answered the question "yes," there were still other landmines, like the statute of frauds question. But the biggest and most important hurdle was the partnership question.

I reminded the jury the critical date was March 9, 2012, when Random House signed the *Fifty Shades* contract. "If The Writer's Coffee Shop was a partnership on that date, and Ms. Pedroza was a partner in that partnership, she is entitled to her share of profits from the sale to Random House of the *Fifty Shades* trilogy."

I later learned, from speaking by telephone with some of the jurors, they were painfully aware of that date and its significance. One said, during deliberations, if certain events came up for discussion that happened after March 9, then they knew it didn't matter for purposes of answering the first question. It gratified me to know I had driven that point home.

Using my handy chart, I moved on to a discussion of the five factors of partnership. I would come back later and track through the evidence I believed supported each, but now I simply wanted the jurors to understand what the factors were and how the analysis worked. I explained there didn't have to be evidence of all five, but the more evidence there was, and the more factors implicated, the stronger the case for partnership.

The first factor was "receipt or right to receive profits." I noted the key was the *right* to receive, not the actual receipt. I predicted Kantner would argue that Jenny had not received *any* profits and told the jurors I had a quarrel with that because the evidence showed the $500,000 advance from Random House was, in fact, divided among the partners. It turned out Kantner did make that argument, so I was glad I addressed it first.

Then I reminded the jury that the fact Jenny hadn't gotten her *full* share of profits was not evidence there wasn't a partnership. Rather, it was evidence she had been cheated. "If Ms. Pedroza had gotten her entire share of the profits," I said, "we wouldn't be here today."

The next factor was "expression of intent to be partners." I acknowledged that just because someone uses the word "partner" doesn't mean there's a partnership, but you had to look at the context in which the word was used. Then it was time to dust off that remark Kantner had said in his opening statement, which sounded jarring at the time.

"I believe it was in Mr. Kantner's opening statement that he talked about walking down the streets in west Texas and saying 'Howdy, partner,' to somebody. What you need to do as you consider the evidence, the things that you've seen and the testimony you've heard and the documents you've seen, ask yourselves, are those 'howdy, partner' moments or are those the kinds of expressions that have some significance to the recipient of the information?"

By way of illustration, I said, "Just to pull one out of the hat, when you sign a contract with a retailer called KOBO as a partnership and you sign it as a partner, are you saying 'howdy, partner' to KOBO, or are you telling KOBO you're a partnership?"

I let that soak in, knowing I could revisit it later to demonstrate its absurdity. One of the jurors later told me he thought it was a "discredit" to Kantner to have trotted out the "howdy, partner" line, as if he was pandering to a Fort Worth jury. I didn't believe Amanda had been merely throwing around the term "partner" as a term of endearment. I thought then, and still think today, Amanda used the word "partner" in the legal sense, and she believed she, Jenny, Jennifer McGuire, and Lea Dimovski were partners in a partnership.

The next factor was "participation, or right to participate, in the control of the business." I reminded the jurors, in what Amanda described as the most important decision Coffee Shop ever made—the sale of publishing rights to the *Fifty Shades* trilogy, the evidence showed it was a joint decision made by the partners. The last two factors were "agreement to share, or actually sharing losses," and "agreement to contribute, or actually contributing, money or property to the business."

Then, as I prepared to go through the evidence in detail for each factor, I switched to storytelling mode. I asked Jackie, our IT assistant, to display the three-act-structure chart on the screen.

"I'm a writer," I said. "I follow the three-act story structure. This case has a three-act structure: It has a set-up, it has a series of complications, and it has a payoff. And the significant date is that date when the Random House contract was signed."

I had Jackie break out the "Set-Up" chart, and I took the jury through the series of events that started with Jenny and Amanda "joining forces" in October of 2009 and ended with Amanda telling Jenny, in early January of 2012, they "had a big problem," because film companies were talking to Erika Mitchell about film rights to her books. Those events included getting an employer identification number from the Internal Revenue Service for Coffee Shop as a partnership—"That's not saying to the IRS, 'Howdy, partner'"—inviting Jenn McGuire to join the partnership, and Amanda telling the full staff of Coffee Shop, "I have 3 other partners in this business."

But things changed when Amanda learned film companies were interested. "I believe it's fair to draw an inference," I said, "that that's the point when the planning started to change things, because big money loomed on the horizon. E.L. James had a contract with The Writer's Coffee Shop, and she couldn't get out of that contract and go to a bigger publisher unless The Writer's Coffee Shop let her."

As I said in my opening statement, "If this were a movie, this is where the ominous music would be queued."

I asked Jackie to break out the "Complications" timeline, the series of events leading up to the magic date when the Random House contract was signed and Amanda, for the first time, dismissed the idea of a partnership and started to assert control of the company. Offers came in from major New York publishers and, sure enough, the author wanted out of her contract. Random House made the winning bid and the partners "agreed" to let the author go. They also agreed that Amanda would sign the Random House contract on behalf of Coffee Shop, but no one could predict what Amanda was going to do next.

"When it comes time to sign the Random House contract, Ms. Hayward contacts Jenny and says, 'I need the employee identification number.' Remember, this is the number they use on all the contracts. It shows up on Amazon. It shows up on the 1099s that go out. Jenny gives her the number. Ms. Hayward signs the contract and then won't let Jenny see it because, she says, 'I signed a nondisclosure agreement with Random House.' Well, come to find out, she didn't sign a nondisclosure agreement with Random House."

In hindsight, I told the jury, it was clear Amanda didn't want the others to see the contract, because then they would have known what she had done: used her personal tax file number, instead of the company's EIN, and directed Random

House to make payments to her account in Australia.

Then, four days after the contract was signed, "A request for information comes in from the *Wall Street Journal*. This is the one where Ms. Hayward tells Christa that the only thing not to say is that Jenny and Jenn are partners because 'we have to say they're business associates for tax reasons.'"

That was the first time anyone ever suggested that Coffee Shop was not a partnership, I told the jury.

"Then Amanda goes off the grid. There's a period of time where she's *incommunicado*. Nobody knows where she is. Then she surfaces full force in June of 2012."

I asked Jackie to display Plaintiff's Exhibit 30 on the screen—the email in which Amanda outlined her plan to restructure the publishing business to make it look like she was a sole trader because "we have to show I'm the owner somehow."

"I refer to this as 'The big con,'" I said, because what followed was not simply changing things for tax reasons. Instead, Amanda created the complicated structure of companies she and her husband owned. Jackie then broke out the "third act" on the screen—the "Pay-Off."

"This is when Amanda comes up with the service agreement for Jenny to sign. What Ms. Hayward doesn't tell her is how she signed the Random House contract using her personal tax file number. Continues to tell her she's got a nondisclosure agreement with Random House. Doesn't let her know she's received the first Random House payment of sixteen-and-a-half million dollars. Doesn't tell her if she signs it, Ms. Hayward is going to take the position that she's now given up any claim she's ever had to anything. That she's waived her claim as a partner if she signs it.

"Jenny doesn't like the contract. Doesn't want to go along with it. But again, she doesn't feel like she had a lot of choice. She trusted Amanda. She did ask some questions. Very concerned about the 'termination without cause' provision.

Amanda's explanation is, 'Oh, I would never do that. I swear on my daughters' lives.'

"And so, Jenny signs it. And sure enough, it's just a matter of months, I think it's a little less than a year, when she's terminated because 'marketing is not working,' and the company is not making money. At which point Ms. Hayward is sitting on over thirty million dollars, which you heard her say she has spent on real estate, she has spent on a gymnasium, she has spent on herself. None of it has gone back into the business. It hasn't gone to the partners. She's spending that money and then pleading poverty as a reason to let them go."

I had been talking for more than 30 minutes, and I knew the worst thing I could do was bore the jury. I sensed that I had them with me, and my gut said it was time to wrap things up and sit down.

But, before I finished, I had one more set of charts I wanted the jury to see.

The first was a pie chart depicting what Jenny's profit share should have been.

"If you assume for the sake of argument that Lea Dimovski, take her at face value, was not a partner and there were three partners, the red represents one-third of the whole. That's what Jenny would have been entitled to as a partner. But what she actually received was one hundred-fifty-thousand dollars—a one-time payment of one-hundred-thousand dollars and then fifty-thousand dollars [for signing the service agreement]."

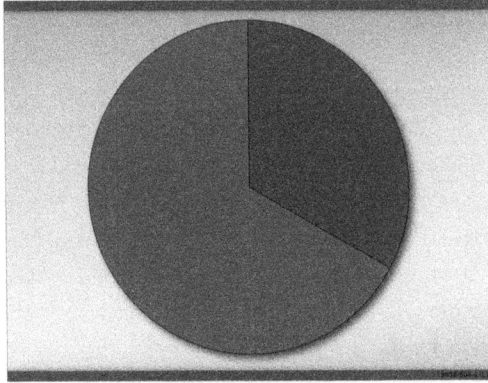

I paused to let that soak in, then asked Jackie to put up the second chart. As it materialized on the screen, you could almost hear a collective gasp as everyone in the courtroom looked at it. "That's what she actually got."

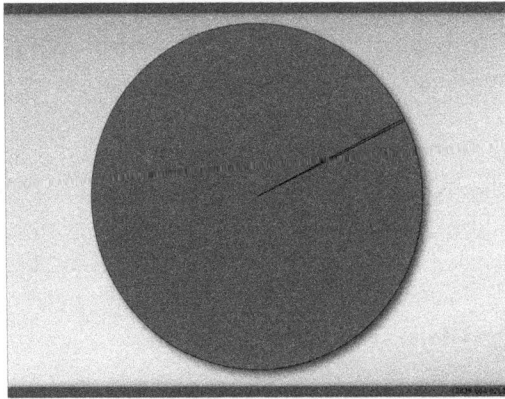

It was striking, no doubt about it, and it represented a stark reminder of the unfairness of what had been done to Jenny. It seemed like a perfect time to end.

"You've heard two different stories," I said. "You get to decide which of those stories is the correct story. And then you get a chance to rewrite the ending. All we're asking you to do is to be fair to Jenny, consider the facts, consider the evidence, consider the partnership factors, and then make your decision. Thank you."

I sat down.

Jenny's Story

When Mike finished his argument, I thought we had already won. I felt as if I were in the climax of a movie where you knew how it would end. Seeing my story played out in the 45 minutes he spoke revitalized a hope that I had not felt in a long time. He often told me that this case was about truth and facts, and that we should win based upon that. I'm sure that the defendants disagreed, but when he sat down next to me, I knew that the truth had, indeed, been told.

I also knew that we still had a long road ahead of us, but I received something better than a judgment that day. I regained my voice. Mike gave me back my strength and a faith in myself that had been ground out over the past couple of years.

I felt alive again.

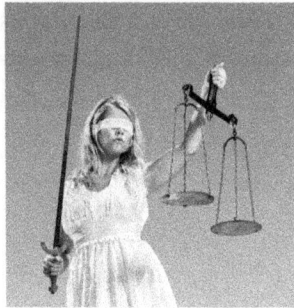

CHAPTER EIGHTEEN: Two Kinds of People

There are two kinds of people in the world: winners and losers.
The trick is to get them together.
　　　　　　　　—Gerald Michaud

Mike's Story

IN LITIGATION, THERE are three versions of the same argument. One is the argument you planned and prepared for. Two is the argument you actually made. And three is the argument you wish you had made. This case was no different. As soon as I sat at the table next to Jenny, I reviewed what I'd said, or thought I'd said, and what I wished I'd said, wondering what I left out, misstated, or left unclear. My best hope was that I knew the facts and the evidence well enough to have coherently put our story together and matched those facts and evidence to an understandable narrative, to help the jury reach a verdict in our favor.

And, I still had another shot, once Kantner finished his argument, to address the jury again—my "close close." That was an advantage to being a plaintiff in a civil lawsuit. You got the first word and the last word, so I wanted to make sure I filled in whatever gaps had been left. I just needed to figure out what those gaps were.

We had been going for some time that morning, between Judge McCoy reading the charge to the jury and then my argument, and now the lunch hour was creeping up. The jurors seemed a bit restless, not surprising, considering plenty of coffee had probably been consumed while the lawyers hammered out the final charge with Judge McCoy before the jury was called in.

Conscious of that, Judge McCoy said as I returned to my place, "All right. Mr. Kantner, I want to give you a full opportunity to close, and in order to do so, I think—why don't we take like a ten-minute break, and then you may do your closing."

Kantner stood and said, "If you like, or I have a break point at about twenty minutes, if you want to take a break. It's your call, obviously."

I wasn't a mind-reader, but I thought I knew what he was thinking. The jury had just spent 45 minutes listening to my side of the story, and he didn't want them to take a break when the last thing they had heard was me. Too much chance for my words to settle into their brains. He wanted to dislodge at least some of what I'd said, leaving his as the last words before the break.

Judge McCoy left it up to the jury. With Kantner's promise of a natural break point coming up shortly, one of the jurors said, "Keep going."

When others nodded in agreement, the judge said, "All right," then turned the floor over to Kantner, who made what I felt was a critical mistake: he failed to honor his promise of a break in 20 minutes and, instead, spoke uninterrupted for nearly an hour-and-a-half. One of the jurors later told me this "left a bunch of pissed-off people" in the jury room. I didn't know if Kantner simply forgot his promise, or if he expected Judge McCoy to cut him off, though how could the judge possibly know what he considered to be his break point?

Kantner stood before the jury, buttoned his coat, and began. "Your Honor, Counsel, ladies and gentlemen of the jury. Good morning, almost good afternoon."

I had no problems yet with what he said. It was, after all, still morning, almost afternoon. My problems started with his next few sentences.

"One of the first questions I asked Mrs. Pedroza was when was the alleged partnership formed? Her answer? Early 2010 was when she claims the alleged partnership was formed. Couldn't be more specific than that. We don't know if it's January, February, March, or April, but that's what she said, early 2010."

That implied that, unless Jenny knew a specific date when the partnership started, then there wasn't a partnership. Except partnerships-by-conduct didn't suddenly appear on a date certain. Rather, it was by reviewing a course of conduct that you reached a determination a partnership was created. What mattered here was simply whether it happened before March 9, 2012, and whether the partnership still existed as of that date.

Kantner then went through various trial exhibits, reiterating his contention that Coffee Shop was merely a hobby not a business. "It stayed a hobby until 2012 when Amanda Hayward decided, you know, we're now making a little money."

When the *Fifty Shades* trilogy came along.

Nobody disputed Coffee Shop started as a hobby, but long before the magic date, it became a business. If it had stayed a hobby until 2012, then it was a unique hobby, one in which the hobbyists signed legally binding contracts with authors, signed legally binding contracts with e-retailers, obtained partnership EINs, provided documents to financial institutions, provided legal documents to authors, and filed partnership tax returns with the IRS. That was unlike any hobby I ever heard of.

After hammering the hobby angle into an illogical mess,

Kantner tried to convince the jury the business was in dire financial straits, so it made sense for his client to fire Jenny from TWCS Operations. "And some of the key testimony, I submit to you was—in particular Mrs. Hayward's testimony and Mrs. Bidwell's testimony about what was not going right with marketing. She [Jenny] was terminated for cause. It wasn't something Amanda enjoyed doing. They had been friends. But she was terminated for cause. The testimony shows you that. And it was not rebutted by the plaintiff."

Not rebutted, that is, unless you discount that, under Jenny's and Christa's efforts, Coffee Shop sold nearly a quarter million copies of the *Fifty Shades* trilogy before closing the deal with Random House, and the company had received about thirty-five million dollars from Random House by the time Jenny and Christa were terminated. All companies should have such problems with marketing.

Kantner then drew this conclusion about Jenny's motive for the lawsuit: "We end up where I thought we would, as I stated in opening. We have a situation where she wants out of the contract she signed, and she wants to enforce a partnership where she offered an agreement to Amanda Hayward and Lea Dimovski, but neither one of them ever signed it. Jenn McGuire did sign it, and we'll talk about that a little bit. But the party being sued in this case never signed that partnership agreement. Never told her she would. In fact, told her the contrary, she would not."

Actually, Amanda told Jenny she would sign the agreement. Told her several times. She simply changed her mind when she saw big money on the horizon. Money, she wanted for herself.

Kantner was simply muddying the water, a common defense tactic. We never asked the jury to enforce the partially-signed agreement. Instead, we asked the jurors to find the existence of a partnership by analyzing the five factors in the

Texas partnership statute. Judge McCoy understood that and included an instruction in the jury charge that "the existence of a formal partnership agreement is not an element that must be proven to establish a partnership."

At this point, Kantner started his own analysis of the partnership factors, pointing out selective excerpts from a handful of exhibits, while ignoring the vast majority that contradicted him. As he talked, I snuck glances at the jury. I saw jurors fidget and squirm, check watches, and look to the clock on the wall—counting minutes and seconds until the promised break. I didn't know if this was the break point Kantner referred to, but it didn't seem to matter, because he blew right past it without slowing down.

"There's great ambiguity about whether there's three or four partners," he said, alluding to Lea Dimovski. He reminded the jury Amanda put up most of the cash at the start and there was no set agreement as to future cash infusions. "So, we have here a situation where there's an alleged partnership. We don't know who's going to put in what. There's no testimony. There's no documentary evidence as to who was going to put in what."

He continued. "So, I submit to you, we don't know for sure who the partners are. We don't know for sure when the partnership started. And we didn't discuss any terms. There's no partnership here."

I actually agreed with him we didn't know for sure who the partners were. We knew who three of them were, but we didn't know for sure whether Dimovski was. Question Number 2 in the Court's Charge asked, "Are the following persons partners in The Writers Coffee Shop?" It then listed four names, with a blank next to each for the jury to answer "yes" or "no"— Amanda Hayward, Jennifer Lynn Pedroza, Jennifer McGuire, and Lea Dimovski. The jury would get to decide how many partners there were.

But this question, like all the others, was conditioned upon the jury having first found Coffee Shop was a partnership, so, the number of partners was irrelevant to whether a partnership existed in the first place. It simply dictated whether Jenny's recovery, assuming a "yes" answer to Number One, would be one-third or one-fourth of Coffee Shop's profits.

Kantner's third prong of "proof" that there was no partnership—"we didn't discuss any terms"—was just as meaningless as the specific date the partnership started, so long as it existed on March 9, 2012, and the number of partners. Texas law expressly said if there was no formal partnership agreement, then the terms were dictated by the statutory provisions of the *Texas Business Organizations Code*. That made Kantner 0 for 3.

Moving on, Kantner seemed to get excited when he incorrectly argued Jenny had not actually received any distribution of profits. Just as I had predicted, he zeroed in on the two-million-dollar advance.

"One-third of two million dollars is six-hundred-sixty-six-thousand-six-hundred-sixty-seven dollars and some cents. She didn't get that because she wasn't a partner. She never received that."

Then it seemed as if an idea suddenly struck him. He bore down on this misguided point, driving the spike into his own case's heart.

"And by the way, while we're on this topic—I'm going to come back to this. Did you hear any testimony from Mrs. Pedroza or see any writing from her in early 2012 saying, 'When am I going to get my six-hundred-sixty-six-thousand-six-hundred-sixty-seven dollars?' Where's the evidence that there was any objection to the fact she was simply being paid a salary and was going to get a one-hundred-thousand dollars bonus? She knew these figures, but she didn't raise a protest about them."

To belabor the point, he carried this same false argument

287

over to a discussion of the service agreement. "Now, another thing that's interesting to me is that Mr. Farris made the comment she would never have signed that service agreement if she'd known about all the money Random House was paying. But Amanda told her in this communication in March, I believe it was, just what the advance was. Again, one-third of two million dollars is nearly seven-hundred-thousand dollars. She knew about that and she signed the service agreement."

Like a dog with a bone, he kept gnawing on the argument. "There's nothing in Plaintiff's Exhibit Sixty-seven, where she talks about, I'm concerned about this termination without cause provision. There's nothing in there—when she's getting ready to sign the service agreement, there's nothing in there about, 'Wait a minute, where is my nearly seven-hundred-thousand dollars? How much more have you gotten from Random House? I want one-third of that.' There's nothing in there. There's not testimony that she raised those subjects with Amanda Hayward at any time, and certainly not before she signed the agreement."

I made a mental note to be sure to address this argument when I closed, including the false premised he based it on. I heard it said from a lawyer with whom I once worked, "The master of the facts, wins." Well, I was the master of these facts.

I was struck by Kantner's repeated references to what the evidence *didn't say*. Just as he incorrectly argued Jenny didn't protest not being paid her share of the Random House advance, he harped on other failures to speak, including by me. "Mr. Farris argued in his closing, well, wait a minute, you can't be a sole trader and be a corporation. And that's true. But what he didn't comment on…"

When talking about when Jenny obtained the EIN and sent it to Amanda, he said, "I submit to you, ladies and gentlemen, what's significant about this document is what she didn't say." And, "Did she hearken back to the July email? No. She didn't say, 'Remember, Jenn, remember when we sent you that email about being a partner and you said you'd go in with us? It's not what she said here. It's not what she said here."

I know sometimes what wasn't said is significant, but a case relying whole-heartedly upon what is absent from the evidence, to the disregard of what actually exists, is a weak case, at best.

When Kantner finished his discussion of the five factors, he went back to his three-pronged attack—how many, when, and what. "The fact is, ladies and gentlemen, when you look at these factors, none of them, none of them, at the end of the day when you balance all the evidence, none of them support a finding that The Writer's Coffee Shop was a partnership. And as I said, there's so many actions she's taken in addition to that. So many things she can't tell us—who are the partners? When was it formed? What were the terms?—that also, I think, argue in favor of a finding of no partnership."

He took the jury through the Court's Charge, just as I had, and proposed the opposite to every answer I suggested. Then he wrapped up with an attack on Jenny. That, of course, was his right, but it ticked me off just the same.

"Mrs. Pedroza is angry. She's angry she got fired and she's concerned—she was concerned last spring that she was going to get sued in Australia, so she sued. She sued in May of 2014 when, by her own admission, that's the first time since January of 2012, over two years previously, that she even said a word about a partnership."

He tracked through a few more points, then wrapped up. "She has received, ladies and gentlemen, somewhere around two hundred thousand dollars for the time she put in. As evidenced by their pie chart, she wants a lot more. But I submit to you she has not shown she was a partner. She didn't take the risk. She didn't act like a partner. She didn't claim to be a partner at times she should have if she had really been a partner. She's simply not a partner.

"And we may feel that Amanda Hayward has been overly

rewarded. We have the same thing in this country all the time. We have multi-billionaires make a lot more than Amanda Hayward. And a lot of people feel like that's just—somehow that's not right.[39] But the issue in this case is whether she's proven to your satisfaction—"

He held his arms out to the side, palms up, mimicking a set of scales. "—and by the way, we don't start here. We start at zero. If you want the scales, we start at zero." He raised one arm and lowered the other, as if a scale had tipped one way or the other. "And the question is..." He began raising the lowered arm and lowering the raised one, until the arm that had been lower was now slightly higher. "...can they get it to here? Before you start putting on evidence, you don't start at fifty-fifty because you haven't presented any evidence. She hasn't done that, and she shouldn't be given a partnership now."

The problem with his scales argument was he acted as if this were a criminal case, where the starting point is a presumption of innocence, which tips the scale in the defendant's favor before the case gets off the ground. Then the prosecution has to introduce evidence to overcome that presumption and, as they place their evidence on the scale, the lower arm starts to move.

But in a civil case, there is no presumption of innocence. There is no presumption on either side. The parties start off equal, and the plaintiff's burden is to prove her case by a preponderance of the evidence. The Court's Charge defined it his way:

The term "preponderance of the evidence" means the greater weight of credible evidence presented in this case...A preponderance of the evidence is not measured by the number of witnesses or by the number of documents admitted in evidence. For a fact to be proved by a

---

[39] Was he really trying to argue that Jenny was a Communist?

preponderance of the evidence, you must find that the fact is more likely true than not true.

So, the arms of the scales start balanced, because both sides start in an equal position. Then both sides place evidence on their respective arms and the question becomes whether, at the end of the trial, the plaintiff's evidence outweighs the defendant's, even by the slightest amount. Just enough to tip the scales.

"All right," Judge McCoy said as Kantner resumed his seat. "I know that Mr. Farris has the opportunity to come back and have the last word, but we're going to take a quick break. His last word will be a quick word, and then y'all can decide your lunch and other schedules."

I took "quick word" as an instruction, but that was my intent to start with. The last thing I wanted to do was to drag things out, especially since we were well past the normal lunch hour and, as much as I knew everyone needed a bathroom break, I was pretty sure all were also hungry.

Jenny's Story

There were times during Mr. Kantner's closing arguments when I seriously wondered if he had listened to the testimony. Or maybe completely disregarding a week's worth of evidence, including admissions from his own client, was just another tactic that I didn't understand. When he went over details, he skewed them to fit his agenda and to create doubt in the jurors' minds, but I found his explanations so off base as to be laughable.

For example, he said, "But I submit to you she has not shown she was a partner. She didn't take the risk. She didn't act like a partner."

Didn't take the risk? So, teaching full-time then working into the nights for the company for more than a year without pay; sacrificing time with my family; and then quitting my career to

291

help with marketing, distribution, banking, payroll, accounts payable and any other freaking thing that was necessary was not a risk? That was madness. My family, my friends, and the company depended on me, and I poured myself into everything that I did. When you take into account that I did all this despite being told that the company was not profitable and could easily fail, while Amanda secretly claimed millions that belonged to the rest of us, I think a very good argument might be made that I took a far greater risk than Amanda.

Mr. Kantner also wondered, talking about the two-million-dollar advance from Random House, why I didn't ask, "When am I going to get my six-hundred-sixty-six-thousand-six-hundred-sixty-seven dollars?" He said, "Where's the evidence that there was any objection to the fact she was simply being paid a salary and was going to get a one-hundred-thousand dollars bonus? She knew these figures, but she didn't raise a protest about them."

This confused the hell out of me. We never got a two-million-dollar check for the advance. Only half of the advance was paid up front, and even that was split between Coffee Shop and the author. That meant five-hundred-thousand dollars came to the partnership, and Amanda, Jenn, and I, agreed that each partner would get one-hundred-thousand dollars, with the remaining amount to be left in the bank for expenses. I didn't directly talk with Lea about this, but I considered her a partner, and so I assumed Amanda would include her in this profit sharing.

Unfortunately, by the time the second half of the advance was paid, Amanda told me she couldn't discuss payments from Random House because of the non-disclosure agreement that she claimed she had signed. She did, however, swear that Random House was not paying correctly, causing a major strain on our finances. So why would I have asked for my supposed six-hundred-sixty-six thousand-six-hundred-sixty-seven dollars when that didn't come close to reflecting my share? Besides, it was his client who had convinced me that we were in dire financial straits and, demanding my share of the profits in that circumstance would have been incredibly self-defeating.

Amanda had also told Jenn and me that, if we signed a service agreement, our signing bonuses and salary would be based on our profits, but paying it out this way would minimize taxes, while allowing the bulk of those profits to continue to draw interest before being paid. I had, in fact, questioned the "termination clause" of the service agreement because of this. How could I be terminated if I had not yet received all of my share of profits? And I didn't even know the amount of those profits. It was a vicious circle that I now recognize in hindsight, but I simply trusted Amanda. Enter the naïve and gullible.

I was also struck by Mr. Kantner's lack of respect for the jurors' need to take a break. As he droned on, everyone in the courtroom (except, apparently, him) could see how uncomfortable they were becoming. When he finally finished, and Judge McCoy told the court that Mike would conclude with a "quick" word after the break, I took that to mean that even she was annoyed. I don't think Mr. Kantner ever recognized the problem as he stood at the lectern, looking quite pleased with himself.

I noticed, though, that he was one of the first out of the courtroom at the break.

Mike's Story

When the jury was brought in at 1:35 PM, I thought they looked a bit more relaxed than they had at 1:25, but a good bathroom break will do that for you.

"Mr. Farris, are you ready to present your 'close close'?" Judge McCoy asked.

I stood. "I am, Your Honor. Thank you."

I walked around the table and stood in front of the jury box. This time I had no notes as a crutch. I knew exactly what I wanted to say. The jury had heard a lot of facts and now, after hearing both arguments, a lot of interpretations. I wanted to remind them the key issue, though, was quite simple.

"I know it's been a long morning already and I promise to be brief." I paused, almost expecting to see eye rolls and to hear clucking of tongues. "And there's a lot of people who'd say as soon as a lawyer tells you that...." I let it hang for a second. Smiles and a few chuckles from some of the jury. "But I promise."

It was time to get serious. "I want to start out by cleaning up a couple of things. I started out with this statement: March 9, 2012 is the key date. Don't be confused by all the things that happened after March ninth of 2012. TWCS is set up as a company. Jenny signed a service agreement with it. That's after March ninth. That's a new and different company. If the partnership existed on March ninth, that Random House contract is a partnership asset. That's all you need to know.

"The partnership was in existence on March the ninth, 2012, and owned the Random House deal. It was a partnership asset. The question is: who were partners on March ninth, 2012? The fact that Jenny went to work for another company is irrelevant to whether she was a partner in the partnership and is entitled to her share of the assets."

Now it was time to address Kantner's misunderstanding of the advance payment from Random House. The one he had gone on and on about, as if it proved Jenny never got any share of profits, and never complained about it, so she must not have been a partner.

"The two-million-dollar advance that Mr. Kantner harped on, that a third of it would have been six-hundred-sixty-six-thousand-six-hundred-sixty-six dollars." So, I missed it by a dollar, big deal. "And why wasn't Jenny screaming for that?

"Look at Exhibit Sixty when you get back into the jury room. Plaintiff's Exhibit Sixty. The deal was paid. It was two million dollars. Half of that went to E.L. James. Half of it went to The Writer's Coffee Shop. So, it's a million dollars for The Writer's Coffee Shop. Half of that paid on signing the contract. Half of that paid on publication of the books. So, the upfront advance payment was five-hundred-thousand-dollars." Not two million, as Kantner had said.

"Jenny testified that she got one-hundred-thousand dollars. She understood from Amanda Hayward that Jenn McGuire got one-hundred-thousand dollars. Amanda Hayward got one-hundred-thousand dollars. She thought Lea Dimovski got one-hundred-thousand dollars. And one-hundred-thousand dollars went into the bank. That's splitting up that advance amongst the partners and putting money in the bank to cover expenses. Don't be confused looking for the six-hundred-sixty-six-thousand."

I paused. Rather than dwell on it as Kantner had, I moved on. I reminded the jurors that they didn't have to find all of the partnership factors.

"The Judge is going to instruct you that there doesn't have to be a formal partnership agreement. The terms don't have to be nailed down before there's a partnership. If it looks like a duck, walks like a duck, talks like a duck, it's duck. If you find enough of these factors to establish a partnership, it doesn't matter when it started as long as it was before March 9, 2012. It doesn't matter what the terms were. It doesn't matter anything else. You get to decide, based upon the facts, whether there was a partnership. The statute says—this is in your instructions—'an association of two or more persons to carry on a business for profit as owners creates a partnership regardless of whether the persons intend to create a partnership.'

"You actually can find a partnership even if everybody in it didn't intend it to be a partnership. The reason for that is, when you're dealing with the world and you're acting like a partnership, you're going to be treated as a partnership. Don't get caught up in whether it started in early 2010 or when the EIN was obtained. Look at the factors and decide, as of March 9, 2012, had a partnership started? If it started before that, and you find that Jenny was a partner in it and Ms. Hayward was a partner in it, they're partners and they own the assets of the partnership."

Next, I addressed the issue that, if answered against us, would totally neuter a partnership finding. "The judge is going to instruct you that every partnership is presumed to be terminable at will unless it was agreed that the contract or agreement would be for a specific time. And you'll remember that I specifically asked Amanda Hayward, 'Was there an agreement to be partners for as long as those writer contracts were in effect?' And she said no. The only other evidence on whether the partnership was terminable at will is that Jenny testified there was no set term and it could have ended at any time. That makes it terminable at will."

And, if so, the statute of frauds didn't apply.

I wanted to end on a strong note, something that would stick with the jury when it retired to deliberate. They had heard the evidence, and they had heard the lawyers, so I wanted something different. The night before, it had come to me.

"I once heard a lawyer from Wichita, Kansas, who spent a period of his life supporting himself as a professional poker player in Las Vegas, say something." That lawyer's name was Gerald Michaud, who went on to be a fabulously successful plaintiff's lawyer in Kansas. A friend and I once spent a weekend with Gerald to get the story of his life for a screenplay we collaborated on.

"He told me one time that there are two kinds of people in the world: There are winners and losers. And the trick is getting them together."

I paused, gathering myself for the big finish. I felt emotions swelling inside me and worried that I might choke up. But if I did, so be it. I believed that strongly in what I was saying.

"Well, I say there's another two kinds of people. There are the naïve and the trusting; and there are the scheming and the manipulative. And when you get them together, this is what happens."

I quickly returned to my place and sat. There was silence in the courtroom for a moment, then Judge McCoy spoke. "All right, ladies and gentlemen, now the time has come for you to go to the jury room and to deliberate."

And just like that, the case was out of my hands and into those of twelve honest souls sitting in the jury box.

Jenny's Story

Mike's closing line rang through the courtroom. It was magic. The jury focused on Mike as he returned to our table and sat down. The defendants' table was silent for the first time since the trial began. It seemed hard to breathe; Mike had sucked all of the air out of the defense's sails. I felt relief, mixed with a new kind of fear. Mike and Brent had been in control up until then, but now my fate rested in the hands of 12 strangers.

CHAPTER NINETEEN: Twelve Honest Souls

There may sometimes be a mistake, but I think the citizens of America who are sworn to uphold their duty in a jury setting are going to try to do their best to do that regardless of the consequences.
—Janet Reno

Mike's Story

THE MOST STRESSFUL part of any trial is after the judge has charged the jury and you have finished your closing argument. Until then, you had at least some control over what happened in the courtroom. You got to pick the jury, question witnesses, present evidence, and even speak directly to the jurors in opening statement and closing argument. Sure, you didn't control the opposing lawyer, nor the judge's rulings, but you had the opportunity to either respond or take steps to compensate for those things. You had some control over the flow of information, and you even had power to shape the story as you saw fit.

I have heard it said one of the perils of a jury trial is the outcome rests on the decision of twelve people whose sole qualifications are United States citizenship and ownership of a driver's license. Not exactly a ringing endorsement of the jury system, though I'll still take it over any other system the world has to offer. But after the judge sends the jury out to deliberate, you can no longer add to the evidence, re-argue to the jury, or remind them what you think the evidence means. That was now the sole bailiwick of the twelve driver's-license-holding U.S. citizens that you selected on the first day, which included people you might not have ideally wanted on the jury, but you ran out of strikes. Or maybe you failed to ask the right question to uncover bias. Or maybe the jury was perfect, but they missed some key evidentiary point you had made. Even worse, maybe you, as the lawyer, failed to make that key point or offer some critical piece of evidence. At this point, you simply had to trust.

Waiting for a jury was a time for second-guessing yourself. That didn't help your case, and it certainly didn't reduce your stress level, but at least it passed the time. It was an age-old, tried-and-true custom for litigators that raised blood pressures, shortened tempers, and tied stomachs in knots.

Before closing arguments, Judge McCoy, in addition to the questions the jurors had to answer, also gave them a set of instructions. It was a standard set of do's and don'ts, some variation of which was typically given to every Texas jury. In addition to orally instructing the jurors, a written copy of those instructions was also included in the Court's Charge.

The general instructions were these:

After the closing arguments, you will go to the jury room to decide the case, answer the questions that are attached, and reach a verdict. You may discuss the case with other jurors only when you are all together in the jury room.

Remember my previous instructions: Do not discuss the case with anyone else, either in person or by any other means. Do not do any independent investigation about the case or conduct any research. Do not look up any words in dictionaries or on the Internet. Do not post information about the case on the Internet. Do not share any special knowledge or experiences with the other jurors. Do not use your phone or any other electronic device during your deliberations for any reason.

Any notes you have taken are for your own personal use. You may take your notes back into the jury room and consult them during deliberations, but do not show or read your notes to fellow jurors during your deliberations. Your notes are not evidence. Each of you should rely upon your independent recollection of the evidence and not be influenced by the fact that another juror has or has not taken notes.

Here are the instructions for answering the questions:

Do not let bias, prejudice, or sympathy play any part in your decision.

Base your answers only on the evidence admitted in court and on the law that is in these instructions and questions. Do not consider or discuss any evidence that was not admitted in the courtroom.

You are to make up your own minds about the facts. You are the sole judges of the credibility of the witnesses and the weight to give their testimony. But on matters of law, you must follow all of my instructions.

If my instructions use a word in a way that is different from its ordinary meaning, use the meaning I give you, which will be a proper legal definition.

All the questions and answers are important. No one should say that any question or answer is not important.

Answer "yes" or "no" to all questions unless you are told otherwise. A "yes" answer must be based on a preponderance of the evidence unless you are told otherwise. Whenever a question requires an answer other than "yes" or "no," your answer must be based on a preponderance of the evidence, unless you are told otherwise.

The term "preponderance of the evidence" means the greater weight of credible evidence presented in this case. If you do not find that a preponderance of the evidence supports a "yes" answer, then answer "no." A preponderance of the evidence is not measured by the number of witnesses or by the number of documents admitted in evidence. For a fact to be proved by a preponderance of the evidence, you must find that the fact is more likely true than not true.

Do not decide who you think should win before you answer the questions and then answer the questions to match your decision. Answer each question carefully without considering who will win. Do not discuss or consider the effect your answers will have.

Do not answer questions by drawing straws or by any other method of chance.

Some questions might ask you for a dollar amount. Do not agree in advance to decide on a dollar amount by adding each juror's amount and then figuring the average.

Do not trade your answers. For example, do not say "I will answer this question your way if you answer another question my way."

Unless otherwise instructed, the answers to the questions must be based on the decision of at least 10 of the 12 jurors. The same 10 jurors must agree on every answer. Do not agree to be bound by a vote of anything less than 10 jurors, even if it would be a majority.

As I have said before, if you do not follow these instructions, you will be guilty of juror misconduct, and I might have to order a new trial and start this process over again. This would waste your time and the parties' money, and would require the taxpayers of this county to pay for another trial. If a juror breaks any of these rules, tell that person to stop and report it to me immediately.

A fact may be established by direct evidence or by circumstantial evidence or both. A fact is established by direct evidence when proved by documentary evidence or by witnesses who saw the act done or heard the words spoken. A fact is established by circumstantial evidence when it may be fairly and reasonably inferred from other facts proved.

From there, the charge went into the specific questions at the heart of the case. The lawyers had been involved in formulating these questions, working with Judge McCoy. Each side submitted its own version, and Judge McCoy ultimately decided how the final version would look. Because the outcome of the case depended upon the specific language in each question, including instructions and definitions, Brent and I carefully and thoughtfully drafted our version, reviewed critically the defense's proposed version, and lodged formal objections if we didn't like the final product. If Judge McCoy included or excluded language one side or the other objected to, that inclusion or exclusion could become an issue on appeal. It would be shame to come this far and lose simply because you didn't put enough thought into the jury questions.

As I noted before, Question No. 1 asked: "Is the Writer's Coffee Shop a partnership?"

The use of present tense in formulating the question was important. Our theory was Coffee Shop existed as a partnership and it had never been dissolved. If so, that meant, not only had it been a partnership during the years in which Jenny was involved, but it remained a partnership even after she was terminated from TWCS Operations. If the jury found Jenny was a partner at the start, then she was still a partner, and she was entitled to her share of profits continuing right up through the dates of the trial. If the question had been worded in the past tense—"Was the Writer's Coffee Shop a partnership?"—then there would have to be a second question for the jury to determine if, and when, it had been dissolved and, if it had, that would have cut off Jenny's rights as a partner at the time it was dissolved.

So, for example, even if Coffee Shop had been a partnership, if it had been dissolved before March 9, 2012, then Jenny would not have been entitled to profits from the Random House deal. I didn't believe that there was any evidence it had been dissolved at all, but to eliminate uncertainty, I needed the question to be submitted to the jury in the present tense—which Judge McCoy did without objection from Amanda's attorneys.

I was confident we had introduced plenty of evidence to the jury to establish all five of the partnership factors required under the *Texas Business Organizations Code*, even though we didn't have to prove all five. One of the instructions to the jury was, "You are not required to find proof of all five of the foregoing factors in order to find that there is a partnership. No single fact may be stated as a complete and final test of partnership." Still, the more factors you proved, the stronger your case.

As we waited for the jury to deliberate, I thought back over the trial, focusing on each of the factors and the evidence we had introduced on each. Surely, we had provided enough evidence on all, or at least most, of the factors.

Surely.

1. Receipt or right to receive a share of profits

To establish this factor, we didn't have to show Coffee Shop actually had profits to share, but simply that there was a *right* by the partners to share profits.

Here's what we introduced to the jury:

- In a March 6, 2012, email, Jenn McGuire discussed the timing of the distribution of profits, in the form of a "bonus," depending upon when the partnership might be dissolved.

- In an email dated February 25, 2012, Amanda wrote to Jenny and Jenn and specifically proposed splitting the profits on a quarterly basis while leaving a minimum amount in Coffee Shop's bank account to draw interest.

- The $500,000 advance from Random House was divided equally among the partners, with $100,000 left in the bank to cover expenses.

- With Amanda's blessing, Jenny prepared a written partnership agreement that, although it wasn't signed by all the partners, reflected the intent of the partners to have the right to share equally in profits.

- Jenny testified, without contradiction from Amanda, that Amanda told her that the "bonus" paid to her when she signed the service agreement with TWCS Operations was a way of getting Coffee Shop profits paid to her but simply structured differently for tax reasons.

2. Expression of intent to be partners

Although Texas law states a partnership can exist "regardless of whether...the persons intend to create a partnership," an expression of intent was nevertheless significant. At the same time, just because a person referred to another as a "partner" didn't necessarily mean a legal partnership existed. The jury would have to examine those "expressions" in light of their context and to decide exactly what their significance was.

The Court's Charge included these instructions on Question No. 1:

The existence of a formal partnership agreement is not an element that must be proven to establish a partnership.

The terms used by the parties in referring to their arrangement do not control and merely referring to another person as a "partner" in a situation where the recipient of the message would not expect the declarant to make a statement of legal significance is not enough.

The term "partner" is regularly used in common vernacular and may be used in a variety of ways. Referring to a friend, employee, spouse, teammate or fishing companion as a "partner" in a colloquial sense is not legally sufficient evidence of expression of intent to form a business partnership. However, the same term could constitute legally sufficient evidence of expression of intent when made in a circumstance that indicates significance to the business endeavor.

It was important to include the instruction that a formal partnership agreement wasn't necessary in order for there to be a partnership. After all, there wasn't a formal partnership agreement here—at least not fully signed by all of the partners—but it made no sense to require a review of the five factors of partnership if the deciding factor was simply whether there was a formal agreement. While the existence of an agreement would dispense with the need to analyze the factors, it was the absence of one that required the analysis.

I anticipated some jurors, who might be unsophisticated in the business world, could get hung up on this point. That was why we had included this question on the jury questionnaire:

Do you believe that a business partnership can only be formed by a written agreement? Answer "yes" or "no." If you answered yes, what is the basis for your belief? If you answered yes: If the judge instructs you at the end of trial that a formal written agreement is not required, will you be able to follow that instruction?"

I spent quite a bit of time discussing that question during jury selection and was comfortable we had managed to seat jurors who promised to follow the judge's instructions regardless of what they believed the law might be. I ran the risk, of course, that the judge wouldn't include the instruction. As it turned out, my gamble paid off because here it was.

The instructions about viewing the context in which the term "partner" was used was equally important to the defense lawyers. If the mere use of the term was enough to prove the factor of "expressions of intent to be partners," then they were sunk. I didn't object to this part of the instruction because I knew it was a fair statement of the law, but I still had an uneasy feeling it offered the jury a way out if it wanted to decide against Jenny. I knew that juries sometimes simply decided who they wanted to win, then tried to answer questions to support their choice. I didn't think there was much competition here as to who was the most likeable between Jenny and Amanda, but there were never any guarantees.

Kantner knew there was a lot of evidence of Amanda calling Jenny, Jenn, and Lea, her partners. That was most likely why he trotted out the "howdy, partner" line during his opening statement. That was also why I attacked that line in my closing argument. There was plenty of evidence that, taken in the right context, reflected a genuine intent by the four women— particularly from Amanda—to be partners, and I didn't want Kantner muddying the issue.

In fact, I thought there was probably more evidence on this factor than any of the others. Here is what we introduced:

- When Coffee Shop issued its first edition of The Writers Coffee Shop Newsletter in January of 2011, it included pictures of the individuals "Behind TWCS" –Amanda Hayward (with the title CEO); Jenn McGuire (with the title Chief Operating Officer); Jenny Pedroza (with the title Operations Director); and Lea Dimov [a shortened form of Dimovski] (with the title Administrative Director).

- In July of 2011, Amanda and Jenny invited Jenn McGuire to be a "partner" with them, and McGuire accepted.

- During a quarterly meeting of Coffee Shop staffers, Amanda stated: "I have 3 other partners in this business" and identified them as Jennifer Pedroza, Jenn McGuire and Lea Dimovski.

- Amanda answered a questionnaire from *Publishers Weekly*, in which she stated she was "one of the founders of The Writer's Coffee Shop."

- Coffee Shop's website held itself as having a CEO and

three other "co-founders."

- Jenny prepared a blog post in which she stated she "co-owned" Coffee Shop with Amanda, who reviewed and approved that language.
- Jenny introduced Amanda to Christa Beebe as her "business partner," without any protest from Amanda.
- McGuire, along with Jenny, signed a written partnership agreement. Amanda promised to sign it, but she simply failed to. She never protested its terms.
- McGuire testified she believed the "partnership" would be dissolved by tax time in 2012, but it was never dissolved.
- McGuire signed an Assumed Name Certificate for submission to financial institutions, identifying Coffee Shop as a "General Partnership" and certifying she was an owner.
- McGuire signed an Authorization for Information and Certificate of Authority as an "Owner, Partner, Officer or Member" of Coffee Shop, for submission to financial institutions.
- McGuire signed a contract with KOBO, Inc. as a "partner" on behalf of "The Writer's Coffee Shop (Partnership)," and provided Amanda with a copy; Amanda did not protest or object to the language.
- KOBO sent invoices to "The Writer's Coffee Shop (Partnership)" on a monthly basis from mid-2011 until October of 2013, without correction or protest from Amanda.
- Jenny obtained, with Amanda's knowledge and consent, an EIN for Coffee Shop as a partnership, which was subsequently used on contracts and tax documents.
- After the EIN was obtained, Amanda emailed that

Coffee Shop was "now a company in the US...."

- Jenny filed, with Amanda's blessing, a partnership tax return for Coffee Shop.

- Jenny and McGuire both included partnership K-1s on their personal tax returns.

- Jenny and McGuire told accountant Paul Varga that Coffee Shop was a partnership and they had another partner in Australia, named Amanda Hayward.

- Jenny testified Amanda told her she had asked Dimovski to be a partner in Coffee Shop and Dimovski accepted.

- After the Random House contract was signed, Amanda gave numerous press interviews in which she told reporters she had "partners" in the United States.

- When Jenny, Amanda, and Jenn discussed, via email, their concerns about losing E.L. James as an author, one of the options they considered was to "make her a partner."

- At conferences promoting Coffee Shop books, Jenny was introduced to the public, without objection or protest from Hayward, as a partner and co-founder of Coffee Shop.

3. Participation or right to participate in the control of the business.

I felt we had particularly strong evidence on this factor, which refers not merely to day-to-day decision-making, but to the right to make executive decisions. Examples that Texas case law gives include exercising authority over operations, the right to write checks, having control over and access to a business's books, and receiving money and managing assets. We introduced evidence Jenny participated in the actual control of Coffee Shop, including:

- Coffee Shop banking was done through a personal account set up by Jenny at USAA Bank. Jenny received money and made disbursements on behalf of Coffee Shop from the accounts.

- Jenny handled the preparation and filing of Coffee Shop's partnership tax return, signed publishing contracts with authors, and signed non-disclosure agreements with authors (including with Erika Mitchell).

- The draft partnership agreement provided the partners were equal partners and "all actions and decisions respecting the management, operation and control of the Partnership" required concurrence of more than half of the voting interests.

- When Erika Mitchell wanted out of her publishing contract with Coffee Shop, Amanda sought the "agreement" of her partners in the decision. Amanda testified this was the biggest decision Coffee Shop ever made.

- When Random House made an offer for the publishing rights to the *Fifty Shades* trilogy, Amanda sought the "agreement" of her partners.

4. Sharing or agreeing to share the losses of the business

It's interesting this is considered one of the five factors of partnership since the *Texas Business Organizations Code* expressly states "an agreement by the owners of a business to share losses is not necessary to create a partnership." Still, it is some evidence of the existence of a partnership. It's also irrelevant there may be no evidence a partnership actually lost money and shared losses; rather, what is relevant is whether the partners "shared or *agreed to share* losses or liabilities." Whether we needed to have evidence of this factor or not, we did. It included:

- When Jenn McGuire was invited into the partnership, Amanda told her she would be responsible for her *pro rata* share of tax liability.

- McGuire testified she knew, by accepting the offer to be a partner, she would be responsible for the company's liabilities.

- Jenny and McGuire claimed their respective share of partnership losses on their tax returns.

- The partners agreed, when it appeared Coffee Shop might finally earn significant income from the *Fifty Shades* phenomenon, to maintain money in the bank to deal with liabilities.

- The written partnership agreement Jenny sent to the partners specifically provided net profits and losses would be borne equally by the partners.

5. Agreement to Contribute or Contributing Money or Property to the Business

This factor can be a bit more nebulous than some of the others. The statute defines "property" as including "tangible and intangible property and an interest in that property." "Money" can include reinvesting profits back into the business and paying, or sharing, expenses. There are cases in which courts held an agreement to reinvest profits into the business, buying equipment for the business, allowing the business to charge items on a partner's personal credit card, making loans to the company, or even working for the company without pay— "sweat equity"—meet the definition of money or property.

Here's what the evidence showed:

- Jenny worked for Coffee Shop without pay for approximately two years.
- Amanda asked Jenny to put up her credit card for the business account, which Jenny agreed to do.
- Jenny, on occasion, paid Coffee Shop debts and was later reimbursed, including paying $14,000 even though Amanda had received more than $16 million from Random House just a few days prior.
- In early 2012, after *Fifty Shades* became a financial success, Amanda suggested to her partners they divide profits on a quarterly basis after first paying expenses out of the money received, so each partner shared proportionately in those expenses.

After running back over these five factors in my mind, I was comfortable with the evidence we had introduced. I strongly believed we were five for five. Now, if only the jury would see it that way.

Jenny's Story

The story Mike had told was true. I should know, because I lived it. Christa and I both felt Mike and Brent had put everything together in the clearest and most concise way possible. My support system of family and friends sat behind me in the courtroom during closing arguments, and they agreed every necessary detail had been presented.

Sitting in the hallway outside the courtroom, waiting on the jury, was the most intense time of my life. To put it in perspective, remember when you were in grade school, and your friends ran to a different section of the playground to talk about you? You knew they were discussing whether you got to play a game with them, arguing for or against you. Some remembered how well you had played the game the other day, while others thought it was unfair that you had been rewarded in class for getting a good grade, so they wanted to cut you out.

Well, that was the same thing with the jury.

I knew they were talking about me and discussing my merits, but there wasn't anything I could do about it. They were either going to find for me or against me. I was never good at waiting around while someone else decided my fate. I was more of an "if I can't fix it, let's just move on" kind of girl. But that didn't mean my stomach wasn't tied in knots.

One of the worst parts of the trial, and now the waiting, was seeing Amanda and her crew in the halls or running into them in the restroom. It helped that Christa and my family were with me every day in court, and their support was priceless. Christa was better at this then I was. She had zero tolerance for people she felt had wronged her or her friends. On our way to court each day, she gave me pep talks about what I should do if I ran into Amanda or one of the others. Most of her suggestions were merely said to make me laugh, but her message was clear: "Don't be intimidated and stand your ground. You deserve your day in court, and the truth is on your side." We even had a playlist of "Court Tunes" to help motivate and keep our thoughts positive. She never batted an eye when our paths crossed with Amanda's group.

Even with all of this support, my mind drifted as we waited for the jury.

I wondered how I had gotten myself into this position. How had I allowed things to go so wrong? How had I not seen what was happening and stood up for myself sooner? I second-guessed each decision I made that led me to that courtroom, but I kept going back to the bottom line: I blindly trusted someone.

If I learned anything, it was to not make that mistake again.

During the trial, my small circle of true friends closed in around me and, to this day, I find it difficult to trust anyone outside of that group. That made me sad at first. Then I realized that getting older meant putting things into perspective. I learned that having a small group of loyal friends when you face adversity is better than having a ton of friends who run away at the first sign of trouble.

Another thought that kept popping up was this verdict meant something to others besides me. A lot of Coffee Shop authors and staffers had reached out to me during the trial. The media reported on important parts of the proceedings and, without fail, with each new story I heard from authors, readers, publishers, editors, and book sellers.

I felt as if I were fighting for all of them, some of whom expressed dissatisfaction with their treatment by Amanda. The sentiment they communicated was they were proud I was standing up for myself. I had gotten to tell my story and, no matter how the jury ruled, I felt like that made me a winner.

I knew, though, that Mike wanted a jury win for me.

It was important to him that I be given what I was rightly entitled to. But he also told me that, no matter what happened, he believed the truth had been told and my voice had been heard. And he told me he believed in me.

That was good enough for me.

CHAPTER TWENTY: Rewritten

Rewriting is the crucible where books are born.
—Cathryn Louis

Mike's Story

BRENT AND I, along with Jenny, Christa, and members of Jenny's family, waited in the hallway after the jury retired to deliberate, while Bob Kantner, Caroline Harrison, and Amanda and James Hayward waited inside the courtroom. It was typical practice that at least the attorneys waited at the courthouse during deliberations in case any questions might arise from the jury that required input from the lawyers before the judge responded with an answer.

The first thing the jury had to do was elect a foreperson before considering the questions posed by the Court's Charge. The initial set of questions from the jury came out in fairly short order. They were in writing and signed by the foreperson. The first said, "*The Plaintiff's copy of trial exhibits is missing a table of contents. Can we get a copy?*" The second said, "*Are there copies of each sides' timelines in the folders? We're having difficulty remembering where we might find them.*"

It was obvious the jury was concerned about the timeline, which was reflected not only by the second question but also by a later question that said, "*Can we ask for the dates the contracts with Amazon, ibook, and B&N were signed and who signed them?*" I hoped the concern about timelines was related to my admonition that the critical date in the case was March 9, 2012, the date the Random House contract was signed. If they were paying attention to dates, I thought that was a good thing.

By the end of the day, the jury had not reached a verdict, which wasn't surprising since they had been deliberating for only about three-and-a-quarter hours. Still, I was encouraged they had not yet reached any conclusion for a simple reason. As I noted before, the first question in the Court's Charge asked, "Is the Writer's Coffee Shop a partnership?" There were ten questions in all, and questions numbers two through nine were all preceded by this instruction: "If you answered 'Yes' to Question No. 1, then answer Question No. [2-9]. Otherwise, do not answer Question No. [2-9]."

I felt sure the jury could have decided in an afternoon the basic question of whether there was a partnership. If they had said "no," then they most likely would have reached a final verdict by the end of the day. The fact they were still deliberating suggested to me they had answered the first question in our favor and had now moved on to the succeeding questions.

Because the judge had a commitment the following morning, deliberations didn't resume until Wednesday afternoon. Brent and I waited at the courthouse alone that day so Jenny could go to work, with our assurances we would call her if the jury came back with its verdict. Sometime that afternoon, the jury sent out another question, this one about Question No. 6 in the Court's Charge.

Question No. 6 asked: "Did Amanda Hayward convert property of The Writer's Coffee Shop?" There was an instruction that followed that said:

To establish a claim for conversion, Jennifer Pedroza must establish the following:

1. *The Writer's Coffee Shop owned or had legal possession of property or entitlement to possession of property; and*

2. *Hayward unlawfully and without authorization assumed and exercised dominion and control over the property to the exclusion of, or inconsistent with, The Writer's Coffee Shop's rights as an owner; and*

3. *The Writer's Coffee Shop demanded return of the property; and*

4. *Hayward refused to return the property.*

As far as the conversion question went, our theory was that the Random House deal, and all of the royalty payments made to Coffee Shop under it, belonged to the partnership and its partners. By taking the payments for herself, Amanda had "converted," or wrongfully taken as her own, assets belonging to the partnership.

The question from the jury sought clarification of the meaning of the words "owner" in subpart 2 and "demand" in subpart 3. What was more significant to me, though, was my earlier supposition was correct. The jurors had, in fact, found Coffee Shop was a partnership because they would not have been considering Question No. 6, or Numbers 2 through 5, unless they had. My confidence level rose accordingly. When the end of the day came and went, and still no verdict, Brent and I were feeling pretty good. At this point, longer was better, because it meant the jury was seriously considering all the questions that had been conditioned upon a positive finding of a partnership.

Thursday morning that confidence level took a nosedive

when we got word the jury had issues with Question No. 9. That question asked whether Jenny had waived her claims by signing the service agreement, and defined waiver as "an intentional surrender of a known right or intentional conduct inconsistent with claiming the right." The defendants had asserted an affirmative defense that, by signing the service agreement, Jenny had waived, or given up, any claims she might have had as a partner in Coffee Shop. So, according to the defense, even if Coffee Shop was a partnership, and even if Jenny was a partner, if she waived her claims, it negated those prior findings.

The jury's questions were:

#1 Please clarify: When Pedroza signed the Service Agreement was she waiving claims prior to the signing date?

Her service agreement uses the word "previous" in several clauses. — caused confusion.

#2 (Service Agreement) Should we go by date signed or date it is backdated to?

The specific language in the service agreement the questions referred to said:

The Service Provider [Jenny] irrevocably releases the Customer [TWCS Operations], its predecessors and its related parties (including without limitation Amanda Hayward) from any other claims, entitlements or interests that it might allege was derived from their previous engagement by the Customer [TWCS Operations] prior to this Agreement.

I had been aware of this language since the start of the case, and I had done considerable research before I filed the lawsuit on the issue of waiver and the effect of release clauses in contracts. I wasn't too troubled by this language for several reasons. First, even though Jenny hadn't signed the agreement until November of 2012, TWCS Operations was created on September 3, 2012, and the contract was made effective as of that date. Since all Jenny was "releasing" was any claim she might have had from a "previous engagement" with TWCS Operations "prior to this Agreement," and since she had never been previously engaged by TWCS Operations prior to its creation, there were no claims to release.

There was also the nonsensical effect of the defense that one had to consider.

Essentially, the waiver defense went something like this: Coffee Shop was not, is not, and never was a partnership, but, by signing the service agreement, Jenny knowingly gave up any claims she might have had as a partner in a non-existent partnership. If also depended on a belief that, knowing she was entitled to millions as a partner in Coffee Shop, Jenny knowingly and intentionally gave up any claim to those millions in exchange for a one-time payment of $50,000 for signing the agreement and monthly payments of $5,000. Nobody in their right mind would believe that.

But the mere fact the jury had sent out questions about No. 9 troubled me. I thought it should have been a no-brainer but, apparently, I was wrong. If the jury answered this one "yes," that Jenny had waived her claims, then it wouldn't matter if Coffee Shop was a partnership and that Jenny was a partner. I couldn't be sure what the intent was behind the questions—whether the jury was seriously considering whether Jenny waived claims that preceded the agreement or only claims that might arise in the future under the agreement—but it sent a shudder down my spine.

So, Brent and I kept waiting—and worrying.

Jenny's Story

I assumed we'd hear from the jury in just a few hours. I mean, that was what happened in the movies. I watched court dramas and, in them, the juries leave, while lawyers talk quietly to their clients in the hall and maybe get coffee. Then an announcement comes that, "The jury has reached its verdict. Will the parties and their lawyers return to the courtroom?" Everyone rushes back to his or her seat, and intense music cues for the climax.

But I found that life doesn't always reflect art. While the waiting was maddening, the second-guessing was worse, and when the jury asked questions, I felt as if the world shifted beneath my feet.

Mike and Brent analyzed every moment that passed, and they were steadfast in their determination to handle me with care. When the minutes turned to hours, they told me this was good news. Mike explained about the first question being a game changer, and the longer the better, so my camp was excited.

However, as the hours clicked on, and the bailiff told us there wouldn't be a verdict that day, my mind immediately went to dark places. The idea that we might lose became more of a reality than it had during the months leading up to the trial. I started to fear that, if we lost, Amanda Hayward would never be out of my life.

Forget about the money; I worried that she would retaliate against my family and me. I wanted to make a clean break, and it seemed as if only a win would accomplish that goal.

I went back to work the second day the jury was out, but I was in a fog. My students knew something was going on. They didn't know what, nor would I talk about it at school, but they knew that their normally happy, excited, and exuberant teacher was withdrawn and hollow. Several wrote me notes with cheerful greetings, telling me they loved me and were glad they were in my class. I still have these notes tucked away. They're one of the reasons I love teaching. Students in my classes knew I loved them. I came to school each day with one thing on my mind: not just to teach the curriculum, but also to make the kids feel like they were part of something bigger than a classroom. I have taught for twenty years, and I always treated my students like part of my family. What I failed to understand until this trial was that they felt the same about me. Those kids held a special place in my heart and, whether they knew it or not, their notes helped me get through those long hours of waiting.

My husband was also a huge factor in my sanity. When I got home each day, he made an effort to not talk about the trial. He asked if I had information I could share about what Mike or Brent had said, but that was it.

We spent our nights watching television, enjoying his home cooked meals, and talking about non-important things that didn't require deep thought. He knew I needed peace, and he headed off phone calls and text messages from friends and family. This was a huge help, and I didn't realize until later how much calm this brought me.

Many people told me I needed to leave my worry in the hands of a higher power.

That was true, but it was easier said than accomplished. I worried, I fretted, but at the end of the trial, it was all up to twelve strangers—and Him. I believed God helped me fight this fight. If he wanted me win, I would win. If he wanted me to lose, I would do it gracefully.

Most of all, I would learn from my mistakes and move on with my life.

That said, waiting for the verdict was hard on all of us. We hoped and prayed that, whatever the jury decided, we could find a way to live in the knowledge that at least I stood up for what I knew was right.

Mike's Story

Shortly after noon on Thursday, February 19, the bailiff emerged into the hallway to tell Brent and me the jury had returned its verdict. We immediately got word to Jenny at school, and she came to the courthouse, where other family and friends had started to gather in the hallway. Inside the courtroom, Bob Kantner and Caroline Harrison waited alone. Their clients had taken an evening flight the night before and were probably still *en route* to Australia.

Brent and I took our places at the plaintiff's table, and Jenny sat behind us, with her family and friends in the gallery. The bailiff asked the lawyers to meet with the judge in her chambers, which was standard practice. In civil cases, the lawyers are generally informed of the verdict before it is officially read in open court. We all followed the bailiff single file and made our way into Judge McCoy's chambers, where she stood behind her desk holding photocopies of the Court's Charge with the jury's answers written on them. Kantner took a seat across from her desk while the rest of us remained standing.

As Judge McCoy passed out the copies, she said something to Kantner to the effect of, "Well, Mr. Kantner, you saved your client twenty million dollars."

At that, I had to suppress a smile. Since the consensus was that each partner's share was likely to be, following an accounting, roughly ten million dollars, and since we had asked for an award of two times the actual award as punitive damages, that meant that, in theory, twenty million was the value of those damages. Neither Jenny nor I cared about punitive damages, and in fact I had not seriously pressed the jury for them. All we wanted was for Jenny to receive her fair share of Coffee Shop's profits. Since punitive damages would not even have come up unless we had prevailed on the main claim, including the waiver

321

issue, I inferred from Judge McCoy's statement that, while punitive damages had not been awarded, we had won.

I quickly scanned the pages to confirm, yes, Coffee Shop was a partnership and, no, there had been no finding of waiver. Out of the corner of my eye, I watched Kantner slowly flip through each page, then start over again, from front to back. It appeared to me he was stunned by the verdict, although that may simply have been a false impression. It's safe to say, though, he did not appear happy.

Brent and I nodded our congratulations to each other. Then, as we filed back into the courtroom for the formal reading of the verdict, I caught Jenny's eye and smiled. Tentatively at first, she smiled back. When I took my seat, I grabbed her hand and squeezed it.

"We got what we wanted," I said.

Tears filled her eyes.

At 12:45 PM on Thursday, February 19, 2015, Judge McCoy entered the courtroom. We all stood as she entered, then remained standing as the jurors filed in and took their places in the jury box.

"All right, everyone be seated, please," Judge McCoy said.

When we all sat, she continued, "All right, we're here to read the verdict, the Court's Charge. And I have looked it over, and I have given a copy to counsel on both sides."

She turned and spoke directly to the jury. "I do want to tell the jurors, I am very impressed by how hard you worked and how carefully you considered everything. I know I mentioned at the end of all the evidence and the end of jury arguments that I notice y'all all paid attention, and I said that's a pretty unusual thing."

I had noticed the same thing and, in my experience, it certainly was unusual that all of the jurors at all times were noticeably attentive. In the past, I had seen jurors whose minds seemed to wander, and some who even nodded off a time or two, but not this jury.

"I think," Judge McCoy continued, "this is just a case where we ended up with a very, very talented jury in the sense that nobody gets schooling on how to become a juror, but y'all really did a very good job considering some of the legal words and phrases and concepts that we put in front of you. So, I want to thank you very much. I could not have asked for more."

She held the verdict in front of her and said, still addressing the jury, "I'm going to read the questions—I'm not going to read the entire question, but I'm going to read the abbreviated version of the questions and see if this is your answer. As I understand, we did not get to the questions that required a unanimous verdict, is that correct?"

She was referencing the question on punitive damages, No. 8, which had a preliminary question (No. 7) that had to be answered unanimously before the question on punitive damages could be answered. Under Texas law, you get punitive damages only if the jury has found, unanimously, that any wrongful conduct by the defendant that caused harm to the plaintiff was committed either by fraud or with malice. Malice was defined as "a specific intent to cause injury," while fraud essentially required either a false statement, or a failure to disclose material information, with the intent that the other party act on either that statement or omission, resulting in harm.

Additionally, the law imposed a higher burden of proof for this question. The typical standard of proof in civil cases is the "preponderance of the evidence" standard, which simply means there was more evidence to establish something than evidence against it. The standard for this question on fraud or malice, though, was "clear and convincing," which was defined as "the measure or degree of proof that produces a firm belief or conviction of the truth of the allegations sought to be established." Not quite as high a bar as the criminal standard of "beyond a reasonable doubt," but higher than the more-likely-than-not "preponderance of the evidence" standard.

I didn't necessarily believe Amanda had acted with malice, as defined legally. I certainly believed she deliberately tried to squeeze Jenny out of money that was rightfully hers, but not necessarily with a specific intent to harm Jenny so much as to benefit herself. The harm to Jenny would merely have been incidental to that. It was my opinion, though, Amanda committed fraud by failing to tell Jenny the terms of the Random House deal or how much the royalty payments were, and by telling Jenny if she signed the service agreement, she would get her share of the profits under the guise of payments from TWCS Operations when she was already scheming to find a way to shut Jenny out. As it turned out, 10 out of the 12 jurors agreed and wanted to answer this question yes, but it wasn't unanimous so they didn't award punitive damages.

Judge McCoy then read the questions and answers, and each time had the jurors confirm aloud that those were, in fact, their answers.

> "Question number one regarding partnership, 'Is The Writer's Coffee Shop a Partnership?'
> Answer: Yes.
> Question number two: Are the following persons partners in The Writer's Coffee Shop? Amanda Hayward.
> Answer: Yes.
> Jennifer Lynn Pedroza.
> Answer: Yes.
> Jennifer McGuire.
> Answer: Yes.
> Lea Dimovski.
> Answer: Yes."

We now knew Jenny was entitled to one-fourth of the profits, not one-third, since the jury had found there were four partners, not three.

"Question number three. This is the question with sort of the double negative. The question was about the partnership's terminability at will. The question was, 'Was The Writer's Coffee Shop not terminable at will?'"

This was the question I had worried about during my closing argument because it was confusingly, but necessarily, worded awkwardly. I needed a negative answer on this one, because a "yes" meant that the partnership was *not* at will, and that would mean that the statute of frauds applied. But a "no" meant that it was at will and the statute of frauds did not apply. Even though I had already read the answer, I still held my breath until I heard it from Judge McCoy's lips.

"Answer: No."

I let my breath back out and the Judge moved on.

"Question number four about duties of loyalty and care. Did Amanda Hayward comply with her duties of loyalty and care to Jennifer Lynn Pedroza?"

These were duties that, by law, partners owed to each other. The instructions for this question were:

You are instructed that a partner owes to the partnership and to other partners: (1) a duty of loyalty; and (2) a duty of care.

A partner's duty of loyalty includes:

1. accounting to the partnership and holding for it any property, profit, or benefit derived by the partner in the conduct and winding up of the partnership business or from use by the partner of partnership property;

2. refraining from dealing with the partnership on behalf of a party having an interest adverse to the partnership; and

3. refraining from competing with the partnership or dealing with the partnership in a manner adverse to the partnership.

4. A partner's duty of care to the partnership and to other partners is to act in the conduct and winding up of the partnership interest with the care an ordinarily prudent person would exercise in similar circumstances. A partner is presumed to satisfy this duty if the partner acts on an informed basis and in compliance with his or her duty of loyalty.

When one of the partners takes forty million dollars in partnership assets without accounting to her partners for it, or even telling them she has received the money, I didn't see how anyone could conclude the partner had complied with her duties of loyalty and care.

Judge McCoy confirmed the jury agreed as she said, "Answer: No."

5. "Question number five about fraud. 'Did Amanda Hayward commit fraud against Jennifer Pedroza in connection with the business of The Writer's Coffee Shop?'
"Answer: Yes."

This was a different question than the one on fraud to support punitive damages. This one simply required a preponderance of the evidence, and 10 out of 12 jurors was sufficient to support it.

6. "Question number six, 'Did Amanda Hayward convert property of The Writer's Coffee Shop?'
"Answer: Yes."

Then came the preliminary question to punitive damages.

7. "Question number seven. This is one requiring a finding of malice. 'Do you find from clear and convincing evidence that the harm to Pedroza caused by the conduct you have found in response to question number four or five resulted from Hayward's fraud or malice?'
"Answer: N/A.

So that question is not answered because it was not unanimous.

8. "Question number eight, question about finding exemplary damages. 'What percentage of ownership interest in The Writer's Coffee Shop, if any, should be awarded to Jennifer Pedroza from Amanda Hayward as exemplary damages for the conduct found in question number five?'
"Answer: N/A.

This was the one that caused me heartburn when the jury sent out questions about it, but that heartburn ceased when I read the verdict in Judge McCoy's chambers.

9. "Question number nine has to do with waiver. 'Did Jennifer Pedroza waive her claims by signing the service agreement? Answer 'yes' or 'no.''

"Your answer was 'no.'"

> 10. "And question number ten has to do with fraud in the inducement. Question, 'Did TWCS Operations fraudulently induce Pedroza to enter into the service agreement?
>
> "And the answer was 'yes.'"

On this last one, I had argued to the jury that part of Amanda's misconduct was to fraudulently induce Jenny to sign the service agreement. Even if the jury had found Jenny waived her claims by signing the agreement, if the jury found Jenny had been induced to sign it by fraud, we could have negated the waiver. After all, if the waiver was based on a fraudulent contract, which was unenforceable, then there couldn't be any waiver. Since the jury had already answered the waiver question in the negative, this question was pretty much a redundancy, but we still got the answer we wanted. Belts and suspenders, as they say.

Judge McCoy confirmed the verdict form had been signed by each of the ten jurors who had agreed on all the answers—unsigned by the two who had agreed on all of the answers except for the fraud questions.

"All right, then the verdict will be officially submitted, and your work here is done," she told the jurors. "What that means is a few things. Number one, you will meet with—at long last, you'll meet the bailiff and she will give you the paperwork necessary so that you can be discharged as jurors. Once you are discharged as jurors, all of the obligations that I read to you previously are not any longer in effect.

"In part, what that means is that you can discuss the matter with other people if you wish. You don't have to. Sometimes lawyers like to wait outside when you're released because they like to talk to you. They're not going to be angry at you or tell you, you know, that they didn't like what you did or question you in the sense of questioning your judgment. Instead, sometimes they like to ask questions to find out what was very effective, what was not effective, which witnesses were believable, certain, you know, techniques.

"You are welcome to talk to them if you wish. If you don't wish to, you don't have to. In Fort Worth, our sort of standard procedure is, when you leave, if they are standing outside and you look them in the eye, make eye contact, then that means that you're willing to talk to them. If you keep your head forward and keep going, no one is going to bother you.

"And again, I can't say more than I said before. Y'all did an outstanding, thorough job, and I'm very, very, very proud. So, thank you very much for your service. You shouldn't have to serve again for two more years. All right. Thank you very much."

The jury was released at 12:55 PM. With that, we were the victors in stage one of the case. The jury had taken my challenge and rewritten the ending to the story. Now would come the stage to conduct the accounting and determine the amount of profits to go into a final judgment. It was also the stage where we would have to fight tooth and nail to preserve what we had won with the jury.

In hindsight, the jury trial was the easy part compared to what was to come next.

Jenny's Story

I later told people that I felt vindicated by the verdict, which I did, but at that exact moment, the feeling was indescribable. When the judge read the jury's answers, my mind blanked. I remember Mike grabbed my hand and, at one point, Brent whispered reassuring words and hugged me. Before the verdict was read, they had told all of us to remain as calm as possible, whether it was good news or bad. I hoped that my family and

329

friends were not making a spectacle. For myself, I focused solely on the judge's words, the hand holding mine, and the arm around my shoulders.

"We got what we wanted," Mike said. I remembered very little after those words. It was as if the only three people in existence were Mike Farris, Brent Turman, and me.

As the jurors filed out, I looked their way. A few caught my eyes, and I tried to express my gratitude with a smile. The judge mentioned how hard the jurors worked during the trial, and up to that point, I hadn't thought much about it. Selfishly, I had just focused on my part of the case, and it was easy to forget that these 12 people—or actually 13, because we had an alternate in case something happened to one of the others—sat in the courtroom day after day, listening to countless hours of testimony. This was time away from their work and their families, yet they listened carefully and took notes. They sifted through evidence and asked solid questions that proved how much they wanted to get this right. I have never had a chance to personally thank them for this service, and I doubt I ever will, but I want to thank them all the same. Not only because we prevailed that day, but also because my plight obviously meant something to them. I was grateful that they took their duty seriously.

After the judge left, I looked at the other side of the courtroom and wished Amanda were there. I wondered if maybe she had anticipated the result and that was why she left the day before. Perhaps she couldn't face the truth, or perhaps she couldn't face me in the light of the truth. I'll never know for sure, but it would have been gratifying to see her reaction.

Immediately after the judge left the bench, family and friends surrounded me. We hugged, cried, laughed, and then hugged some more. Relief wasn't immediate, but rather was a slow burn as it dawned on me what a major obstacle we had overcome. But, as Mike warned me, our journey wasn't over yet. To see this through to the end, he and Brent would have to deal with all types of legal maneuvers. But that was for tomorrow.

For today, we celebrated.

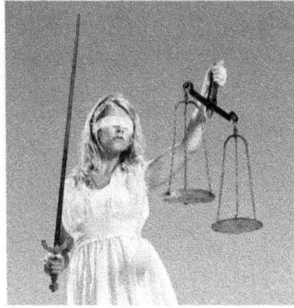

PART IV: WHAT'S PAST IS PROLOGUE

CHAPTER TWENTY-ONE: The Calm before the Storm

If you spend your whole life waiting for the storm you'll never enjoy the sunshine.

—Morris West

Mike's Story

WHEN THE TRIAL ended and Judge McCoy dismissed the jury, Brent and I didn't wait around to talk to any of the jurors. I had their contact information and figured I could call them later, something I did about a month later. Instead, we left the courthouse and took Jenny, Christa, and their family members, who had arrived to support Jenny as the verdict was read, to a late, but celebratory, lunch.

It was a very upbeat group in the restaurant as we re-lived the highlights and lowlights of the trial and basked in what could only be seen as a complete vindication for Jenny. She had been wronged, had stood up for herself, and had now been proven right. As relieved as I was to have prevailed and justified my law firm's faith in my judgment in the viability of this contingency case, I was almost overcome with happiness for Jenny. I have often said, in talking about Jenny and Christa, this was the first case in over three decades of lawyering in which I had full confidence everything my clients told me was the truth, and there was usually a document or email somewhere, often preserved on Christa's smartphone, to back it up. In fact, I sometimes wondered if they even knew how to tell anything other than the truth. Any time we talked about the case, or when they testified at deposition, the temporary injunction hearing, and the trial, it seemed as if it had never occurred to either of them to hedge, fudge, or otherwise shade the truth. One of the jurors whom I later called made this observation, as well. She told me Jenny and Christa didn't appear to be judging the effect of their answers when they testified, but they simply answered questions.

That honesty had now been rewarded.

After lunch, Brent and I returned to the office, where the firm arranged an impromptu celebration in the main conference room. I had, of course, texted some of the partners from the courthouse to announce the jury's result, and I got the sense they had been waiting impatiently for Brent and me to arrive so we could fill in more details. While it was fun to accept the congratulations of the other lawyers, I was already thinking ahead to the next steps I knew we had to take.

In *The Tempest*, Shakespeare wrote, "What's past is prologue." Nowhere is that truer than in litigation. The storm of trial had ended, but it was a mere foreshadowing of what was yet to come. The trick was to enjoy the sunshine before the dark clouds gathered again.

The end of a trial always brings with it a feeling of great relief, which is enhanced even more if you've won, as we had—but relief either way because it's over. The fifteen- and sixteen-hour days, the sleepless nights (I averaged three to four hours of sleep a night during the trial), the headaches, and the anxiety were at an end. Unfortunately, it's only a temporary respite because, after taking a deep breath or two, it soon becomes time to either preserve what you've won or to begin the process of taking back what your opponent has won.

There are a lot of ways to lose what you've won at trial. We had already survived the first two attempts to have the win taken away when Judge McCoy denied two motions for instructed, or directed, verdict Kantner had made during the trial. Next up, presumably, would be a motion for judgment notwithstanding the verdict or, in the Latin, *non-obstante veredicto*, commonly called a motion JNOV. This was the same vehicle Judge McCoy hinted at when she said she was going to submit an issue to the jury on the statute of frauds over the objections of the lawyers and she "would consider post-verdict any objections to the answer."

If we survived a JNOV motion, and I knew Kantner would file one, the defendants were sure to appeal. An appeal would bring into question the entire trial and place every action I had taken, or ruling the judge had made, under a microscope to see if any "reversible error" had been committed. I was sure mistakes had been made; they always were. The question, though, would be whether those errors were of such a magnitude as to have improperly affected the evidence presented to the jury and rendered their verdict erroneous.

The minefield that stretched out ahead was deep and wide and would probably consume the rest of the year and probably the year after. If Kantner filed an appeal, we could be looking at two or more years before things were actually final. The good news was we had won at trial. It's difficult to overturn a jury verdict on appeal, and I would much rather be on the winning side, trying to preserve my victory, than on the losing side, trying to snatch victory from defeat. Barring any legal rulings that might have been "reversible error," the standard for appealing a jury verdict was whether more than a "scintilla" of evidence existed to support the verdict. A scintilla meant there was nothing more than an iota, or crumb, of evidence, so if there was more than a crumb or iota to support the jury findings, the verdict would stand up. On top of that, any questions about the evidence would be resolved in favor of supporting the verdict, so an appeal from a jury trial would be an uphill battle for Kantner.

Even though we didn't yet have a final number for damages, it made sense to at least get a partial judgment entered. I wanted to lock in the findings of the existence of a partnership and Jenny's position as a partner in that partnership, as well as the legal wrongs that had been committed by Amanda—fraud, conversion, and breach of partnership duties. So, I needed to file a motion for that.

We also needed to have an accounting of Coffee Shop's profits, which would require both sides to appoint experts to examine not only Coffee Shop's financial records, but also records of the Australian proprietary companies Amanda had set up, and maybe even Amanda's personal financial records. We would have to rely either upon cooperation from Bob Kantner and the good will of Amanda Hayward, or a court order. I didn't think Kantner would voluntarily agree to turn over his client's financial records, especially if he filed a JNOV motion. He would want that resolved before moving on with the accounting and that would simply delay matters, so I was convinced we needed a court order to head off delay.

In our pleadings, we had asked the court to impose a constructive trust over any assets traceable to payments from Random House in order to preserve those until we had a final judgment and could begin steps to collect. A constructive trust was an equitable remedy under Texas law that allowed a court, if a party has been unjustly enriched at the expense of another, to impose a trust on assets in the hands of that party that the court believes rightfully belonged to the other.

I was concerned that Amanda would try to hide the remaining money from the Random House royalty payments and to insulate any property she had purchased with that money. Oh, sure, we had a temporary injunction ordering her not to dispose of assets traceable to the payments but, given that she had already been found to have committed fraud and to have converted money belonging to Jenny, I didn't trust her. We wouldn't have a final number for Coffee Shop's profits until the accounting was completed, but we knew Jenny's share was in the neighborhood of ten million dollars. I wanted something to specifically preserve at least that much, so I knew we needed to file a motion asking the court to impose a constructive trust.

I also thought ahead to the likelihood that, even if we won on appeal, Amanda wasn't likely to just hand over payment. In order to collect once we had a final judgment, we would probably have to take steps to make it enforceable in Australia. Because there wasn't a treaty between the United States and Australia that allowed a simple process for statutorily enforcing each other's judgments, we would have to file a new lawsuit in Australia.

To succeed in that lawsuit, we would have to prove:

(1) the U.S. judgment was final;

(2) the U.S. judgment was for a fixed sum of money or an amount that could be readily calculated;

(3) the parties to the U.S. judgment were the same parties to the common law action in Australia;

(4) the U.S. judgment was less than 12 years old; and

(5) the Australian resident had submitted to the jurisdiction of the U.S. court.

It was number five that had worried me at the start. Fortunately, Amanda made the strategic decision to engage Texas counsel for the Fort Worth lawsuit, and she appeared and contested the case, so she had submitted to U.S. jurisdiction.

To get started on the Australia end of things, one of the firm's senior partners and I left the celebration in the conference room, went to his office, and placed a call to the Australian lawyers who had assisted us in serving our Texas lawsuit on Amanda in Australia. We wanted to alert them we had won at trial and wanted them on standby to act as our local counsel "down under" when we got a final judgment.

The firm wanted to capitalize on the win as a marketing opportunity, to showcase its expertise and success in publishing law, so it arranged to issue a press release through a Dallas PR firm. I had already given a couple of television interviews back when we first filed the lawsuit, but they seemed necessary since the TV stations were intent on running stories with or without my input. I figured it was best to get our perspective out there if it was going to be news anyway, and it clearly was going to be.

I was a little concerned about how a press release would be received, because the case wasn't over. This had merely been round one, with a long way yet to go. I didn't think it was seemly to appear to be gloating when the possibility always existed that things could still go sour, so I reviewed, and edited, the release to ensure that it was straightforward and accurate.

Late that afternoon, this release went out on the Internet, with my name and number as the contact, and quickly made its way around the globe:

Fifty Shades of Grey Publishing Partner Wins Lawsuit
Plaintiff Entitled to Book Royalties

Dallas, TX (February 19, 2015)...In a verdict with blockbuster implications, a jury in the case of Pedroza v. Hayward and TWCS Operations Proprietary Ltd awarded a victory to Jennifer Lynn Pedroza in a dispute over royalty rights for the publishing phenomenon **Fifty Shades of Grey***.*

The original publisher of the trio of books was The Writer's Coffee Shop, an independent publisher of e-books and print-on-demand books. The plaintiff, Jennifer Pedroza was one of four original partners in the start-up company that published **Fifty Shades of Grey**. *The Writer's Coffee Shop eventually sold the publishing rights to the book to Random House.*

Today's verdict confirmed that Jennifer Pedroza was a partner in The Writer's Coffee Shop. The jury determined that fraud had been committed by Ms. Amanda Hayward and TWCS Operations Proprietary when they induced Ms. Pedroza into a Service Agreement, and also deprived her of her share of one of the most successful book deals in history. To date **Fifty Shades of Grey** *has sold more than 100 million copies and is currently on the* **New York Times** *best seller list.*

Damages will be assessed at a later court hearing after a forensic audit determines Ms. Pedroza's appropriate share of royalties. Ms. Pedroza was represented by the Dallas law firm of Vincent Lopez Serafino Jenevein, P.C.

-end-

The PR firm later reported that the press release was picked up by over 850 websites worldwide (in the United States, United Kingdom, Spain, Germany, France, and Canada) with an estimated potential exposure of 50 million readers. Calls came rolling in over the next few days. I spoke with reporters from the Fort Worth *Star-Telegram*, *Publishers Marketplace*, *Texas Lawyer*, *The Wrap*, *Law 360*, *The Guardian*, and *The Sydney Morning Herald*. Articles popped up in print and on the Internet. *Texas Lawyer* ran an article online on February 23, followed by another in its print edition, under the headline "Woman Wins 'Fifty Shades of Grey' Verdict." The article recited that "A Tarrant County jury found a Fort Worth-area woman was a partner in the company that originally published the 'Fifty Shades of Grey' trilogy, paving the way for her to receive a share of royalties

338

from the sale of the racy books."

The Sunday edition of Fort Worth's *Star-Telegram* contained a front-page story headlined "Woman wins suit over 'Fifty Shades of Grey,'" complete with pictures of both Jenny and Amanda, above the fold and, on the continuation of the story inside, a photo of Jenny and Christa. The article, by veteran reporter Max Baker, who would attend many of the post-trial hearings and cover every step of the case from that day forward, started with the line, "Color Arlington resident Jennifer Pedroza fifty shades of happy." He went on to write:

The jury deliberated for about 10 hours over three days before determining on Thursday that Pedroza was defrauded by Amanda Hayward, her Australian partner in an e-publishing business that originally released what would become a New York Times bestseller.

State District Judge Susan McCoy will determine how much Pedroza eventually gets after an accounting of the financial records connected to book sales is completed. Records on the royalties have been sealed, but earlier estimates were that her share could be $10 million to $20 million.

Baker also noted that he spoke with me, and that I told him that "the verdict is only 'the first step'" but that "his client feels 'vindicated.'" As for Bob Kantner, Baker wrote, he "said his clients decided not to comment to the press and will 'litigate the case in the courts.'" When I read that, I couldn't help but wonder whether Kantner was aware we had already litigated the case in the courts and Jenny had won. Baker also said, "Kantner did not respond when asked if his clients would appeal the verdict." I thought I already knew the answer.

The *Hollywood Reporter*'s "Hollywood Docket" included an entry that said:

A Texas woman, who once co-owned a small, online publishing company that originally held rights to Fifty Shades of Grey, has reportedly

339

emerged victorious at a jury trial. According to the Fort Worth Weekly, Jenny Pedroza sued Amanda Haward [sic] for breaching a partnership. Together, the two ran The Writer's Coffee Shop. Pedroza claimed she was told to sign an agreement to restructure the company, which resulted in Pedroza being cut out of profits when Fifty Shades publishing rights were sold to Random House.

That wasn't completely accurate—we had deliberately *not sued* for breach of a partnership agreement, instead claiming a partnership had been established by conduct—but it was close enough, I guess. It made the more important point that Jenny had been victorious.

The *Houston Chronicle*, in an article headlined "'50 Shades of Grey' lawsuit could earn Texas woman millions,'" got to the heart of the lawsuit when reporter Craig Hlavaty wrote Amanda Hayward "reportedly earned millions from publishing the novel-turned-movie '50 Shades of Grey,' but cut Pedroza in on only a small portion of the profits."

The website *www.author.com* noted that, not only had Jenny won, but:

What's particularly ironic is that Pedroza may not have filed suit at all had Hayward not tried to shut her down after she gave an interview to a local paper, which was covering a new soap business she and a partner (who had also been employed at TWCS) had started. It was after Hayward's threat to sue that Pedroza filed suit. Oops.

Oops, indeed.

Most articles were fairly straightforward in their reporting, but others were more tongue-in-cheek, like www.reportingtexas.com, which said, "No whips or chains were involved but an independent Texas publisher of the e-book version of 'Fifty Shades of Grey' slapped around a former colleague in court for duping her out of royalties." Along this line, once a final judgment was entered in January of 2016, *The Onion* picked up the thread, with comments from "commentators" that included, "I hate to see the close-knit erotica community wracked by this kind of scandal;" "Defrauding your business partner completely undermines the novel's themes of empathy and generosity;" and "Good for her [Pedroza]. All of our teachers deserve to be making a comfortable living from royalty disputes."

The story even made the rounds in Australia. The site www.booksandpublishing.com.au headlined an article "US jury finds Australian publisher of 'Fifty Shades' defrauded partner out of royalties." One of the most informative stories on the case would also come from Australia, from noted journalist and best-selling Australian author, Caroline Overington.

In August of 2012, just a few months after Coffee Shop sold the *Fifty Shades* publishing rights to Random House, and only one month prior to Amanda's creation of the complicated business structure she used to strip Jenny of her share of profits, Caroline wrote a feature in *The Australian Women's Weekly* about Amanda and the publication of *Fifty Shades of Grey*. The article was titled "The Female Porn Boom: Fifty Shades of Lust" and posed the question: "Is the novel *Fifty Shades of Grey* the new Viagra for Australian women—or is it turning us into a nation of porn addicts?"

Caroline interviewed Amanda for the article, whom she described as "business-savvy" and "the kind of jolly person that keeps pet turtles." She wrote that Amanda said, "[S]he knew straight away that *Fifty Shades* would be popular because 'I was speaking with E.L. [James] for a year before she signed with us. She already had a large group of readers following her—I was one of them."

What was most interesting to me about the article, though, was Amanda's recounting to Caroline of the origins of Coffee Shop. The article said:

Amanda…went online a few years ago, looking for tips on how to be a romance writer. She came across a world of other would-be writers, most of them women, many of them stay-at-home mums, who also longed to write romance, and linked up with them.

It was, she says, a "bit of fantasy, a bit of fun" ——a dreamy escape from her "other life" as a wife and mother. Amanda made some firm friendships in cyberspace, and over time, she and some partners started The Writer's Coffee Shop…."

Caroline first contacted me in the summer of 2015 while she was living in Los Angeles, holding down the U.S. west coast office of *The Australian Women's Weekly*. She wanted to, in effect, write the sequel to that article, so she made arrangements to fly to Dallas for a day. She met with Brent and me at my office for several hours, where we talked about the case and allowed her to browse some of the file materials. Then Brent and I drove her to Fort Worth for a lunch of Mexican food at Joe T. Garcia's and, afterward, to meet with Jenny for an off-the-record discussion at Jenny's school.

Caroline's article was published in November under the title "Fifty Shades of Greed." A subheading offered this description of the article: "It's the most lucrative book ever brought out by an Australian publisher, but instead of triumphant joy, the team behind the *Fifty Shades* trilogy is at loggerheads."

Caroline introduced her article this way:

There can't be many red-blooded Australian women who didn't read Fifty Shades of Grey, so who is ready for the sequel? Not what happened next for the virgin and her billionaire boyfriend. This is what happened next for the Australian mum and her Texan friends who published the book in the first place.

Maybe you heard they made a million dollars? That's not quite right. They actually made US$39 million and counting, so they all *went out to celebrate.*

Kidding! That would be the Hollywood ending. In real life they ended up in court, fighting over the cash. Interested to know who came out on top? Well, the trial took place in Texas, so strap yourself down for a wild ride.

Caroline recounted some of the history from her prior article, noting Amanda became active in a fan fiction website where "one of the first women" she connected with was "a bubbly blonde fourth-grade teacher called Jenny Pedroza from Fort Worth, Texas." After recounting the history of The Writer's Coffee Shop and the relationship between Jenny and Amanda up until the time Amanda "fired" Jenny from TWCS Operations and the interview Jenny gave to the *Fort Worth Weekly*, the article said, "What happened next would rock Jenny's boat as surely as if the billionaire Christian Grey had walked into it." After Amanda had her lawyer send Jenny a threatening cease-and-desist letter, Jenny "got a fright" and went "looking for a lawyer of her own."

To this day, she believes that Mike Farris came to her via divine intervention: not only was he the Texan son of a Baptist minister, he's also a writer, with five novels to his name. Mike gets this stuff and he couldn't wait to get stuck in."

In interpreting the trial, Caroline said, "Amanda struggled from day one," and "Amanda's lawyer, Bob Kantner, didn't do much better..." For my part, she picked up on the storytelling style I used. "Mike Farris took the literary approach." She quoted my argument about two stories being told, and the jury's opportunity to decide whether they wanted to rewrite the ending. "Rewrite the ending they did," she said, as the "jury found for Jenny."

Upon hearing this, she [Jenny]wept. Amanda did not, telling The Weekly: "This case is not over". She intends to appeal, which in turn means that we can expect at least one more chapter and quite a bit more pain.

Jenny's Story

One of the first things Christa and I did on the way to lunch was to call Jeff Prince of *Fort Worth Weekly*. Without his article about two crazy women selling soap, none of this would have happened. He answered right away and wished us congratulations. I expressed how thankful I was for him and his article, and I promised to send everyone to read his work. Throughout this ordeal, I learned that, even though bad things happened, good ultimately won out. Jeff probably never dreamed his article would have the impact it did, but I was thankful for his help and always will be.

As the press release went viral, I found my name splashed on newspapers all around the world, and I saw my name over and over across the Internet. My husband and I received many random phone calls, but we refused to answer any number we didn't know. I felt the same way about the press as Mike, that talking now seemed like gloating and that we still had a long way to go.

One exception was when Mike asked if I would meet with Caroline Overington, from Australia. He really liked her work, he said, and he felt like she was "good people"—the highest praise a Texan can bestow. I was hesitant to talk with her because I was teaching, and I was worried any unnecessary publicity about winning a trial over what some called "mommy porn" might get me in trouble. Mike got Caroline's assurances the meeting would be off the record—she simply wanted to meet me and get to know me a bit as she worked on a story about the case, but she wouldn't quote me. I spoke with my principal, who granted permission.

Mike and Brent arrived at the school one afternoon with Caroline, and I could see they were both comfortable with her. She was able to see where I worked and she asked some insightful questions. Telling a beautiful, smart, and very put-together woman I had been a naïve fool wasn't easy, but she put me at ease. If Mike and Brent trusted her, I knew I could, too.

One really surreal moment came on the Sunday after the verdict when my husband and I went to our local coffee shop. Neither of us thought much about being out in public, but we both noticed a few stares in our direction. When we finished our coffee and were leaving, I saw it. The Fort Worth *Star Telegram* sat in the newspaper section and, upon further inspection, was in the hands of at least five other customers. Smack dab on the front of the paper was a picture of me, beneath a headline that screamed "Woman wins suit over 'Fifty Shades of Grey.'"

Mick pointed to the paper, we gave each other big eyes, threw our trash away, and scuttled out of the coffee house. Once we were safely tucked into our car, we started laughing.

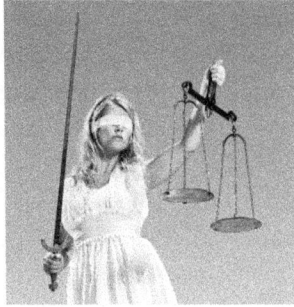

CHAPTER TWENTY-TWO: New Storm Clouds Gather

There are some things you learn but in calm, and some in storm.

—Willa Cather

Mike's Story

MY FIRST VOLLEY after trial was to file a Motion for Partial Judgment and a separate Motion for Application of Equitable Remedies, which the court set for hearing on April 23. The first motion was the simpler of the two, and it simply asked the Court to enter a partial judgment capturing the findings in the jury's verdict. Specifically, I asked for a formal declaration that Coffee Shop was a partnership and Jenny, as one of four partners, was entitled to twenty-five percent of Coffee Shop's profits.

I also wanted the partial judgment to state Jenny was entitled to recover her attorney's fees, with the amount to be determined at a later hearing, and to deny the defendants' counterclaims. Lastly, I wanted it to state an accounting would be performed, although I would also address that in the second motion.

The motion for "application of equitable remedies" was more complicated. In it, I asked the Court to actually order the accounting and for the defendants to provide "all relevant books, records, accounts, and other documents…in their possession that are necessary to perform the accounting." I also asked the Court to impose a deadline for turning over those documents, as well as to set a hearing date to determine the amount of profits.

Most of that should have been non-controversial, though I anticipated resistance from Kantner in producing the documents. In fact, he had already been dragging his heels. As I left the courtroom after the jury returned its verdict, he told me he would contact me to get the accounting started. After several weeks' delay, I contacted him and he told me he would need at least three to four months to gather the necessary financial records. Keep in mind these were largely documents he had originally been ordered to produce nearly a year earlier in connection with the TRO.

The real crux of the second motion, though, was for the imposition of a constructive trust on all money or property that could be traced to Random House royalty payments. The Texas Supreme Court long ago defined a constructive trust this way:

A constructive trust is a relationship with respect to property, subjecting the person by whom the title to the property is held to an equitable duty to convey it to another, on the ground that his acquisition or retention of the property is wrongful and that he would be unjustly enriched if he were permitted to retain the property.[40]

Another Texas Supreme Court case held, "Actual fraud, as well as breach of a confidential relationship, justifies the imposition of a constructive trust." [41] We had jury findings that Amanda

---

[40] *Talley v. Howsley,* 176 S.W. 2d 158, 160 (Tex. 1943).

[41] *Meadows v. Bierschwale,* 516 S.W.2d 125, 128 (Tex. 1974).

obtained all of the Random House royalties, including Jenny's share, by breaching her partnership duties, which are fiduciary in nature, and by committing fraud against Jenny. Those findings entitled Jenny to a constructive trust, which I asked the court to impose on the Random House royalty payments and any properties bought, or investments made, with the money. That included four houses and a gymnasium in Australia, as well as various investment and bank accounts. There was also an additional payment not yet due from Random House, so I asked the judge to order it to be paid into the court's registry when the time came.

I figured we would be in for a fight over this motion. I was right.

On the afternoon of Monday, April 20, Bob Kantner filed his Motion for Judgment Notwithstanding the Verdict, asserting the same statute of frauds argument he had asserted in a motion for summary judgment before trial and two motions for directed verdict during the trial, all of which had been denied. Because the hearing on my motions was set for 1:30 PM on April 23rd, and the JNOV motion was filed after 1:30 on the 20th, the JNOV technically didn't meet the three-days-notice requirement of the Local Rules of Tarrant County, so it wasn't set at the same time as my motions.

Brent and I drove to Fort Worth during the lunch hour on the 23rd, stopping to eat along the way, then headed up to the courtroom. Kantner was there, as expected, but he now had a new co-counsel, David Keltner from the Fort Worth law firm of Kelly, Hart, & Hallman, LLP. I had never met David before, but I knew of him by reputation. He was a former justice on the Fort Worth Court of Appeals, and one of the most prominent, and pre-eminent, appellate attorneys in Texas. A very distinguished-looking white-haired gentlemen who had been practicing law since 1975, his appearance told me that appeal was a certainty, not merely likely.

Also present in the courtroom were Random House's lawyer and Max Baker of the Fort Worth *Star-Telegram*.

All the lawyers rose as Judge McCoy entered and took her place on the bench. Imagine my shock when she said she would be hearing not only my two motions but also Kantner's JNOV motion. I quickly got to my feet and said the JNOV motion hadn't been scheduled, and in fact had been filed only the Monday before, less than 72 hours earlier. Judge McCoy seemed surprised, and she asked if I would waive the notice requirement. I hadn't specifically prepared for the motion, nor had I yet filed a response to it, but if I waived the notice, as she seemed to want me to, I didn't think she would treat me unfairly. And specific preparation or not, I knew the arguments and I knew the law.

I thought for a moment, then said, "I'm ready, so I'll waive the notice."

She nodded, then went formally on the record. "Good afternoon, everybody. We're here on Cause No. 153-272310-14, Jennifer Lynn Pedroza, et al., versus Amanda Hayward, et al. We have today pending before us Plaintiff's Motion for Partial Judgment; Motion for Application of Equitable Remedies, which, after reading it, as I understand, it's requesting a constructive trust, and there were responses and replies; as well as we also have filed a Motion for Judgment Notwithstanding the Verdict filed by the defendants. And it was pointed out to me before we went on the record that that motion for JNOV was not set for today's hearing. It was filed on Monday of this week being, I guess, the 20th. Today is Thursday, the 23rd. I guess there's technically three days."

I stood behind the lectern, realizing that this was my last chance to object. Instead, I said, "I got it about four o'clock in the afternoon, so technically it was a little less than three days, but I am prepared to argue the motion."

I started with my motion for partial judgment, which was pretty straightforward. I focused mostly on our request that the judgment state Jenny was entitled to recover her attorney's fees. The provision of the *Texas Civil Practice & Remedies Code* on declaratory judgments provided that a party who prevailed on a claim for declaratory relief was entitled to recover attorney's fees. The jury found Coffee Shop was a partnership and Jenny was a partner, which was the "declaration" we asked for, and now I wanted to ensure an award of attorney's fees.

In response, Kantner argued we had asserted a lot of other claims, such as claims for fraud and conversion, that were not part of any declaratory relief. According to him, we simply "tacked on" the declaratory claim in order to recover attorney's fees that wouldn't otherwise be allowed. He also argued that, if the partnership finding got wiped out by the statute of frauds in his JNOV motion, then there was no declaration left and so Jenny shouldn't be allowed to recover.

I didn't buy it—all of the claims depended upon a declaration that there was a partnership. Unless there was a partnership, there wouldn't be any fraud; unless there was a partnership, there couldn't be any breach of partnership duties; unless there was a partnership, there couldn't be any conversion of partnership assets. Every subsequent answer to the questions in the Court's Charge was contingent upon a positive answer to the first one, which asked if Coffee Shop is a partnership. So, the finding of partnership was all that was necessary for a full award of attorney's fees.

Judge McCoy didn't buy Kantner's argument, either. "I don't believe this is a case where that has just been simply tacked on for the purpose of getting attorney's fees," she said, "because I think it's been a request from the beginning to determine if the plaintiff was a partner. And, as a matter of fact, that was the very first question asked upon which all of the other questions was predicated...I believe that the judgment should contain a declaration that the plaintiff was a partner and the judgment is going to be, in part, a judgment for declaratory relief. As a contingent matter on that, I believe that attorney's fees come with it."

I moved on to the motion for an accounting. "That was something that we all agreed to before the trial," I said, "that if the plaintiff prevailed, we would have the accounting. In fact, I think one of the last things Mr. Kantner said to me after the jury came back was 'I'll be in touch within the next couple of weeks about getting the accounting started.' Well, now we're two months later and the accounting has not started, and now what they're saying is we need a minimum of ninety to one-hundred-twenty days to even get documents together to produce for the accounting, which, in my opinion, is ridiculous on its face. We sought the documents in discovery in this case. Before the trial started, we discussed the fact that there would be an accounting. It's been two months since the trial. Nothing has been done and now they want another four months." [42]

Judge McCoy granted my motion for an accounting and said, "I'm going to give you guys thirty days to exchange the information that you need. And work together on it, please. After thirty days, I don't want any new information to pop up to suddenly change somebody's numbers. I mean, unless there's some real good reason that I would say, oh, yeah, I can understand why that didn't get produced before. If there's any contentious documents that either of you think you need or he's asking for and you don't think he should get, y'all call me and we can try to do a quick hearing, even if it has to be by telephone. But within thirty days, y'all exchange what you need to exchange, and then thirty days later we're going to have a hearing."

---

[42] That delay thing again.

The guts of this day's hearing involved my request for a constructive trust, which Kantner vigorously contested through some, in my opinion, intellectual tap dancing. There was still a payment left to be made by Random House, I said, and "based upon the numbers that we have so far, if the total is in the neighborhood of thirty-nine—let's say forty million dollars just for round figures, Pedroza would be entitled to a judgment, in our opinion, against Ms. Hayward for ten million dollars."

I asked that a trust be imposed for at least that amount, either in the form of equitable liens on real estate in Australia or, if there was sufficient cash still available, that ten million dollars be paid into the registry of the court. I also expressed concern Amanda had already dissipated a lot of the funds and had been either hiding assets or acquiring properties in Australia in order to shelter them. When Kantner, as part of his argument, told Judge McCoy she didn't have jurisdiction over properties in Australia, she perked up.

"This is not us doing something underhanded or not being candid," Kantner said. "This notion of assets being outside the jurisdiction of the Court was brought to the Court by the plaintiff and acknowledged by the Court in the [temporary injunction]. So that's point number one. Now—"

Judge McCoy cut him off in mid-sentence. "Let me go back to this 'outside the jurisdiction of the Court.' I do agree with you as a statement, I mean, literally, my jurisdiction does not go all the way to Australia. It does not reach Australia. And I don't disagree that that was in numerous writings that the plaintiffs have filed, particularly at the beginning.

"One of the things that I've really enjoyed the most about this case—and I don't want to beat a dead horse here—but one of the things I've really enjoyed most about this case is when you have really good lawyers on both sides who fight hard but fight fairly. I never really have to worry about whether or not the money is going to slip through my fingers or whoever's fingers.

And I have always admired the fact that I could at least put that little concern away somewhere else and not worry about the fact that all the money is going to disappear. And because I think your client knows that she is within the jurisdiction of the Court, I have never had the feeling that she was going to go and hide it in some offshore account or something. But—so that has just been one of those things I've never worried about.

"I understand that you may have been quoting something that the plaintiff may have said from the very beginning, but that is the first time I went, 'Uh-oh, do I need to be worried about this?' And, you know, I guess I'm just going to ask you, is that something that we need to be worried about?"

"I don't think so, Your Honor," Kantner said, the beginning of a less than positive assertion Amanda had not been hiding assets, but rather more of a separation of himself from her actions. "I have no reason to believe that Amanda Hayward or TWCS Operations has done anything with the Random House moneys that were covered by this Court's order other than what's permitted in the Court's order."

"That's what I thought."

But "having no reason to believe" is not the same as a positive assertion that a client has not done anything wrong. Kantner continued his answer, putting the onus on Amanda, and off of himself. "There's certainly no evidence that they've presented to the contrary. What I'm representing to the Court as an officer of the Court is that I have no reason to believe that money has been used for any improper purpose." A minute later, he added, "I appreciate the Court's concern, but I have absolutely no reason whatsoever to believe that they have or that they intend to, and certainly wouldn't participate if I had any reason to believe they did."

In other words, Kantner had no reason to believe—repeat, no reason to *believe*—repeat *absolutely no reason whatsoever to believe*—that Amanda had improperly used any of the Random

House royalties and, if she did, she didn't provide him any evidence she did, and he didn't have anything to do with it if she did. Back to Shakespeare and protesting too much.

After Kantner argued his JNOV motion, and I responded, Judge McCoy ruled at the end of this nearly-three-hour hearing. She granted my motion for partial judgment and the motion for an accounting, overruled the JNOV, then turned to the constructive trust. She started by addressing the upcoming royalty payment due from Random House, telling its attorney to have his client place the money in an interest-bearing escrow account, rather than in the registry of the court, not to be disbursed until further order from the Court.

Then she said, "I'm going to enter an order that says that the defendant shall maintain ten million dollars, which can include the amount that's in the escrow account from the April payment from Random House. And it can be, I guess, in property, in cash. What I was trying to do is I was trying to create a fund of cash that came close to that amount. But shall maintain ten million in either accounts or property that shall be unencumbered until the time—I guess I'm going to take this in steps until the hearing when we have the accounting."

Even though an order granting the constructive trust would not be signed for more than a month—Kantner and I, of course, fought over the proposed language—Max Baker of the Fort Worth *Star-Telegram* reported on the hearing the following Monday, April 27. The headline proclaimed "Judge wants $10 million set aside for possible award in Fifty Shades lawsuit," and the article led off with, "A state district judge wants $10 million in cash or investments to be set aside for a potential award after a Tarrant County jury ruled earlier this year that an Arlington woman was cheated out of royalties from the blockbuster novel *Fifty Shades of Grey*."

Baker noted, although records on the royalties were sealed,

"[I]t was divulged that the e-publishing business that Hayward, Pedroza and two other women formed, which originally released what would become an international blockbuster, made up to $40 million." He also noted, "[Judge] McCoy expressed some concern about her ability to encumber property and cash in Australia. She said that during the trial, because of the attorneys' reputations, she set aside worries that the 'money would disappear.' Nonetheless, McCoy decided to honor a request from Farris to have the $10 million put into a fund."

Baker quoted me as saying, "We were pleased with the judge's ruling. We think it is in keeping with the facts at the trial and the law in Texas that allows for these kinds of remedies."

Nicely understated, I thought. He also included a statement of my concerns about disappearing assets. "During the hearing, Farris mentioned that Hayward now lives in a house worth $4.8 million and that she owned a gym and several other houses. 'Our concern is that we have no way to follow the money once it gets to Australia without going to Australia and following legal steps down there,' Farris said Monday."

As for Kantner? Baker wrote that he "declined to comment Monday, saying that his clients don't want to 'litigate this in the press.'"

The media in Amanda's part of the world also caught wind of the hearing. Writing in the *Sydney Morning Herald*, reporter Linda Morris said:

> A Sydney publisher of the *Fifty Shades of Grey* trilogy is facing a multi-million-dollar payout after a jury found she committed fraud against her Texas partner.

Noting that author E.L. James was at the top of *Forbes* magazine's list of highest-earning authors for the year ended June 2013, she continued:

Hayward is also a wealthy woman.

Her personal investment interests identified by Pedroza's lawyer include a gymnasium, a hairdressing salon and a consultancy business.

Pedroza's claim for 'equitable remedies' refers to five properties including Hayward's $6 million [in Australian dollars] home in Dural, and a commercial property in South Windsor. Proceeds from book sales, presented in court by Pedroza's lawyer as "Exhibit One", were estimated at around $US30,000 per month.

An attempt by Hayward's lawyer, Robert Kantner, to set aside the jury verdict failed in court. An appeal is expected.

On May 5, Judge McCoy signed a partial judgment that I prepared. It was always a tricky business preparing orders because, even though most judges reviewed them and, if necessary, made edits, the draftsman essentially took on responsibility for any errors in the language. If an order or judgment you drafted gets overturned on appeal because of faulty wording, there's no one to blame but yourself.

The Partial Judgment said:

PARTIAL JUDGMENT

On February 9, 2015, the trial of this case began. Plaintiff Jennifer Lynn Pedroza ("Pedroza") appeared in person and through her attorneys and announced ready for trial. Defendants Amanda M. Hayward ("Hayward") and TWCS Operations Proprietary Ltd. ("Operations") appeared in person and through their attorneys and announced ready for trial.

A panel of twelve qualified jurors was selected, and the case proceeded to trial. The jury heard the evidence and the arguments of counsel. The parties concluded evidence on February 13, 2015, when the parties through their respective attorneys announced in open court that they had presented all their evidence and rested. The Court submitted questions, definitions, and instructions to the jury on February 17, 2015. In response, the jury made findings that the Court received, filed, and entered of record. The jury's verdict, as reflected in the Court's Charge, is expressly incorporated into this Partial Judgment for all purposes.

After considering the evidence, the testimony received, the arguments of counsel, and the jury's verdict, the Court renders partial rather than final judgment as follows:

1. Pursuant to Chapter 37 of the *Texas Civil Practice & Remedies Code*, the Court declares that The Writer's Coffee Shop ("Coffee Shop") is a partnership.

2. Pursuant to Chapter 37 of the *Texas Civil Practice & Remedies Code*, the Court declares that Plaintiff Pedroza is a twenty-five (25) percent partner in Coffee Shop and is entitled to twenty-five (25) percent of the net profits of Coffee Shop.

3. The amount of the net profits of Coffee Shop will be determined pursuant to the Court's Order for Accounting and Pedroza's share will be included in a later Final Judgment.

4. Pursuant to Chapter 37 of the *Texas Civil Practice & Remedies Code*, Pedroza is entitled to recover her reasonable and necessary attorney's

fees.

5.   Pedroza is entitled to recover 25% of the net profits of Coffee Shop due to the jury's findings of Hayward's fraud, failures to comply with partnership duties, and conversion of partnership property.

6.   Defendants Hayward and Pedroza [sic][43] take nothing by way of their counterclaims against Pedroza.

7.   The amount of Pedroza's reasonable and necessary attorney's fees are not decided in this partial judgment but shall be determined at a later date and will be included in a later Final Judgment.

SO ORDERED this [5th] day of [May], 2015.

[Susan McCoy]
Honorable Susan Heygood McCoy, Judge Presiding

It took a bit longer to finalize the orders for the accounting and for the constructive trust because—surprise, surprise!—Kantner and I had disagreements over the language.

Judge McCoy made modifications of her own to the language and then finally signed both orders on May 29. Predicated on the jury's verdict, the constructive trust order said...

---

[43] One of those errors in drafting that I was talking about. I fixed this when the Final Judgment was signed.

ORDER ON PLAINTIFF'S APPLICATION FOR CONSTRUCTIVE TRUST

A jury trial was conducted in this case, beginning on February 9, 2015, and on February 19, 2015, the jury reached a verdict that included the following findings:

- The Writer's Coffee Shop ("Coffee Shop") is a partnership.
- Plaintiff Jennifer Lynn Pedroza ("Pedroza") is one of four partners in Coffee Shop.
- Defendant Amanda Hayward ("Hayward") did not comply with her partnership duties of loyalty and care to Pedroza under the Texas Business Organizations Code ("TBOC").
- Hayward committed fraud against Pedroza in connection with the business of Coffee Shop.
- Hayward converted property of Coffee Shop.

On April 23, 2015, the Court considered Pedroza's Motion for Application of Equitable Remedies (the "Equitable Motion"), which included a motion for application of a constructive trust. After considering the Equitable Motion, the arguments of counsel, and the above findings in the jury's verdict, the Court orders as follows:

IT IS ORDERED that the royalty payment from Random House (the "Random House Payment") that is due for royalties earned from the sale of the Fifty Shades of Grey trilogy in the period ending with December 31, 2014, shall be placed by Random House in an interest-bearing escrow account in the United

States, and the name on the account, the account number and the name and address of the institution holding the account shall be provided to counsel in this case. In the event Random House determines that it is not feasible to set up such an interest-bearing escrow account, Random House shall retain the Random House Payment until further order from this Court.

IT IS FURTHER ORDERED that Defendants shall designate $10 million (in United States dollars) in assets (the "Assets") traceable to any royalties paid at any time by Random House for the sale of the Fifty Shades of Grey trilogy, or any other funds received in connection with the business of Coffee Shop, or properties purchased with said royalties or funds, for retention by Defendants (as ordered below) during the pendency of this case. Such Assets are to be designated by location, account number, address, or any other reasonable manner by which the Assets, including the amount or value of such Assets, can be identified and located with specificity. The Assets may be in cash, property, or otherwise, or any combination thereof, but shall include the Random House Payment referenced above, as well as whatever funds may remain from Random House royalty payments previously made for the royalty period ending June 30, 2014, and funds in an investment portfolio at WestPac Private Bank (which was identified by Hayward at her deposition in this case, and is more particularly identified in Hayward's answer to Interrogatory No. 23 of Plaintiff's Second Set of Interrogatories to Defendant Hayward). To the extent any properties purchased with the referenced funds or royalties are currently encumbered, the Defendants shall first designate unencumbered properties.

IT IS FURTHER ORDERED that the Defendants shall maintain the Assets and may not transfer, move, dispose of, further encumber, assign, sell, alienate, deplete, conceal, or otherwise dispose of the Assets until such time as a hearing on the profits of Coffee Shop can be held, or until such time as this Order may be extended.

IT IS FURTHER ORDERED that nothing in this Order shall prevent the Defendants from paying legitimate business expenses of The Writer's Coffee Shop incurred after the date of this Order, as well as attorney's fees and expenses incurred in this case after the date of this Order. The Defendants shall provide an accounting to the Court and to the plaintiff of any such payments on a monthly basis, such accounting to be provided on the first day of each month.

So ordered this [29th] day of [May], 2015.

[Susan McCoy]
Honorable Susan Heygood McCoy
Judge Presiding

As we'll see, the constructive trust would prove to be a serious point of contention between the parties, and Judge McCoy, throughout the remainder of the year 2015.

Jenny's Story

The constructive trust. The trust that was constructive. Constructiveness in a trust. Any way I looked at it this was confusing. Mike broke it down by explaining that this might help ensure that Amanda had the money available when it came down to a final judgment.

Up to this point, it was safe to say the defendants had not been forthcoming about where the money had gone. Remember James's "drop of water in a bucket" statement? Apparently forty million dollars had just evaporated. That worried me, but I had faith in Mike and Brent.

At the end of my time with Coffee Shop, I wrote Amanda an email on October 31, 2013, about finishing our book *Mistakes*.

I would really like the opportunity to complete this project on my own. Could I have the rights to the book and the series released back to me? I will be self-publishing, and don't intend to make a fortune, but I would like to finish it.

She replied:

Jenny I'm sorry I can't do that. I don't want my name on anything that is associated with that book, because of the way you wanted to finish it. The reason we never finished it is I didn't like where you were going with it. Which is why we didn't continue.

I thought also about continuing this book on my own and decided it wasn't worth our friendship fall out.

I'm sorry that this has all happened I wish it hadn't, but I can't give you that I'm so sorry. My name is on the first of the book series and that is why I pulled it off the market as I knew it was never going to be finished. Even if we took my name off the book for future sales it will always be there somewhere.

These would be the last words we every spoke, or wrote, directly to each other. I felt it ironic that our friendship started with her encouraging my writing and ended with the failure of our book supposedly being my fault.

Mr. Kantner was correct about one thing: I was angry. I felt completely helpless at first, as if I were a nothing that could be easily discarded, and I was distraught. I didn't really understand until much later how angry I was. Looking at the constructive trust order, which recited I was a partner in a partnership but I had been defrauded, I understood my anger. No matter what happened from that point on, the world knew the truth. I didn't need to be angry anymore. I had been vindicated.

Amanda had tried to take everything away from me, including my love of writing, but she had failed.

CHAPTER TWENTY-THREE: The Storm Rages

It is not the light that we need, but fire; it is not the gentle shower, but thunder. We need the storm, the whirlwind, and the earthquake.
                                    —Frederick Douglass

Mike's Story

I LATER FILED a second motion for application of equitable remedies and asked Judge McCoy to actually require the defendants to deposit assets into the registry of the Court. She had declined to do that at the April 23 hearing, saying, "Placing money in the registry of the Court really opens up a can of worms that I don't feel comfortable with. Not to say I would not do it if the situation warranted it."

But she had also expressed concerns maybe the defendants hadn't complied with the temporary injunction, even though Kantner said he "had no reason to believe" they hadn't. I thought his protestations lacked conviction. Amanda maintained an investment account she said contained seven million dollars, but when Judge McCoy asked Kantner about the amount, he said, "Your Honor, I wouldn't take that as a fact." He explained that the seven-million-dollar figure was based on "deposition testimony at some point in the past," but "I don't think we should make assumptions that there's seven million dollars in that account today."

That seemed to me to be an admission, wishy-washy though it was, money that was supposed to have been frozen by the temporary injunction had been spent. If not, it should still be there. I was afraid money would continue to bleed out of that account unless it was kept in the Court's registry.

In the meantime, the accounting was underway on Coffee Shop's profits, and we finally got the necessary financial records from Kantner. We knew this would be a battle of the dueling experts, with our side hoping for a high number for the value of those profits, while the other side would try to keep the number lower. We hired, as our expert, an accountant with a Texas-based accounting firm whose expertise, with his CPA, JD, and experience as a former special agent for the FBI, was forensic and litigation services, specifically forensic accounting and white-collar crime investigations. On the other side, Kantner hired the name partner of a major accounting firm, who was the partner in charge of his firm's Forensic, Litigation & Business Valuation Practices section.

Both experts were given the same financial records to review and the same deadline to produce reports. Kantner's expert's report inadvertently omitted one of the Random House payments and came up with a range of profits that depended upon whether you also included some unsubstantiated expenses that I disagreed with, and that not even he would verify as accurate. If you added that omitted Random House payment, then his range for Jenny's share of Coffee Shop's profits was from $10,560,667, on the low end, to $10,724,667, on the high. Remarkably, the number our expert came up with was $10,690,648—in the upper portion of that range.

I emailed Bob Kantner on August 3, pointed out the omitted Random House payment, and said, "Provided your expert will agree that the 12/8/14 payment (of $1,357,285) should have been included, we can agree on the figure of $10,724,667 [which was the high number from his expert] as the proper dollar amount for the judgment damages."

Kantner asked me to provide evidence of that omitted Random House payment, which I did, even though he already had a full listing of the payments and it was clear this was simply an oversight on his expert's part. I didn't hear anything else from Kantner after that, so it appeared we would need a formal hearing on the accounting, even though his expert came up with a number that I was willing to agree to.

We gathered again in Judge McCoy's courtroom on August 7, 2015, for a hearing on my second motion for application of equitable remedies, with the ubiquitous Max Baker of the Fort Worth *Star-Telegram* also in attendance, as was Random House's lawyer. After an hour of fairly contentious arguing, the judge issued her ruling.

"My interest is not necessarily in tracing down every penny of where the money went, although some of my orders have required an accounting over time. My interest is in making sure there's money to satisfy the judgment. And I have hesitated to require the ten million, plus or minus, to be put in the registry of the court until now. But just because that might be a cumbersome, difficult thing to do, it doesn't necessarily mean it's the wrong thing to do. And given, not my concerns that attorneys or a party are playing hide the ball, but given that my interest is in making sure that the judgment can be satisfied that was entered in this court, I am going to order that the money be placed in the registry of the court."

Kantner wanted clarification as to "which money," and Judge McCoy explained, "I believe that I required that ten million be designated in my previous order. So that's the amount that I'm going to ask be placed in the registry of the court. Ten million dollars."

I also asked the judge to sanction the defendants for what I felt were violations of her prior orders, but she declined. "I'm not granting any sanctions. And my order for the ten million to be placed in the registry of the court should be construed as being an order granting the equitable remedy, not an order granting sanctions."

Before an order could be signed, Bob Kantner and David Keltner promptly filed a motion to reconsider the ruling on this second motion for application of a constructive trust, and that hearing was held on August 26, the same date scheduled for hearing on the accounting. Keltner, instead of Kantner, argued the motion to reconsider, complete with PowerPoint presentation. A minor part of his argument was that the defendants considered the constructive trust, as ordered, to more closely resemble an "attachment," which was a legal procedure that permitted a party to seize another party's assets, and which would require the posting of a bond, but, he argued, no bond had been ordered.

Then he moved on to the guts of his argument, which was that Amanda didn't have ten million dollars in cash. "Our real complaint, Your Honor," he said, "is the liquidation factor to be able to post them in the registry." He went on to argue, "[N]o Texas authority permits forced liquidation as part of a constructive trust. If you were to order that, you would be the first court in Texas to do that."

After listening for a while, Judge McCoy posed a series of questions to Keltner. The first was, "I'm looking to your expertise in appellate matters because—if the money is put in the registry of the court, is there still always going to be a requirement of having a supersedeas bond?"

A supersedeas bond was something that a defendant who'd had a judgment entered against her could post, either in cash or with a court-approved bond, that would supersede, or halt, any efforts by the judgment plaintiff to collect while a case was on appeal. If no supersedeas bond was posted then there was nothing to stop the plaintiff from seizing the defendant's assets even while an appeal was pending. What the judge was asking Keltner was whether he thought, if his clients put ten million dollars in the court's registry, they would still have to provide a separate supersedeas bond during an appeal.

After a rambling answer that diverged from the question, Keltner concluded, "I think I'm anticipating where you're going. If I'm missing this, I apologize. I think where you're going is, we wouldn't have to supersede if we've got ten million dollars posted."

"You correctly read my mind," Judge McCoy said.

The judge then asked, "Since I haven't yet signed an order regarding placing the money in the registry of the court, I haven't yet crystallized exactly what that money would be comprised of. I haven't signed anything. So, are there ways to put money in the registry of the court other than cash?"

"Not given the financial circumstances of my client as I understand it," Keltner said. "Mr. Kantner may be able to answer that more correctly than I can, but as I understand it, no, from a practical standpoint. In other words, do they have ten million dollars in cash to put in the registry of the court? I think the answer to that is no."

I found that answer to be incredible, since Amanda had received approximately forty million dollars from Random House. Her Australian accountant testified at his deposition that he treated those payments as capital gains which meant, under Australian law, fifty percent of it was exempt. So, she had received roughly twenty million tax-free. As for the other half, the highest tax rate in Australia was forty-five percent, so she likely kept more than ten million of that half tax-free. That meant it was probable she had received, and not paid taxes on, more than thirty million dollars—yet she couldn't come up with ten million to satisfy the constructive trust? Remarkable.

I knew, from my research of public records in Australia, Amanda had acquired—or, rather, companies she had set up that were owned by her husband, James, had acquired—nearly fifteen million dollars' worth of real estate. I also knew, at one time, she maintained seven million dollars in an investment account, although when Judge McCoy asked Kantner about the amount at the April 23 hearing, he had said, "Your Honor, I wouldn't take that as a fact." It sounded as if Amanda was spending money like crazy and finding creative ways to disguise it, so that her lawyers could now argue, "Gee, our client just doesn't have that kind of money and it's mean of you, Judge, to expect her to."

"Because we don't have an order yet setting out exactly what that means, putting aside ten million dollars in the registry of the court, is there a way to use real property as a portion of that ten million dollars?" Judge McCoy asked.

"I'm going to give you a legal answer, not a factual answer," Keltner said. "The legal answer is yes, that has been done before in some circumstances." The problems were practical, he said. "From a legal standpoint, a candor reply to be answered, yes, there very much could be a way to do that. I think practically there may not be, but from a legal standpoint, to be honest, the answer to that would be yes."

When I took the floor to rebut Keltner's argument, I zeroed in on his complaint that real estate and investments might have to be liquidated in order to come up with ten million dollars. "The defendants have characterized our application for constructive trust, and asking money to be paid into the registry of the court, as asking the Court to order liquidation of assets. We haven't asked for any assets to be liquidated. We have asked for money to go into the registry of the court. If assets have to be liquidated to do that, to be blunt, my thought on that is if you are going to walk off with forty million dollars, thirty million of which belongs to other people, ten million of which belongs to

Jenny Pedroza, and you want to use that money to buy real estate, you can't really complain when the Court says 'give Jenny her money back.'"

After about thirty more minutes of argument, Judge McCoy was ready to rule. "I've read the *Wheeler v. Blacklands Production Credit Association*[44] case from the Fort Worth Court of Appeals in 1982 carefully, and I do not want to go afoul with it or any other Texas case law. I am not going to withdraw my prior order about placing ten million dollars in the registry of the court...but here is what I want to make absolutely clear. In so doing, I am not asking Ms. Hayward to liquidate any assets. I'm not pointing to any assets that she has to liquidate. She can designate or use whatever money or property that she has, or has a right to, to get to the ten million dollars...to be sure I did not violate the *Wheeler* case, I'm not trying to get Ms. Hayward to put aside or use all of her assets. It is just the approximate ten

---

[44] That case held that there was no hard-and-fast rule as to what a constructive trust had to look like and that courts had broad discretion in setting them up. It cited the Texas Supreme Court case of *Meadows v. Bierschwale*, 516 S.W.2d 125 (Tex. 1974), which said: "Moreover, there is no unyielding formula to which a court of equity is bound in decreeing a constructive trust, since the equity of the transaction will shape the measure of relief granted...'[i]n order to satisfy the demands of justice, courts of equity will indulge in presumptions and even pure fiction.'" In doing so, though, there "must of necessity be specific property, the subject of the inequitable transaction, before a constructive trust may be imposed. Definitive, designated property, wrongfully withheld from another, is the very heart and soul of constructive trust theory." *Wheeler* upheld a constructive trust on properties that the judgment defendant had obtained wrongfully, but it reversed the portion of it that was imposed on assets that the defendant already owned and that had nothing to do with the transaction that was the subject of the lawsuit.

million dollars that will—the exact dollar figure to be determined, but approximately ten million dollars that belongs, according to the jury's finding, to Ms. Pedroza.

"So, to be absolutely clear, she can use property as part of that ten million dollars, and she can handle it either by selling it, mortgaging it, giving title to the district court. I am not asking her to liquidate any assets. I don't want more than ten million dollars to be placed in the registry of the court."

Once the money was in the court's registry, she said, there would be no requirement for a supersedeas bond on appeal. She also said the final payment due from Random House should continue to be kept by Random House, as her prior order had said, but Amanda would get credit for it toward the ten million dollars. She instructed me to prepare an order reflecting her ruling, run it by Keltner, and then submit it to her to sign.

Judge McCoy next turned to the issue of the accounting. I stood and approached the lectern and told her about how close the numbers were, and how our expert's number was actually lower than their expert's high number. Rather than slug it out with a protracted hearing in front of Judge McCoy, with each side's experts testifying, she suggested we try to work something out.

The lawyers went into a separate room off the courtroom to talk—something we could have already done had Kantner responded to my email about the omitted payment. But now, with the help of David Keltner, who I found to be reasonable, we decided to, in effect, split the difference between our number and their lower number.

It didn't make sense to fight over what was, in the grand scheme of things, a negligible amount. So, after some discussion, we agreed to a profit number for Jenny of $10,634,587.

Coming up with an order from this hearing was not so simple.

When the lawyers ultimately submitted something to Judge

McCoy, she rewrote portions of it, then signed it on September 15.

ORDER ON PLAINTIFF'S SECOND MOTION FOR APPLICATION OF EQUITABLE REMEDIES AND MOTION FOR SANCTIONS AND DEFENDANT'S MOTION TO RECONSIDER

On August 7, 2015, the Court considered Plaintiff Jennifer Lynn Pedroza's Second Motion for Application of Equitable Remedies and Motion for Sanctions, and on August 26, 2015, the Court considered Defendants Amanda Hayward's and TWCS Operations Proprietary Ltd.'s Motion to Reconsider. After considering the motions, the evidence, and the argument of counsel as well as the jury's answers to the questions in the Charge of the Court (including the jury's finding of a partnership between Plaintiff and Defendant, a finding that defendant did not comply with her duties of loyalty and care to Plaintiff, as well as finding Defendant committed fraud and conversion against Plaintiff) the Court finds that the elements required for a constructive trust have been met. The Defendant has been unjustly enriched and benefitted by her actions as found by the jury at the trial of this matter. Specifically, Defendant has received the $40+ million in royalties from the sale of the trilogy of books known as *Fifty Shades of Grey* trilogy (the res) which were owned by the partnership. Therefore, Plaintiff's Second Motion for Application of Equitable Remedies should be GRANTED as provided herein, that Plaintiff's Motion for Sanctions should be DENIED, and that Defendants' Motion to Reconsider should be DENIED.

IT IS, THEREFORE, HEREBY ORDERED that Plaintiff's Second Motion for Application of Equitable Remedies is GRANTED, and a constructive trust is imposed, as follows: Defendants are ORDERED to deposit into the registry of the Court, by the close of business on September 25, 2015 $10,000,000.00 (Ten-Million and no/100 dollars) in U.S. dollars from the funds traceable to any royalties paid at any time by Random House for the sale of the *Fifty Shades of Grey* trilogy, or any other funds received in connection with the business of The Writer's Coffee Shop.

This Court does not specify which asset or assets Defendant should use to satisfy this Order (whether property, cash, investments or otherwise) other than the fact that it is to be paid out of the funds traceable to the royalties from the *Fifty Shades* trilogy; nor does this Court in any way require Defendant to liquidate any property or asset. In so Ordering, the Court does not consider this Constructive Trust to be a substitute for any supersedeas bond that may be required in the event of an appeal, but instead intends it to be a Constructive Trust to prevent unjust enrichment of the Defendant.

The Court allows but does not require for this amount paid into the Court's registry to include, or take into account, the final royalty payment ("Final Royalty Payment") due from Random House. Pursuant to this Court's Order on Plaintiff's Application for Constructive Trust, entered on May 29, 2015, the Final Royalty Payment has been withheld and retained by Random House. The Court ORDERS that Random House shall continue to retain the Final Royalty Payment until further order of this Court.

IT IS FURTHER ORDERED that Plaintiff's Motion for Sanctions is DENIED.

IT IS FURTHER ORDERED that Defendants' Motion to Reconsider is DENIED.

Signed the [15th] day of [September], 2015.

[Susan McCoy]
Judge Presiding

The defendants' lawyers quickly filed a petition for a writ of mandamus from the Fort Worth Court of Appeals, which asked the appeals court to order Judge McCoy to withdraw this order. They contended the order overreached by not specifically identifying the source of the ten million dollars to be paid into the registry, although the order actually benefitted the defendants because it let them designate for themselves the source of funds, rather than be forced to comply with a designation by the Court.

On October 26, the appeals court ordered Judge McCoy to withdraw her September 15th Order. I disagreed with that decision then, and I still do today. I thought it ironic that a large part of the reason why the higher court reached this conclusion was because of Judge McCoy's effort to be fair to the defendants.

The Court of Appeals opinion said we had "failed to show that the $10-million-cash res[45] of Respondent's[46] constructive

---

[45] This is a Latin term that *Ballantine's Law Dictionary* defines as: "The thing. The real thing. A transaction. An affair. The subject matter of a trust in a sense of the property held under trust. The subject matter of an action in the sense of the property or status involved."

[46] In a mandamus action, the "respondent" is the particular judge who entered the order that is being attacked, so in this case that meant Judge McCoy. However, because the order was based upon relief

trust was the same property—or the proceeds from the sale thereof or revenues therefrom—that was wrongfully taken from her." [47] The opinion also said:

> Pedroza's failure to meet her burden of strictly proving an identifiable res constituting the same property – or the proceeds from the sale thereof or the revenues therefrom – that was wrongfully taken from her (royalties paid to Coffee Shop) is demonstrated from Respondent's order itself. The order states that "[t]his Court does not specify which asset or assets Defendant should use to satisfy this Order (whether property, cash, investments [,] or otherwise) other than the fact that it is to be paid out of the funds traceable to the royalties from the Fifty Shades trilogy." [Emphasis added.] A constructive trust cannot attach to unidentified assets, "[d]efinitive, designated property, wrongfully withheld from another, is the very heart and soul of the constructive trust theory." Wheeler, 627 S.W.2d at 851. In order to fasten a constructive trust on property owned by the defendant, some particular property must be identified.

The court's theory seemed to be, because the order didn't specifically identify properties or accounts, but simply left it up to the defendants to figure out where to find the money, then it wasn't a proper constructive trust.

In my original motion for application of equitable remedies, I identified five specific properties Amanda bought

---

we had sought on behalf of Jenny, then Jenny is identified as the "real party in interest."

[47] *In re Hayward*, 480 S.W.3d 48 (Tex. App. - Fort Worth, 2015, orig. proceeding).

using Random House Royalties. My motion said:

> When the beneficiary can point to the specific property that was purchased or inherited, or to its mutation, the tracing burden is met." Peirce v. Sheldon Petroleum Co., 589 S.W.2d 849, 853 (Tex. Civ. App. – Amarillo 1979, no writ). Hayward testified in open court at the temporary injunction hearing in this case, as well as at her deposition, that she paid for, in whole or in part, the following property for her personal benefit using Royalties:
>
> - A house in Dural, New South Wales, Australia.
> - A house on Kenthurst Road in Dural, New South Wales, Australia.
> - A house in Kenthurst, New South Wales, Australia.
> - A commercial property in South Windsor, New South Wales, Australia
> - A house in Cherrybrook, New South Wales, Australia.
>
> Collectively, the foregoing are referred to as the "Properties." Pedroza is entitled to a constructive trust on the "Properties."

My motion also identified some specific investment accounts and businesses into which we had traced money from the Random House payments, which I listed on an exhibit:

> In addition to a constructive trust on the Properties, Pedroza is entitled to a constructive trust on the entirety of the businesses, accounts, and funds

376

identified on Exhibit 1, as well as any investments, whether in WestPac Bank or otherwise, or any other accounts or funds that include Royalties (collectively the "Investments").

My motion asked Judge McCoy to impose an equitable lien on those properties and accounts and to order any cash or funds traceable to the royalties be paid into the court's registry. When the initial order didn't require placing anything in the registry, I followed up with my second motion and asked the judge to take that extra step, which resulted in the second order. It was that second order, not the first, that had been attacked in the mandamus action.

The second order specifically identified the "$40+ million in royalties from the sales of the trilogy of books known as *Fifty Shades of Grey* trilogy (the res) which were owned by the partnership." The deficiency, according to the Court of Appeals, was the order didn't specifically identify properties or accounts, even though that benefitted Amanda. As the saying goes, "No good deed goes unpunished."

I wasn't terribly concerned by the court of appeals' decision because, even though the second order had to be withdrawn, the first order remained in place. More importantly, we were now only two weeks away from a hearing on our application for attorney's fees. That was the last step (or at least so I thought) before a final judgment, after which there were actions we could take to tie up Amanda's assets and accomplish what we had been unable to accomplish with the second constructive trust order: require assets to be deposited in the registry of the court.

Following the August 26 hearing, Judge McCoy gathered the lawyers in her chambers to discuss what was left in the case, including attorney's fees. Fees in a contingency case are weird because the attorneys get paid an agreed-upon percentage of the recovery, but they still have to keep track of their time, at a reasonable billing rate, to prove the value of those fees. You can't just say we're entitled to have X amount added to the final judgment because that's the math. So, Brent and I kept track of our time from the start of the case and regularly provided Kantner with copies of our fee statements, which contained a breakdown on the dates legal work had been done, a description of the work, and the number of hours spent, with a running total at the end of each statement.

As of the beginning of August, I had just under 1,300 hours in the case, while Brent had just under 800 hours. My hourly rate ranged between $400 and $475 per hour, depending upon the stage of the case, while Brent's ranged between $250 and $325 per hour. I told Judge McCoy that I estimated the updated total through the prior week to equal about $785,000. I added I also intended to apply a multiplier to that, since the law permitted it. If we could reach an agreement with the defendants' lawyers, I would ask for a multiplier of 2X to bring it up to $1,570,000, which, based upon a judgment amount of $10,634,587, would result in an award of attorney's fees of less than 15%.

Kantner said he would consider it, and he thought we could reach an agreement. He asked if I would provide him with an update on our fees, along with a calculation of pre-judgment interest, and I agreed. Since attorney's fees and the amount of pre-judgment interest were the last things we needed to nail down before entry of a final judgment, it looked like we were almost there.

Two days later, on August 28, I emailed both Kantner and Keltner and said:

As promised, here is a breakdown of our attorney's fees. We have already provided fee statements through the end of July 2015, which, on a lodestar calculation[48], total $753,103.50. Through Friday, August 21, the total increased to $784,678.50. Adding fees for this week and estimating a few more to at least wrap up the judgment, we can simply round off to $800,000 if you are agreeable. As I told the judge, we will ask for a multiplier of 2, which would bring the total up to $1,600,000. Please let me know by the end of business on Wednesday of next week (Sept. 2) if you will stipulate to those fees.

Bob asked me to provide a pre-judgment interest number, as well. Based on the net profits number the parties stipulated of $10,634,587, pre-judgment interest at 5% breaks down to $1,456.79 per day. By my calculation, that brings the total of pre-judgment interest, as of August 28, to $665,753.03.

That would bring the total of a judgment as of today's date to $12,900,340.03 − $10,634,587 + $665,753.03 pre-judgment interest + $1,600,000 in attorney's fees. Of course, pre-judgment interest will continue to accrue at the rate of $1,456.79 per day until a judgment is actually signed.

Kantner responded by email on Tuesday, September 1, and said:

I have sent my thoughts on Pedroza's claim for prejudgment interest and attorneys' fees to David [Keltner], but David had an oral argument today and may have another commitment this week.

May we aim to respond to your inquiries re interest and fees on Friday, rather than tomorrow?

Of course, I agreed to that two-day extension[49] but then, on Friday, Kantner emailed:

Defendants are not going to stipulate on fees...As for prejudgment

---

[48] Lodestar is simply multiplying the number of hours by the billing rate.

[49] There's that delay thing again.

interest, I do not dispute your calculations, but I cannot find any statutory basis for an award of prejudgment interest on the claims on which Pedroza prevailed. Will you please tell me what you are relying on?

I was flabbergasted! Could he really believe that our fees, at less than 15% of the total, weren't reasonable? And it was well-established law in Texas that a Plaintiff who prevailed in a lawsuit was entitled to recover pre-judgment interest. In a landmark ruling I felt sure all trial lawyers in Texas knew, the Texas Supreme Court held this:

The primary objective of awarding damages in civil actions has always been to compensate the injured plaintiff rather than to punish the defendant. . . A law that denies recovery of prejudgment interest frustrates this goal. If a judgment provides plaintiffs only the amount of damages sustained at the time of the incident, plaintiffs are not fully compensated. They have been denied the opportunity to invest and earn interest on the amount of damages between the time of occurrence and the time of judgment.[50]

What this meant, then, was yet another couple of hearings—one would be an evidentiary hearing in which both sides would put on experts to testify as to the reasonableness of our attorney's fees and, after that, a hearing for entry of a final judgment *including* an award of pre-judgment interest. Kantner's refusal to agree accomplished only two things. One was to run up the amount of fees on both sides, including what Amanda's lawyers charged her. The other was more delay in entering a final judgment, which correspondingly meant a delay in our being able to begin collection efforts. That, I feared, would give

---

[50] *Cavnar v. Quality Control Parking, Inc.*, 696 S.W.2d 549, 552 (Tex. 1985).

Amanda more time to hide assets, which might have been the goal all along.

We started an evidentiary hearing on attorney's fees on November 20, which lasted from 1:35 PM until it was adjourned at 3:20 PM, and it was resumed, and finished on December 10. I hired, as an expert, an attorney with whom I had previously worked whose expertise was in business and commercial litigation. Kantner relied upon a prominent Fort Worth attorney who had been a former president of the State Bar of Texas.

I was the first witness, and I introduced our fee statements, identified the work we had done, and testified that the "lodestar" calculation (hours multiplied by rate) was $873,458.50 as of the date of the hearing. I stated my opinion that, under Texas law, those fees were reasonable. I then requested a multiplier, not of two-times, but three-times because Kantner had dragged this thing out, forcing more work to be done and unnecessarily delay a conclusion. Asking for a multiplier of 3X gave Judge McCoy room to compromise and at least allow 2X.

In order to support what I asked for, I had to prove the time and labor required; the novelty and difficulty of the questions; the level of skill required; the effect on other employment by the attorney; the customary fee; whether the fee was fixed or contingent; time limitations imposed by the client or the circumstances; the amount involved and the result obtained; the experience, reputation, and ability of the attorney; the undesirability of the case; the nature and length of the attorney's relationship with the client; and awards in similar cases.

Kantner's attack on our requested fees was twofold:

(1)   He argued we failed to "segregate" our fees, which meant we failed to separate legal work done solely for Christa Beebe and against TWCS

381

Operations. Because the only basis for recovering fees was the declaratory judgment we obtained for Jenny against Amanda, he contended any work unrelated to that claim was not recoverable.

(2)   He contended our fees were not reasonable.

Less than two weeks after the second day of the hearing concluded, Judge McCoy issued a letter ruling, just before Christmas. Her letter noted that, while much of the work Brent and I had done involved claims other than the declaratory judgment, the same work had to be done for both it and other causes of action. She wrote, "[T]he Defendants even admit in their Motion for Summary Judgment on Statute of Frauds, that all of Plaintiff's other causes of action are based upon the premise that TWCS is a partnership, where Plaintiff is a partner." She deducted only the amount of $10,857 for what she felt was work done solely on behalf of Christa's claim.

At the end of her letter, she addressed my request for a multiplier.

I find that this case does warrant an "adjustment" upward of Plaintiff's Lodestar figure. Among other things I find [it] notable that the case was taken on a contingency fee basis, and the outcome was risky. Plaintiff had signed the Service Agreement waiving her rights to more money, a notable hump that Plaintiff had to overcome. Defendant had two other "partners" who testified that there was no partnership, which is a major issue for plaintiff to overcome, as well. The case involved international issues, given that the money and the Defendants were in Australia. Plaintiff was required to spend time and large amounts of money to travel to

Australia to take depositions (the costs for which Plaintiff is not seeking reimbursement). The recovery was one of the highest recoveries for a Plaintiff in Tarrant County ($10M+) in the last 5 years. Taking into account all of the above, I believe this case warrants an upward adjustment (multiplier) of the Lodestar figure. While Plaintiff requests a multiplier of 3, I believe that a multiplier of 2 is more appropriate.

Plaintiff is awarded her attorney's fees of $873,458.50 minus the amounts for work on Christa Beebe's case ($10,857.00), for a total of $862,601.50. That figure with a multiplier of 2 equals $1,725,203.

Kantner continued his opposition to pre-judgment interest, even after I directed his attention to the *Cavnar* case, so I filed a motion for entry of judgment, which was set for hearing on January 28, 2016. Just when I thought this was the last issue for this phase of the case, the defendants filed a second motion for judgment notwithstanding the verdict, which was set for the same date. David Keltner argued the JNOV motion and, just after he finished and I was gathering my notes to approach the lectern, Judge McCoy said, "Mr. Keltner, I'm going to overrule your motion for JNOV."

Over the years, I found I was at my most eloquent the less I said. As a young associate, I once had a hearing on a motion for summary judgment that I had filed. After I made my argument and then my opponent finished his, the judge started questioning the other lawyer about his position. I was too inexperienced to understand that the judge questioning the other side, but not me, was a good sign. When I felt like it had been too long since I had last spoken, I tried to interject what I felt sure was a brilliant bit of insight to save the day, but the judge cut me off with this admonition: "You've already earned your nickel, Mr. Farris. Better let it lie."

So, I was more than happy for Judge McCoy to overrule Keltner's motion without my having to open my mouth.

Next came my motion for entry of judgment, and Kantner argued against any award of pre-judgment interest, but Judge McCoy overruled him and granted my motion in full. She then immediately signed an order denying the defendants' motion for JNOV, as well as a final judgment (after filling in blanks for the pre-judgment interest amount and attorney's fees for any future appeal), both of which I had prepared and brought with me—just in case.

FINAL JUDGMENT

On February 9, 2015, the trial of this case began. Plaintiff Jennifer Lynn Pedroza ("Pedroza") appeared in person and through her attorneys and announced ready for trial. Defendants Amanda M. Hayward ("Hayward") and TWCS Operations Proprietary Ltd. ("Operations") appeared in person and through their attorneys and announced ready for trial. A panel of twelve qualified jurors was selected, and the case proceeded to trial. The jury heard the evidence and the arguments of counsel. The parties concluded evidence on February 13, 2015, when the parties through their respective attorneys announced in open court that they had presented all their evidence and rested. The Court submitted questions, definitions, and instructions to the jury on February 17, 2015. In response, the jury made findings that the Court received, filed, and entered of record. The jury's verdict, as reflected in the Court's Charge, is expressly incorporated into this Final Judgment for all purposes.

After considering the evidence, the testimony received, the arguments of counsel, and the jury's verdict, the Court previously rendered partial judgment on May 5, 2015, and now renders final judgment for Pedroza and against Defendants as follows:

1. Pursuant to Chapter 37 of the *Texas Civil Practice & Remedies Code*, the Court declares that The Writer's Coffee Shop ("Coffee Shop") is a partnership.

2. Pursuant to Chapter 37 of the *Texas Civil Practice & Remedies Code*, the Court declares that Plaintiff Pedroza is a twenty-five (25) percent partner in Coffee Shop and is entitled to twenty-five (25) percent of the net profits of Coffee Shop.

3. Pedroza shall recover from Hayward the amount of $10,634,587 as her share of Coffee Shop net profits, plus pre-judgment interest in the amount of five percent (5%) per annum, in simple interest, accruing from the date this action was filed on May 29, 2014, until the date of final judgment, at a per diem rate of $1,456.79, in the total amount, as of the date of this final judgment, of [$888,642.87].

4. Pedroza shall recover post-judgment interest on the amounts set forth in Paragraph 3 at the rate of five percent (5%) per annum, compounded annually. The post-judgment interest shall begin to accrue on the date following the date of this final judgment and shall continue to accrue until this judgment is satisfied in full.

5. Pursuant to Chapter 37 of the *Texas Civil Practice & Remedies Code*, Pedroza shall recover from Hayward and TWCS her reasonable and necessary attorney's fees in the amount of

$1,725,203 for services rendered through the entry of final judgment in this matter. In the event of an appeal by the Defendants to the court of appeals, if the appeal is unsuccessful, Pedroza will be further entitled to an additional [total $50,000] in attorney's fees; in the event of an appeal to the Supreme Court of Texas, Pedroza will be entitled to an additional attorney's fees of [$15,000] for filing or responding to a petition for review, [$25,000] for briefing on the merits, and [$10,000] for oral argument. The court finds these fees to be equitable and just.

6. Pedroza is entitled to the equitable relief set forth in this Court's May 29, 2015, Order on Plaintiff's Application for Constructive Trust, which Order, and the relief stated therein, is incorporated into this Final Judgment by reference as if fully set forth therein.

7. Defendants Hayward and TWCS take nothing by way of their counterclaims against Pedroza.

8. All costs of court spent or incurred in this cause are adjudged against Hayward and TWCS.

9. All relief requested in this case and not expressly granted in this final judgment is denied. This judgment finally disposes of all parties and claims and is appealable.

SO ORDERED this [28th] day of [January], 2016.
[Susan McCoy]
Honorable Susan Heygood McCoy
Judge Presiding

News media around the world picked up the story of the final judgment. Locally, Max Baker of the Fort Worth *Star-Telegram* wrote:

Five years after Fifty Shades of Grey *became an international bestseller, Jennifer Pedroza of Arlington is getting closer to cashing in on the erotic novel's success with an $11.5 million payday.*

Saying it was time to "put the case to bed," Tarrant County District Judge Susan McCoy signed an order Thursday awarding Pedroza $10,634,587 in royalties. A jury said last year that Pedroza was cheated out of her portion of the earnings by Amanda Hayward of Australia, a partner in a business that originally published the book.

Including pre-judgment interest of $888,643 assessed from the day the lawsuit was filed in May 2014, Pedroza could receive $11.5 million. McCoy also ordered Hayward to pay Pedroza's $1.7 million in attorney's fees.

In Australia, the outcome was reported using Australian dollars instead of U.S. dollars. A *Sydney Morning Herald* headline proclaimed "Fifty Shades of Grey publisher Amanda Hayward ordered to pay $18.5m to partner." The story began:

A US judge has ordered Australian publisher Amanda Hayward to pay more than $18.5 million in compensation, costs and interest to her former business partner in a long-running stoush[51] over profits from the runaway erotic bestseller Fifty Shades of Grey.

The huge award comes after a Texan jury last year found Hayward had cheated Jennifer Pedroza, a primary school teacher from Fort Worth, out of her share of earnings from the book.

---

[51] This was a new word for me. It's an Australian term that means a fight or brawl.

Jenny's Story

Christmas of 2015 was a joyous occasion for my family because we had much to celebrate. My dad was alive, Christa and I had new jobs, and we were moving on with our lives. Mike and Brent were hard at work and, hopefully, a judgment awaited in the near future. But, while life went on, I would never be the same mentally. I didn't become cynical and reclusive but, rather, I grew less trusting. Gone were the blinders that prevented me from seeing the hidden motives of others. I now knew that everyone had an agenda, and it was up to me whether to be a part.

When Mike and Brent called after the hearing on the final judgment, I was elated. This was it. The moment when a judge placed a value on Amanda's destruction of our friendship. Most of my friendships are priceless, but Amanda and I were apparently worth eleven-and-a-half-million dollars, plus attorney's fees, bringing the number to over thirteen million. Forty million dollars divided four ways, and she could have saved three million dollars just by allowing her partners their fair share—and kept some good friends to boot. How sad was that!

During one of her visits to my house, she had given me a small wooden sign, which I kept above my desk. The sign read, "You'll always be my best friend…You know too much."

Well, there you go.

CHAPTER TWENTY-FOUR: The Final Calm

...storms that rip up the world as you know it, and leave, like a sacrifice, a rainbow to make you forget what has come before.
—Jodi Picoult, *Picture Perfect*

Mike's Story

IT TOOK LONGER to get a final judgment entered following trial than it took to get to trial in the first place, but we were finally there. Unfortunately, having a judgment and collecting a judgment were two different things. I knew Amanda was good for it; after taxes, she had likely cleared more than thirty million dollars. I knew she spent millions on real estate, but that real estate was 8,600 miles away, literally on the other side of the world. That's why I asked the constructive trust to require ten million dollars to be paid into the court's registry or real estate deeds be deposited. I wanted to get at least some assets into my hemisphere.

A second problem was much of the Australian real estate had been acquired in the name of one of the companies she had established, SpoiltOne Investments Proprietary Limited, which was solely owned by her husband James. I saw this as a transparent attempt to move money out of the reach of

389

creditors. She and James jointly owned their residence in Dural, New South Wales, which she bought for $4,780,000 Australian dollars (roughly $3.8 million U.S. today), and a second house in Cherrybrook, New South Wales, which she bought for $1,000,000 Australian (roughly $780,000 U.S. today).

According to public records in Australia, though, there were three other properties that were *not* in her name: a gymnasium in Windsor, New South Wales (bought for $2,565,000 Australian dollars), and two additional houses in Dural, New South Wales (one bought for $2,254,321, and the other for which she paid $391,000 as a down payment against a purchase price of $1,995,000 AU). That meant that she had spent nearly eleven million Australian dollars on real estate, but less than six million of it was in her name. I had no idea where the rest of the money was.

Although the judgment wouldn't be final for 30 days after it was signed (and that could be extended for an additional 75 days if the defendants filed a motion for new trial, which they did on February 29), there were still things we could do in the interim. Texas has what is called a "turnover" procedure that allows a judgment creditor, which Jenny now was, to ask the Court to order the judgment debtor, in this case Amanda, to "turn over" property "in the debtor's possession or is subject to the debtor's control" to a sheriff, constable, or receiver, or the Court may "otherwise apply the property to the satisfaction of the judgment." [52]

This procedure could give me another shot at accomplishing what I had tried, and failed, to do with the second constructive trust: get money and/or property into the registry of the court. That, in turn, might pressure Amanda into thinking it was preferable to reach a settlement than to continue fighting.

---

[52] The Texas turnover statute is found at §31.002 of the *Texas Civil Practice & Remedies Code*.

I filed the motion for turnover on February 8, and filed an amended motion on February 22, and asked Judge McCoy to order Amanda to turn over all bank accounts she controlled by paying their balances into the court registry, and to turn over any deeds to property she owned or controlled, either solely or as a joint tenant with James. I also asked that Random House deposit the final royalty payment, which it had been holding as required by the first constructive trust order, into the registry. A hearing was held on March 10, and I had an inkling in advance how Judge McCoy was going to rule when I realized she had asked someone from the Tarrant County District Clerk's office, which controlled the court's registry, to be present. Why would she have asked for that unless she intended to order *at least something* into the registry?

The hearing lasted nearly two hours and, at the end, Judge McCoy granted the major part of my motion. As usual, Kantner fought with me over the language of the order I ultimately submitted to the judge. Random House's lawyer got involved, adding language that affected the payment his client would have to make. His concern was, since the contract between Random House and Coffee Shop directed Random House to make royalty payments to Coffee Shop, payment to any party other than Coffee Shop might breach the contract, and then Random House might be sued for breach.

The order, finally signed on May 6, said, in part:

The Court **GRANTS** Pedroza's Amended Motion for Turnover to the following extent:

1. ...This Court hereby directs that Random House deposit the Final Royalty Payment due pursuant to the Random House Contract directly into the Court's registry by delivering to the Tarrant County District Clerk a check

made payable to the Tarrant County District Clerk. The Clerk shall hold such funds in an interest bearing account pending further order of this Court. This Court further directs that Random House make all of the tax withholding and reporting required in connection with the Final Royalty Payment to the Original Publisher in a manner consistent with the withholding and reporting that Random House has made in connection with the previous payments made to the Original Publisher under the Random House Contract. Finally, this Court directs that the deposit of the Final Royalty Payment into the Court's registry shall discharge Random House (to the extent of the payment and the amount withheld and paid to the IRS) of its obligation to make the Final Royalty Payment to the Original Publisher for income generated during the Initial Term (as those terms are defined in the Random House Contract).

2. Defendant Amanda Hayward shall – on or before May 16, 2016 – turn over to the Tarrant County District Clerk's Office the deeds that reflect her joint tenant interest in the properties at:

4 Yuruga Road, Dural, New South Wales, Australia; and
22 Worthing Place, Cherrybrook, New South Wales, Australia.

The Tarrant County District Clerk's Office shall take

possession of the deeds and keep them in a safe place pending further order of this Court.

3. Defendant Amanda Hayward shall – on or before May 16, 2016 – pay into the Court's registry the balance, as of the date of this Court's ruling, in the following accounts:

WestPac Private Bank Cheque Account ending in 5988; and

Commonwealth Bank Streamline Account ending in 3951.

4. Hayward shall pay the balance of these two accounts to the Tarrant County District Court Clerk by delivering to the Clerk a check or checks made payable to the Tarrant County District Court Clerk. The Clerk shall hold such funds in an interest bearing account pending further order of this Court.

5. Defendant Amanda Hayward shall – on or before May 16, 2016 – provide a list of assets which would be available to satisfy the Final Judgment in this case. The list shall include investments, money, bank accounts, and real property that is available for the purpose stated herein.

6. Defendant Amanda Hayward is enjoined from transferring, moving, disposing of, alienating, depleting, destroying or concealing any nonexempt property.

I took Amanda's deposition, again, on April 6, this time to learn information about her assets and to see if she had anything else we might go after to satisfy the judgment. Rather than fly to Australia, it was conducted via video conference from Bob Kantner's office at Jones Day.

To hear her tell it, Amanda was a penniless pauper, and her sole major assets were the two houses she co-owned with her husband. As for the other assets, including that investment account she once said contained about seven million dollars, she testified they were not under her control because she had simply given all the Random House money to her husband, James.

"So, did you just lose it [money coming in from Random House] all?" I asked.

"No."

"Did you give it to your husband?"

"Yes."

"Did you get anything in exchange for giving it to your husband?"

"No."

"So, when you gave him sixteen point five million or fifteen point seven million dollars, you didn't get sixteen point five million in exchange. Is that correct?"

"Correct."

"The same thing on the fifteen point seven million. When you gave it to your husband, you didn't get anything of comparable value in exchange, did you?"

"No."

I moved on to the investment account. *"That investment account we talked about a while ago, that had at least at one time seven million, is that in the name of SpoiltOne Investments?"*

"I believe so."

"That was money from the Random House deal, correct?"

"I believe so."

"Again, was that money that you simply gave to your husband to

put in an investment account?"

"Correct."

"Did you receive anything of value in exchange for giving that to him?"

"No."

Incredible!

Prior to the deposition, I had learned from Australian public records that James Hayward recently sold two of the houses owned by SpoiltOne Investments. Amanda confirmed this but, unbelievably, claimed she didn't know what James did with the sale proceeds. Millions more simply vanished!

I believed those sales violated the temporary injunction, which prohibited any sale or disposition of assets that had been acquired with money from Random House royalty payments. I planned to use Amanda's answers to set up yet another action we might take in this case, depending upon how our efforts went to collect the judgment in Australia. What I had in mind was to file a new lawsuit under Texas's Uniform Fraudulent Transfer Act[53], which defined a "fraudulent transfer" as a transfer of property or assets by a debtor to another person or entity "with actual intent to hinder, delay, or defraud any creditor of the debtor" or, if the transfer was made "without receiving a reasonably equivalent value in exchange," leaving the debtor without sufficient assets to satisfy debts. Amanda had just testified she gave the Random House payments to her husband, got nothing in return, and now didn't have enough assets to satisfy the judgment. I intended to ask the Court to set aside any transfers Amanda made to James, so she would, once again, be the legal owner, and then we could go after those assets in her hands.

---

[53] The statute is found in Chapter 24 of the *Texas Business and Commerce Code*.

I let Bob Kantner and David Keltner know of this possibility in a letter I sent to them on April 8. In that letter, I said:

Ms. Hayward's testimony at her deposition on Tuesday, which at times was absurdly unbelievable, has made several things clear: (1) Ms. Hayward and her husband James conspired to fraudulently transfer funds that Ms. Hayward received from Random House with the intent to hinder, delay, or defraud creditors; (2) The sales by James Hayward of the houses at 33 Kenthurst and 5 Coolalie Place, on October 22, 2015 and December 16, 2015, respectively, violated the temporary injunction in this case.

...

We intend to proceed with an action to set aside fraudulent transfers of assets from Ms. Hayward to her husband / SpoiltOne.

I didn't have any problem telegraphing my intent because I wanted to put pressure on their client. Besides, I thought the logical next steps were obvious. I figured Kantner and Keltner already knew it; I might as well let them know I knew it, too.

Jenny's Story

I characterized this as the "wait and see" time. Each time we made a move, the defense lawyers made a counter-move, and more days passed by. It was particularly frustrating knowing that, with every day that went by, money slipped through our fingers. Mike and Brent worked hard to plug the leaks, but Amanda's bucket overflowed. We worried that, before long, the money would be so hidden that not no one could find it. And maybe that had been the intent all along. How can that be right?

Still, I maintained faith, having come this far, things would work out in the end.

396

Mike's Story

On April 27, David Keltner filed a Notice of Appeal with the Fort Worth Court of Appeals. In the Civil Docketing Statement, he listed the issues to be raised on appeal as "Statute of frauds and release for recovery; no evidence of partnership; attorney's fees excessive." Other than the attorney's fees question, these were the same issues that made up their motion for summary judgment, two motions for directed verdict, and two motions for judgment notwithstanding the verdict, as well as the motion for new trial, all of which had been overruled, so I wasn't terribly worried, other than by the delays it would cause in finalizing the case.

That same date, we took the first steps to start enforcement of the judgment in Australia. Working with Australian lawyers who had assisted us before, we had "*caveats*" filed in the real estate records in Australia. In Texas, we have something called a *lis pendens*, which can be filed in deed records to put the world on notice that a particular piece of real estate is involved in litigation, which might affect the title and ownership of the property. It puts potential buyers on notice that title to the property is in dispute.

Somewhat of an equivalent in Australia, a *caveat* can be filed by any person who has "any estate or interest in land" and, when it is filed, it, in effect, creates a lien on that property and prevents the owner from disposing of it. The Australian attorneys filed caveats on the two properties Amanda co-owned with her husband, the same ones Judge McCoy had ordered the deeds to be delivered to the Tarrant County District Clerk. This was probably a case of "belt-and-suspenders"—two remedies to accomplish the same goal—but, even though Kantner delivered those deeds, I was still concerned Amanda might try to sell the houses, in violation of Judge McCoy's order. After all, the temporary injunction, which applied not only to Amanda but also to "any other person or entity acting in concert or participation" with her, hadn't prevented James from selling two houses that had been bought with Random House money and which should have been frozen by the injunction. The injunction and turnover order in Texas were the belt, the *caveats* in Australia the suspenders.

Although the defendants filed a notice of appeal, they didn't file a supersedeas bond, which meant there was nothing to stop us from trying to collect the judgment, even while it was on appeal. My plan was to register, or "domesticate," the judgment in Australia, then to force Amanda into bankruptcy and turn over enforcement of the judgment to an Australian bankruptcy trustee.

Throughout the case, I had become a bit of an expert on Australian law, from partnership law to how to enforce a U.S. judgment in Australia. I probably knew just enough to be dangerous. Now I was also becoming an expert, or at least a semi-expert, on Australian bankruptcy law. As with my prior letter telegraphing the actions I planned to take to enforce the judgment in Texas, I gave Amanda's lawyers notice of my intentions in Australia. By letter dated April 4 (two days before I took the post-judgment deposition of Amanda), I told Kantner and Keltner:

We have attorneys standing by in Australia to take any necessary steps to assist [in enforcing the judgment]. That may include registering caveats with the registrar of deeds in Australia under the authority of Section 74 of the New South Wales Real Property Act of 1900 and obtaining freezing orders[54] so as to preserve the status quo until the judgment in this case becomes final. When the judgment is final, we intend to then pursue collection of the full judgment in Australia following the

---

[54] The Australian equivalent of injunction orders.

procedures set forth by the Supreme Court of Australia in Benefit Strategies Group v. Prider. We believe the requirements of that case have been met, particularly since Ms. Hayward did not contest jurisdiction in the United States, but instead submitted to the Texas Court's jurisdiction.

On May 24, I wrote David Keltner another letter, outlining my plans in more detail. I wasn't making idle threats but was honestly laying out my intentions so he would know, first, I was serious and, second, I had familiarized myself with the steps I would have to take. I reminded David that I had previously told him I was going to begin the procedure to register the judgment, then told him:

Once it is registered, we intend to make an application to an Official Receiver to issue a bankruptcy notice and to file a creditor's petition for bankruptcy against Ms. Hayward. I'm sure Ms. Hayward's Australian attorneys can confirm that, under Australia's Bankruptcy Act of 1966 [the "Act"], a creditor owning a final judgment in the amount of $5,000 or more can take these steps. [Act at §§ 41, 44] Under Bankruptcy Regulation 13.03, a bankruptcy is recorded on Australia's National Personal Insolvency Index, a public record, and remains there permanently. [https://www.afsa.gov.au/resources/npii]

I'm certainly not an expert in Australian bankruptcy law, but my understanding is that the bankruptcy court may then direct the trustee to take control of the debtor's property and take certain actions. [Act at §50] That includes taking control of legal proceedings, which are stayed unless the trustee elects to pursue them and the creditors elect to fund those proceedings. [Act at §60]

The trustee also has the following powers and authority:

- *To require production of books and records of the debtor and any associated entity; "associated entity" is defined broadly enough in the Act to include James Hayward and SpoiltOne Investments Proprietary Ltd. [Act at §§ 5B and 5C]*

- *To have access to books of an associated entity. [§77A]*
- *To take action to void "undervalued transactions" as well as "transfers to defeat creditors." [Act at §§ 120, 121]*
- *To take steps to discover property that may be used to satisfy creditors. [Act at §81] We believe the trustee will be interested in discovering the amounts paid by Random House to Ms. Hayward that have previously been unaccounted for....*
- *To examine the debtor and any associated entities (such as James Hayward and SpoiltOne) under oath about their financial affairs, and to require them to produce their books for examination. The Act specifies that "an examination under this section shall be held in public." [Act at §81(2)] Creditors may also take part in this examination. [Act at §81(8)]*
- *Once the trustee has gathered all of the debtor's property, he may sell assets as necessary, including property that is jointly owned, and apply the proceeds to the claims of the creditors. [Act at §116] At the end of the proceeding, the debtor is then discharged but the discharge "does not release the bankrupt from a debt incurred by means of fraud or a fraudulent breach of trust to which he or she was a party...." [Act at §153(2)(b)]*

We are already in the process of registering the judgment in Australia. If we take the route of placing Ms. Hayward in bankruptcy, we will make claim for the full amount of the judgment, which, by my calculations of the post-judgment interest, is currently $13,433,120.20 (US); that is $18,672,037.08(AU).

None of the things that could happen to Amanda Hayward, and her husband, in an Australian bankruptcy would be pleasant. The one potentially the most devastating was the fact that the trustee would take over all legal actions, which in this case would have been the appeal. The trustee would then decide whether to pursue the appeal, but only if the creditors agreed to fund it. It appeared Jenny would be the only major creditor, and maybe the only creditor, period. What were the odds she would agree to fund an appeal from a judgment in her favor?

On June 9, our Australian attorneys filed an action in the Supreme Court of New South Wales to register, and enforce, the judgment that had been entered by Judge McCoy.

The Sydney office of Kantner's firm, Jones Day, immediately got the proceedings delayed, then filed a motion to stay the whole shebang pending the appeal in Texas. They argued that, since the case could potentially be reversed on appeal, it wasn't proper to proceed with registering the judgment in Australia.

My understanding of Australian law, though, was a foreign judgment merely had to be final, which this one was, and the fact that it was appealed shouldn't prevent its registration in Australia, particularly since a supersedeas bond had not been filed. The Australian judge, called a "Senior Registrar," imposed a briefing schedule to hash out this question, requiring Amanda's lawyers to "file and serve all the evidence upon which they intend to rely by 28 July 2016."

We then had until August 11 to respond, and the motion was set for hearing on August 29.

While all of this was going on in Australia, and while still waiting for the trial court's record to be filed with the appeals court (which would trigger the start of timetables for filing briefs), David Keltner and I had been hard at work trying to settle the case.

In mid-summer, the parties reached an agreement. By the end of September, settlement papers had been signed, the appeal had been dismissed, the action to register our judgment in Australia had been dismissed, the *caveats* had been released, and all was at an end.

As with virtually every other aspect of this case, even settlement was big news. Max Baker led off an article in the Fort Worth *Star-Telegram* this way:

Five years after the smutty novel Fifty Shades of Grey *became an international bestseller, the two women fighting over its riches have finally put the case to bed.*

Jennifer Pedroza, a Fort Worth elementary schoolteacher, is settling out-of-court with Amanda Hayward, her former Australian partner in the business that originally published the book, for an undisclosed amount.

Both Keltner and I contributed quotes for the article:

"All I can tell you is that everyone is satisfied with the settlement," said Michael Farris, the attorney representing Pedroza, who lives in Arlington. "I can't comment on what she is getting, one way or the other."

David Keltner, an attorney representing Hayward, wouldn't talk about the total amount.

"It is a good settlement from both parties' standpoint," Keltner said.

Reuters picked up on the *Star-Telegram* article and released a report of its own, which began:

A Texas woman who claimed she was cheated out of royalty money from the erotic "Fifty Shades of Grey" novels has reached a settlement with her former business partner, bringing an end to their lengthy legal battle, their lawyers said on Friday.

Both articles were picked up by other media outlets, and the news made it way around the globe.

The case was finally over.

PART V: FACING THE FUTURE

EPILOGUE: Lessons from the Storm

When you come out of the storm, you won't be the same person that walked in. That's what the storm is about.
—Haruki Murakami

Jenny's Story

LAST YEAR, MY son read one of my all-time favorite novels, *To Kill a Mockingbird* by Harper Lee. Since it had been a while since I last cracked the pages of this classic, I read it along with him. It made me realize Mike Farris was my Atticus Finch. Before I met him, I had given up.

Amanda Hayward tried to take everything away from me, and I thought she had succeeded, but, on a daily basis, my mom reminded me to trust in God. I believed from our first meeting that divine intervention brought Mike into my life. He took on my case because he believed in *me*. He believed I had been wronged, and he used his calm intelligence to fight a fight on my behalf when neither of us knew what the outcome would be.

In the beginning, the world seemed against us, but as more and more of the story emerged, I re-claimed my power, and the truth prevailed. I could finally hold my head up knowing that, with the help of Mike, Brent, Christa, Mickey, and a hoard of good family and friends, I found justice.

In writing this book, I hope other people will learn from my mistakes. Learn that the best of intentions can go awry and, in business, it's always a good idea to "get it in writing." Be vigilant, keep your eyes and ears open, and don't be blinded to the truth. Listen with your heart, but also listen with your head. As the old saying goes, if it sounds too good to be true, it usually is. A corollary to that might be, if it doesn't sound right, it probably isn't.

The settlement was a breath of fresh air. Both Mr. Keltner and Mike told reporters that it was a good settlement, and I was satisfied. More than anything I was relieved I could finally put this behind me and move on with my life without Amanda's shadow hanging over my every move. A part of me wished I had never met Amanda Hayward, but there was another part of me that celebrated the fact I made it through and made some damn fine friends in the process.

As Polonius said in *Hamlet*, "This above all: To thine own self be true."

Mike's Story

Lying in a hospital bed in early 2013, after the sudden onset of Guillain-Barre Syndrome, I knew I would recover; it was just a question of how quickly the GBS could be arrested and reversed.

I knew I would get on my feet again; it was just a question of when I would walk again. And I knew I would practice law again; it was just a question of whether I would ever again find a case that would provide me with any real satisfaction.

It turned out the answers to those questions were:

(1) Five days;

(2) Three weeks; and

(3) Yes.

I have always believed lawyering is a noble profession, but not every lawyer, nor every case, is noble. With Jenny's case, I was able to rediscover the spark that sent me to law school in the first place, and I regained the satisfaction I got from helping someone who genuinely needed my help. Once the settlement agreement was signed and the case dismissed, I retired at the end of September, 2017.

My legal career had been filled with highs and lows, peaks and valleys. I felt blessed my final case was a high—not just a peak, but probably the pinnacle.

Litigation, which is adversarial by its very nature, didn't really fit my personality. I sometimes said I was the Rodney King of litigation, with the attitude of, "Can we all just get along?"

But there are some things worth fighting for, and I believe Jenny's case was one of those things. Now that it's over, though, I'm ready to stop the fighting, at least in the legal arena. I'm through with briefs and pleadings and depositions and hearings and trials.

As the old spiritual says:

I'm gonna lay down my sword and shield, down by the riverside; ain't gonna study war no more.